C. J. CADOUX

THEOLOGIAN, SCHOLAR AND PACIFIST

C. J. CADOUX

THEOLOGIAN, SCHOLAR AND PACIFIST

ELAINE KAYE

EDINBURGH
1988

© 1988 Elaine Kaye

Published by members of the Cadoux family

Produced and marketed by
Edinburgh University Press
22 George Square, Edinburgh

Set in Linoterm Plantin
by Speedspools, Edinburgh, and
printed in Great Britain by
Redwood Burn Ltd, Trowbridge

British Library Cataloguing
    in Publication Data
Kaye, Elaine
C. J. Cadoux : theologian, scholar and
pacifist.
1. England. Congregational churches. Cadoux,
Cecil John, 1883-1947
I. Title
285.8'092'4

ISBN 0 85224 603 X

Contents

	Partial genealogy of the Cadoux family	vi
	Foreword by Theodore Cadoux	vii
	Preface	xiii
I	Early life	1
II	At the Admiralty 1902–1911	10
III	Mansfield 1911–1914	28
IV	Mansfield: war and marriage 1914–1915	44
V	War and peace: the founding of a family and the making of a scholar 1916–1919	57
VI	Bradford: teaching 1919–1920	70
VII	The search for truth: writing 1920–1924	81
VIII	Light and shade: the mid 1920s	95
IX	*Catholicism and Christianity*; looking to the future 1928–1929	106
X	Smyrna 1930	120
XI	Last years in Bradford 1930–1933	131
XII	Return to Oxford 1933–1934	141
XIII	In defence of liberal theology 1934–1939	151
XIV	Christian pacifism re-examined 1939–1940	166
XV	War years 1940–1945	176
XVI	New Testament scholar	191
XVII	Last years 1945–1947	203
	APPENDIX A. The Cadoux Papers	214
	APPENDIX B. Published works of C. J. Cadoux	215
	APPENDIX C. C. J. Cadoux Memorial Lectures	219
	APPENDIX D. Published works of Arthur Temple Cadoux	220
	Index	221

Partial Genealogy of the Cadoux Family

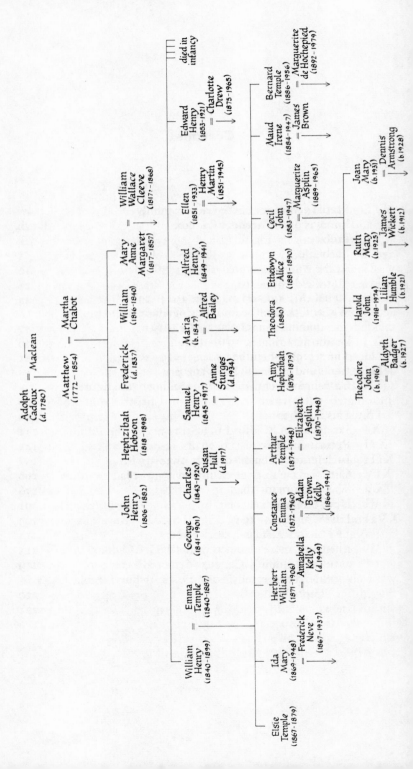

Foreword

My first duty in introducing the reader to this account of my father's life and work is one of apology to those of his many friends who are still alive, for not having furnished them with such an account long ago. To the majority who have died no apology, alas, can be made. It was always my intention to write his life myself, but for various reasons I never progressed beyond the study and analysis of the material. I am therefore all the more grateful to Miss Elaine Kaye for accepting the task and accomplishing it so successfully. She has tackled the immense mass of evidence with admirable perception, discrimination and diligence, so as to reduce it to a well-proportioned, balanced and sympathetic narrative and appreciation of my father's achievements and qualities. In a wider perspective she has recalled the social and religious climate of an age now rapidly receding, and illuminated issues which still exercise the Christian world today.

I must also, on her behalf and that of my sisters and myself, express our thanks to Mr A. R. Turnbull, Secretary of the Edinburgh University Press, who has placed all its resources at our disposal on generous terms and so enabled the book to appear.

It remains for me to attempt my own appreciation of my father's character, which more than in most cases has been an example admired, but too little followed, by his son. What I say will naturally here and there repeat, or be illustrated by, Miss Kaye's narrative: if it differs at all, no criticism is intended.

My father said more than once that he felt himself, like Wordsworth, to be 'else sinning greatly, a dedicated spirit'. The quotation was well-worn but expressed exactly his strong sense of duty. Opinions may differ as to whether this feeling of being dedicated is possible without religious faith: it surely requires at the least a faith in something far more important and exalted than oneself, the service of which has a prior call on one's whole endeavour. In his case it certainly was his Christian faith which, nurtured in a pious Victorian home, came to full measure through the inspiration, as he recalled, of a work by another dedicated man, Leo Tolstoy. It was as an apostle of that faith that he lived and worked, conversed and wrote, suffered and rejoiced.

His writings reveal a true controversialist, who relished the deploying of trenchant arguments, and came down heavily, and when called for with generous indignation, on irrelevance and evasion. 'Who', he wrote (*Philip of Spain* p.109), 'can read the story of Alva in the Netherlands and be impressed by *his* sufferings?' He refused to let his opponents get away with what he called 'question-begging labels', as when critics dismissed Zwingli's view of the eucharist as 'a *mere* commemoration' (*Christian Worship* p.149). In defence of the pacifist allegedly shown up by the dictum 'Qui facit per alium, facit per se' as sheltering behind the warrior, he ripostes 'But an assertion is not necessarily true because it can be quoted in the form of a Latin tag' (*Christian Pacifism Re-examined* p.181). He could poke gentle fun at the extravagant language of some of his Barthian opponents, for example T. F. Torrance's picture of 'God striking in desperate anguish at the seat of evil' (*The Presbyter* IV 2 (May 1946) p.28). But views that he held to be wholly pernicious were condemned with unqualified severity: new doctrines of sex-morality drove him to recall Jesus' words 'Whoever causes one of these little ones to stumble, it were better for him if a millstone were hung about his neck, and he were cast into the depths of the sea!' (*A Pilgrim's Further Progress* p.177). He believed passionately in the efficacy of rational discussion as a means of resolving differences, and was frankly puzzled by those who appealed to its limitations, though of course he recognized that all reasoning must be based ultimately upon axioms incapable of proof. To his opponents he was always scrupulously fair. The convinced Protestant could write a chapter on 'The Advantages and Merits of Catholicism', and the pacifist enjoin his sons to 'cultivate a good soldierly bearing'. In personal exchanges he was unfailingly polite, earnestly seeking to convince, not to humiliate, and persisting in spite of rebuffs. One of his mottoes was 'Suaviter in modo; fortiter in re'.

From his youth he was fascinated by history, especially ancient history; and he early acquired that total respect for the evidence that marks all his contributions to the history of the Christian church from the life of its founder to his own day. His models were the great Victorians: Macaulay, Grote, Motley, Lecky: and when they were attacked for making moral judgements, as by Butterfield, he sprang to their defence. Grote's *History of Greece*, in twelve volumes, he read through three times. In planning the treatment of any matter he would first set out the divisions of the theme in logical order, often on a single large sheet, and then methodically assign the evidence and other material to each division, with scrupulous attention to detail, though sometimes with excessive support from quotations expressing views similar to his own, helping to swell the footnotes which were a conspicuous feature of his works (as of Grote's).

A careful stylist himself, he was very sensitive to the power of words, and deeply affected by moving passages from his favourite English reading – Shakespeare, Milton, Wordsworth, Tennyson, and above all the Bible; though in interpreting the Bible he preferred, for reasons of accuracy, to use modern translations; for the same reason his own translations of ancient texts were often so literal as to be stilted.

His system of values placed the utmost emphasis on personal relations – between friends, fellow-worshippers, husbands and wives, parents and children, and especially between Man and God. His sense of the fatherhood of God drew strength from his recollections of his own father. He had little appreciation of the value of forms and symbols in Christianity – architecture, music, the liturgy, vestments. But he could, on occasions, enjoy a dignified ceremony: he was proud to wear the scarlet and grey robe of a Doctor of Letters in the Sheldonian Theatre at Oxford when he and his two sons graduated on the same day in 1939, and when he took part in the Encaenia within a few weeks of his death.

His own tastes in art, music and literature had been formed early, and did not alter much. From his childhood he practised drawing with pen and pencil – portraits of friends and young people, sketches of buildings and scenery, not without merit; he left some exquisitely-drawn maps illustrating ancient and biblical history. He found Ruskin a congenial instructor, and adopted so wholeheartedly his opinions on architecture as to blind himself permanently to the virtues of the classical styles. As for music, his ear was true and his voice good: in the Boys' Brigade he was often called on, when an instrument was lacking, to introduce the singing of a hymn with a solo rendering of the first couplet: and in a number of tunes he was master of the bass part. He could divert the family by whistling a tune with perfect accuracy, and then deliberately and excruciatingly flattening the last note. His appreciation of music was, however, limited. He could never understand why in his later years the Victorian hymn-tunes he had grown up with were dismissed as sentimental: for him that would be no defect. In fact, his scheme of duties allowed no time for listening to music as a recreation, and he knew few of the works of the great composers. In literature, too, he remained a romantic: the revived interest in Donne, Dryden, Pope, etc. left him cold. He read all the great Victorian novelists, but few twentieth-century authors, though in his last years he found P.G. Wodehouse refreshingly diverting.

These limitations, joined with his total abstention from alcohol, his vegetarianism, and strict views on sexual morality, might seem to suggest an austere and joyless man: nothing could be more wrong. He had a hearty enjoyment of the simple pleasures of physical exercise, natural scenery, food and drink, and especially of family life and personal friendship, a lively sense of humour, and a boyish delight in the preposterous and absurd. He was an excellent conversationalist and story-teller, and no one ever found his company other than entertaining. He was unfailingly courteous, and to women the perfect gentleman. His strong moral sense made him frequently critical of the conduct and opinions of others, but with few exceptions his total sincerity and warm-hearted concern disarmed any resentment.

His love of method and of the ordered life penetrated into every department of his activity. He showed the same carefully planned efficiency in, for example, the pressing and mounting of wild flowers, the packing of a rucksack or suitcase, or the organization of the commissariat of a Boys' Brigade camp, as in the preparation of a treatise or discourse.

His last years were clouded by ill-health, sorrow and anxiety. The eventual fulfilment of his great ambition, so often disappointed, to return to Mansfield, did not bring with it the expected measure of satisfaction. The years which followed, though not without their joys and triumphs, were overcast by personal differences, and by the not infrequent bouts of illness which interrupted the performance of his duties. He was grievously disturbed by the darkening world scene, and when it came the tragedy of the Second World War. Always soft-hearted, he could lie awake at night haunted by this or that instance of suffering inflicted by battle or persecution. There were family worries too: for instance, his younger son for a time believed lost, then for four years a prisoner of war. Constitutionally he had always been liable to depression and anxiety, and though he strove through prayer and meditation for mental peace, he never wholly achieved it. His observance since youth of regular hours, daily exercise and a sober diet, his compliance, albeit reluctant, with the restrictions imposed by the doctor, and my mother's devoted care might delay, but could not prevent the premature failure of his heart and vascular system, assisted, no doubt, by his propensity to worry about this and everything else. The fact is that his feelings were so sensitive and his consciousness of duty so keen and unremitting that he was never able thoroughly to relax. This combination, to be sure, gave him the motive and the means to achieve so much, but it also used up his psychosomatic resources too rapidly to allow of a long span of life. He faced his approaching end with a mixture of confidence that he was in the hands of a beneficent God, and a touch of defiance – half jocularly, he dismissed evasion of the prospect with a favourite quotation: 'Should such a man as I flee?'

He died in the height of his mental powers, when he had much still to contribute. He had, for example, projected a discussion of legalism in religion, had collected a mass of material for a study of man's duty to animals, had contemplated a book of his sermons, under the title *Eternal Things*, and had written part of the second volume of his history of Smyrna. Had he been spared for a few more years, he might well have completed all these projects, and made valuable contributions towards the solving, or at least the better understanding, of some of the religious and ethical problems of the post-war world. He would have followed with close interest and concern the further careers of his children, and witnessed the birth of more of his nine grandchildren. Others would have benefited from his wisdom. But his health could not have been other than precarious, and there would have been much to distress as well as to delight him. We cannot perhaps entirely regret that his life ended when it did.

27 Gayfield Square,   Theodore John Cadoux
Edinburgh,
April 1987.

Preface

This book has arisen out of a longstanding connection with the Cadoux family. My father, Harold Kaye, was a student under C.J. Cadoux at the Yorkshire United Independent College in the 1920s, and our two families later developed a friendship which has continued ever since. Though the book has its origin in that friendship, it has developed into a critical biography, with some attempt to assess the significance of C.J.Cadoux's thought, much of it relevant to issues being debated today.

Dr Theodore Cadoux has been unstinting in his help and meticulous criticism of the text, and has undertaken much of the practical work connected with the publication of this book. I should like to thank him and his two sisters, Ruth Wickett and Joan Armstrong, for all their support and encouragement, and Aldyth Cadoux for kind hospitality when I began work on this project.

I owe a considerable debt to Professor John McManners, now of All Souls College, Oxford, for his generous help and advice with the text.

I should also like to acknowledge kind help from the following: Kenneth Anderson, Dafydd Ap-Thomas, Alma Bartholomew (Librarian of Mansfield College, Oxford), Malcolm Bligh, Wilfred and Joan Bligh, Sir Francis Boyd (for permission to quote from his Smyrna diary), Denis Britton, Lilian Cadoux (Mrs Harold Cadoux), George Caird, Geoffrey Carnall, Margaret Cullen, W.T.Pennar Davies, Harry Escott, John Fenton, H.W.Fuller, Alan Gilderdale, Harold Greenwood, Rachel Heaton (for permission to quote from unpublished letters of her father, C.H.Dodd), Donald Norwood, Geoffrey Nuttall, Mary Osborn, Margaret Sykes, Roger Tomes, Anthony Tucker, Kenneth Wadsworth, Alec Whitehouse, Harold Wickings and George Williams. And I wish to thank the Governing Body of Mansfield College, Oxford, for permission to quote from the College records.

Finally, I wish to thank my sister, Rosalind Kaye, for her support and wise advice; and I dedicate this work to the memory of my mother, Kathleen Kaye, who gave valuable criticism in the early stages of this work, but who sadly did not live to see it completed.

Oxford, April 1987   ELAINE KAYE

Early life
1883–1902

CECIL JOHN CADOUX was born on 24 May 1883 in Smyrna (now Izmir), Turkey. His father, William Henry Cadoux, was a member of the British trading community in Smyrna, merchants who were taking advantage of the development of trade between Britain and the Levant.

The family were originally Huguenot refugees from France. The name Cadoux is French, and is still fairly widespread in France. Two families of this name appeared in Britain in the course of the eighteenth century. One of these is now represented only by descendants in the female line; some of them have taken the name Cadoux-Hudson. The other is that from which Cecil John came. Almost certainly both had a common origin in a single family of Huguenots who left their home in South-West France (where Protestantism was particularly strong), after the revocation of the Edict of Nantes in 1685 had made it difficult for Huguenots of any standing to remain. This family was of the middle class; it numbered, while in France, at least one pastor and one advocate. They wrote their name de Cadours or simply Cadours; it was, in fact, the name of a small town, still so called, about 20 miles north west of Toulouse. Members of the family lived in those times in the neighbouring towns of Monfort, Mauvezin, and Montauban, and there is still a Protestant of the name at Mauvezin. Elsewhere in France the name was borne by Catholics as well as Protestants, and, perhaps because of a different, or more than one different, derivation, was eventually spelled Cadoux. Those who emigrated to Britain adopted this spelling and their descendants have all kept the French pronunciation; they have also, with varying degrees of conviction, adhered to Protestantism.

Cecil John's family can be traced back as far as an Adolph Cadoux, who set up as a surgeon in Edinburgh about 1770 and married a Miss Maclean. After his (probably premature) death in 1780 his widow moved to London, where her only son Matthew (1772–1854) worked as a clerk in William Deacon's Bank. Of his three sons only the eldest, John Henry (1806–1882) – Cecil John's grandfather – lived beyond his twenties.

Dissent, independence and a strong moral conscience ran strongly in the Cadoux veins, and Cecil John inherited his full share. Two of his relatives were, or had been, Congregational ministers. John Henry, his grandfather, served as minister of Wethersfield Congregational Church, Essex, for 32 years. Edward Henry (1853–1921), his uncle, trained for the ministry at Spring Hill College (forerunner of Mansfield College, Oxford) and was in the year of Cecil John's birth about to embark on his first pastorate at Warsash, near Southampton. Though William Henry, Cecil John's father, remained in commerce throughout his life, he twice gave serious consideration to taking up more specifically religious work.

William Henry originally went to Smyrna as the first British manager of MacAndrews and Forbes,[1] one of the firms which arranged the export and sale of Turkish goods to London. He was principally concerned with the export of cotton, emery stone and fruit. When he married in 1866, he took his bride out to Smyrna with him. He established a good reputation during his 19 years there, a reputation which stood him in good stead when he came to set up his own business.

William Cadoux's wife was born Emma Temple, daughter of Josiah Temple, Keeper of the Guildhall, London, in succession to his brother and father. The Temple family lived in Camberwell in comfortable style. William and Emma had met at the wedding of a mutual friend in April 1861, and apparently fell in love at first sight. William Cadoux was employed by a Quaker stockbroker at the time, but was plagued with doubts as to whether working on the Stock Exchange was 'entirely consistent with Christian principles'; he wondered whether he should act on an inner prompting to become a missionary. The prospect that he might come to such a decision dismayed Emma's father and delayed the engagement, but not for long. By September they were engaged and William had abandoned his missionary aspirations; but it was another five years before they were actually married.

When Cecil John – always known in the family circle as Jack – was born in May 1883, his parents were both 42. They already had a considerable family. There were five surviving children: Ida was thirteen, Herbert eleven, Constance ten, Arthur almost nine, and Ethelwyn (Effie) almost two. Two other daughters, one of them the

---

[1] See R. S. Harrison *A History of MacAndrews and Forbes Company 1850-1950* (1953).

eldest child, had died within a month of each other in 1879, and another died within the following eighteen months. Two further children were to complete the family circle within the next four years.

Fifty years later, the eldest surviving daughter, Ida, wrote her memory of the days preceding Cecil John's birth:

> About 3 days before, Mother had a very bad attack of asthma one night, so bad that the old Nurse – defying all convention and the Turkish night patrol – stumbled through the Smyrna streets at midnight to fetch Mr Eppstein – Maurice – and another medical Dr Levi Prinski Scott. Maurice very kindly walked to the other end of the town to fetch our Eichstorff. I can well remember poor F[ather] sobbing and praying – while we four stood around shivering in our nighties expecting her to die every moment.

However, Emma Cadoux's ninth baby arrived safely, and mother and son soon grew stronger. Two months later the new member of the family was baptised by Maurice Eppstein, the acting British Chaplain in Smyrna, and was registered as a British subject.

On the day of Jack's baptism – 24 July – William Cadoux resigned from his service with MacAndrews and Forbes, on the grounds of ill health. It meant returning to England and an uncertain future, but there were relatives to offer help. Early in August, the family furniture was sold by auction, and on the next day the whole family sailed for Liverpool in the ss 'Osiris'.

Jack cannot have remembered anything of Smyrna, but he was proud of having been born there and later wrote a history of the city; in the preface to that published work[1] he referred to it as 'inexpressibly dear as the place where my revered parents had their home for seventeen years'. He regretted deeply the substitution of Turkish names for Greek ones after the first world war, and he refused to call his birthplace 'Izmir'; 'this alteration of geographical names not only occasions difficulty to map-users, but is a needless aggravation of the nationalistic pride and aggressiveness which were generated by the Great War and its aftermath'. It was always Smyrna to him. His return visit to the city in 1930 was a kind of pilgrimage as well as a search for information and proved a happy and rewarding experience.

When the Cadoux family returned to England in 1883 they stayed temporarily in a small rented house in Countesthorpe, Leicestershire, accommodation found for them by William Cadoux's younger brother, Charles. They then began house-hunting in London, first in Blackheath and then in Croydon. In late October, they moved into Mead House in St James's Road, West Croydon – a substantial

[1] C. J. Cadoux *Ancient Smyrna* (1938), p.xiv.

four-storey semi-detached house in a residential area.

When William Cadoux had recovered reasonable health and re-established the family home in England, he began systematically to study for the Congregational ministry, following the example of his father and younger brother. His diary for 1884 lists his regular hours of work (a habit which his son inherited in full degree). Though working largely on his own, he received some help from the Reverend George Rogers, the retired principal of Pastors' College, who had once been an assistant to John Clayton at the King's Weigh House Church in the City of London – now a man of 85. This period of study lasted for a year, until William Cadoux began to realise that the ministry might not after all be his vocation. He thought it over at length, and in the autumn of 1885 wrote a paper, 'Why do I think that the exclusive ministry of God's word presents conditions which make it impossible for me to enter it as a sole occupation?'. He listed four reasons: he doubted his ability to preach regularly over a long period, he doubted his own strength for the task, he realised that a stipend of £120 per annum (the probable salary of an inexperienced minister) would not be sufficient to support his family, and he noted that there was no shortage of Congregational ministers. Finally, he concluded that 'by remaining in business I am not precluded from serving God'.

So William Cadoux returned to business. In May 1886 he set up on his own at 52 Lime Street, starting with his saved capital of £472 5s 9d, together with £1000 borrowed from his brother Alfred. He returned to the London-Smyrna trade, this time finding purchasers for goods shipped from Smyrna to London. His son, Arthur, who joined him in the business for a time, wrote that 'there is no doubt that his excellent reputation in Smyrna was a great asset', though 'it was an uphill struggle and his reputation for honesty kept away as much Levant business as it attracted . . .'. According to Arthur, he refused, on principle, a very lucrative offer for the sale of opium to the Dutch government, for smoking in their colonies. He traded chiefly in dried fruits, beans, barley, valonia, rugs and carpets, antimony ore and whetstone. In 1888, he became the selling agent for the Orient Trading Corporation's liquorice paste in the United Kingdom. The business seems to have done well, and the family was reasonably well provided for materially.

We do not know which church the family attended in Croydon, only that for a short period William Cadoux was appointed super-intendent of West Croydon Baptist Sunday School. We also know that he acted as corresponding secretary in England of the Greek Evangelical Union for seamen in Smyrna.

4

The family circle increased again in England. Maud was born in June 1884, and Bernard in December 1886. But a tragic loss occurred six months later. William's wife, Emma, was taken ill at the end of June 1887, and Effie, Jack and Maud were sent to the Eppsteins at Hackney, for the duration of her illness. She did not improve, and on 18 July she died at home in the presence of her husband and four eldest children of 'mitral disease of the heart'. 53 years later Connie wrote to Jack on the anniversary of their mother's death:

> It was a very hot July afternoon and we four elder ones were all in the room; Father too and the trained nurse who was a dear. Our poor darling Mother was just lying back in an easy chair practically unconscious and I just remember the nurse telling us it was all over after an hour or two of sad watching on the part of us four awestruck children.

She added:

> Don't repeat all this, it is too sacred.

Jack was only four, and the youngest child, Bernard, was only seven months old. The loss of his mother at such a young age cannot but have deeply affected Jack, though it was not something he talked or wrote about. He was always a person who needed to give and receive affection in large measure, and as he grew up he had to search for what he had missed in other ways.

William Cadoux seems to have accepted his loss stoically and continued to build up his business. The organisation of the household was now taken over by Emma's sister, Beatrice Temple, and by the two eldest girls, Ida and Connie; there was other help with the domestic work. Materially the household carried on as before, and the elder children looked after the younger ones.

Soon the family moved to North Park, another part of Croydon, and Jack was sent to Stamford House School. A further tragedy hit the family two summers later when they were on holiday on Hayling Island. Effie was taken ill with a white patch on her throat; five days later she died of diphtheria at the age of nine.

Herbert, the eldest boy, had joined his father in business at Lime Street, but after his mother died he moved to a post at Messrs Simons Bros, Steel and Iron Forging Company, and Arthur, now thirteen, joined the family business instead. In 1888 Herbert went out to Oudjari in the Caucasus; he stayed for eight years, working for the Orient Trading Corporation, and living a lonely, hard-working though interesting life. Long letters came from him to Jack and other members of the family. He showed a flair for and consuming interest in languages, and mastered as many as he could. In April 1893 he wrote, 'I am pursuing my Persian studies which I find eased by my knowledge of Tartar as a great many words are the same'; in June 1894 he wrote, 'I am the only white man in the place that can converse and write Russian and speak Tartar fluently'.

Herbert took seriously his position as the eldest brother, and offered to contribute towards the education of his younger brothers. For instance, in August 1893, he wrote home:

> Is Arthur still intent on college or university? If he cares to attend any lectures at King's College on any subject in the evening classes I wouldn't mind paying for a year the class fees.

In fact, it was some years yet before Arthur took up serious, sustained study, though his interest in social and theological issues was already lively and informed.

In 1894 the family moved again, this time a few miles north east to Catford – the reason is not clear. The house was 28 Vancouver Road, half-way between the stations at Catford and Forest Hill. Nearby, seven minutes' walk away, was a newly established public school for boys, St Dunstan's College. It had a large, impressive building, and had already established a sound educational tradition. It owed its existence to bequests made to the parish of St Dunstan-in-the-East, in the city of London, the income from which had recently been allocated for the establishment of a school as the result of a settlement in the Court of Chancery in 1883. It first opened its doors on 1 October 1888, and soon had 400 day boys and 40 boarders. In September 1894 Jack Cadoux became a pupil there.

He did well at school academically, particularly in languages. At the age of fourteen, he was already showing special aptitudes; his father wrote to him (26 March 1897) from Brooklyn, on one of his regular business trips:

> My dear little boy, it is no use your getting angry with your master, and saying that he gases. Surely if he is talking about the lesson, there must be something to be learned from it. I am glad to see you are first in English, you don't say where you are in French. If you really *are* doing your best in arithmetic it cannot be helped that you are 20th, though I would like to see you higher. *However try on.*

He was not only winning prizes for English and foreign languages, but also for drawing, for which he undoubtedly had a gift. Indeed for some time he nourished an ambition to be an architect.

But the subject which fired his imagination most was ancient history. As he wrote later on, 'I was mad then, as I always have been, on Ancient History'. Throughout his life, ancient history was an absorbing interest, and a subject to which he made a notable scholarly contribution.

He took the University of London matriculation examination in the summer of 1899 and was successful. When he entered the sixth form after the holiday he began to specialise in languages – French, Latin and Greek – a grounding which served him well in later years.

Seven years later he wrote about his schooldays in a memo about his earlier life:

> Owing largely to my own fault, my school experiences were not of the happiest. Though keen and interested in the work I never thoroughly entered into the games and for some time I had had the painful consciousness that it was too late to make a start. I was a prefect and in the VI but this, if anything, served but to make my mistakes more evident. However I found much to take an interest in at school, and now that the past is passed, I take pleasure in recalling my schooldays to mind.

He made many friends there, and some of them remained friends for life. There was Fred Baggs, who became a commercial traveller and whose schoolboy letters to 'Amicus Jackricus' survive among the Cadoux papers; A.C. Bouquet, who later became a prolific writer on a wide range of theological and religious issues; Greville Hart; and others.

Two of the masters, especially, earned his respect and even veneration – R.W. Philpott and R.S. Bate, and he renewed contact with them in later years. Their photographs, along with those of his Mansfield tutors, hung on the walls of his study as those to whom he owed most in the development and formation of his mind. He always felt a great sense of loyalty and gratitude to his teachers; *pietas* was a strong instinct in him.

William Cadoux's ill-health had now returned, and his condition rapidly deteriorated during the summer of 1899. He recalled Herbert to help run his business which he could no longer manage alone; when the family went on holiday to Margate, William Cadoux had to be wheeled along the front in a bath chair. The summer and autumn brought no alleviation, and finally on 20 November he died while staying at Ventnor, on the Isle of Wight, of a pleural effusion; he was only 59.

Throughout his life, Jack retained the utmost respect for his father as a kind and devout man. The Bible which his father had given him when he was seven years old had inscribed on the front page the quotation, 'Casting all your anxiety upon Him, for He careth for you' (*I Peter* 5.7); it was a dedication to which he frequently referred in later life, and a great source of strength to him.

His father had held the evangelical beliefs common to Non-conformists of his time. He knew the Bible well, but had little knowledge of Biblical criticism. He was essentially a fundamentalist who accepted the literal teaching of the Bible. In an article[1] written a few months before his own death, Jack Cadoux wrote that he hoped that modern fundamentalists would have the good sense to deal with their belief in eternal hell fire in the same way as 'my fundamentalist father did – namely, never rub it in, but put all their stress on the redeeming love of God, and leave it at that'. As he grew older, Jack could not accept his father's fundamentalist beliefs, but was able to reconcile his acceptance of Biblical criticism and liberal theology with loyalty to his father by making a distinction between the 'foundation-realities' (his father's faith) and 'doctrine' (reflection on that faith and experience), which the Christian mind was free to sift, re-formulate or even abandon as its grasp of truth developed and expanded. This was to form the theme of a good deal of his later thought.

Herbert was now the head of the family of seven. He had already made, and was to continue to make, many sacrifices for his family. He had left Oudjari at the end of 1896 because he could not work happily with his superior. Since 1897 he had been working in Rhodesia for Rhodesia Transport Ltd, and then as a surveyor; he enjoyed the freedom and outdoor life, and it was hard to give all this up when his father summoned him to help in London. Jack wrote later that 'compliance with his father's entreaty must have been a sore trial and sacrifice for him . . . Almost at every step, he was thwarted and his inclinations and ambitions denied to him'. Now at least Herbert was free, when he had seen the family settled again, to go back to the Levant. Ida, now thirty, had married Frederick Neve in 1896; they lived in Tonbridge and were expecting their first child. Beatrice Temple had now left the Cadoux household to get married, and so Connie, now 27, was left to run the home. Arthur was 25; after a serious illness he had moved to South Africa, but corresponded regularly with Jack. Then there were the three youngest children still at school – Jack who was 16, Maud 15 and Bernard 12. An old friend who was now the headmaster of Reading School offered to complete the education of Jack and Bernard. Herbert, now in charge, accepted the offer as far as Bernard was concerned, but let Jack remain at St Dunstan's. Jack wrote later:

> In January 1900 the younger brother with whom I had so long lived and quarrelled without ever appreciating what he might

[1] In *The Christian World* 6 February 1947.

have gained by solid sympathy and friendship was parted from me to become glorified in my eyes as boarder at a large public school in true storybook style.

There were now more changes. The family moved about a mile away from Vancouver Road to Derby Villas in Forest Hill. It was decided that Jack should leave St Dunstan's after one year in the sixth form (thus ruling out the possibility of a university career for the time being) and prepare for the competitive examination for junior appointments in the supply and accounting departments of the Admiralty. For this purpose, he now began to travel up to London every day to the Strand School (a part of King's College) so that he could attend the civil service day classes from September 1900. He did not particularly enjoy it, for 'the building was dark and dismal – the faces all strange – the work uninteresting – my attempts at gymnastics humiliating'. He wrote a depressed letter to Arthur, who in reply 'gave me a piece of advice which I should have done well to follow – "Forget not the ample smile" . . . "It taketh at a jump ditches that solemnity hath to wade . . ."'. But if he did not enjoy it, at least he was successful; after four terms there he had risen to first place in most subjects, and had come second out of 35 candidates in the competitive entrance examination for the Admiralty. Towards the end of January 1902 he received a letter telling him that he had been appointed an Assistant Victualling Store Officer at the Admiralty in Whitehall, and ordering him to report for duty to the Director of Victualling on the 30th.

He was a serious young man who drove himself hard. He had a large measure of idealism and a burning desire to live a good life and to persuade others to do the same. He was also an avid reader; Bernard complained in a letter from Reading School, 'Why don't you write? Ancient History, I suppose . . . I shall have to sneak all your books before you go [on holiday] but even if I did, you'd buy some more down there'. But he was not a loner and as much as reading he loved discussing and arguing, and if possible, persuading others to see the truth as he saw it.

II

At the Admiralty
1902–1911

FOR THE NEXT nine and a half years, Cadoux's working days were spent as a civil servant at the Admiralty. It was not a career which particularly appealed to him, though he did the work well and was liked and respected there. The greatest satisfaction in his life came not from his daily work but from his reading and study, and his work with boys in the Boys' Brigade and Sunday School. He worked prodigiously hard and in much of his spare time lived the life of a scholar.

Every weekday he travelled up to Whitehall from Forest Hill, with occasional spells working at Portsmouth. He began by working in the victualling department, then moved to accounts, finally returning to the victualling department. It became his responsibility to supervise a group of men older than himself, all working in the same room; the piles of books in use at any one time provided a convenient screen for other activities, and Cadoux had a hard time trying to persuade or exhort his staff to work to his own exacting standards. He confided little to his diary (begun in 1903) about his work, except to express doubts about it and to long for other work which would not 'grate upon conscience as the Admiralty does'.

Like many who became prominent pacifists in the early part of the twentieth century, Cadoux was influenced both by the impact of the Boer War and by the writings of Tolstoy. In 1901, while the Boer War was still continuing, he began attending a Young Men's Class on Sundays at Trinity Congregational Church, Catford. The leader of the class was a Mr Hoyles; 'the South African war was still in progress and my dissatisfaction with patriotism gathered much force from my hearing Mr Hoyles' opinions expressed in the class', Cadoux wrote in a memo of 1906, and when Mr Hoyles died in June of that year, 'I felt I had lost a kind friend and a wise adviser'.

1901 was the year in which the word 'pacifist' was first used, at an international peace conference held in Glasgow, though a more precise meaning of the word, and of the variant 'pacificist' which the

British representatives tried to establish in opposition to the French invention of 'pacifist', had to await the experience of individuals in two world wars.[1]

Cadoux's concern about the violence and hatred implicit in the mindless patriotic jingoism expressed by many during the Boer War was further stirred, as happened to many sensitive, thoughtful people, by reading Tolstoy's later works. Tolstoy's *Resurrection* was finished in 1899 and led to his formal excommunication from the Russian church early in 1901. Herbert Cadoux, by this time in Baghdad, obtained a copy and read it; he wrote to his brother in August 1903 and recommended that he read it 'more or less in private'. Cadoux bought a copy the same day as Herbert's letter arrived and started on it at once.

That autumn he suffered from feelings of depression. 'Got the utter pip', he wrote in his diary on 13 November – it was one of his favourite expressions – '. . . life seemed void of joy, interest and human sympathy'. This was no doubt partly influenced by the recurrent ill-health which beset him at this period of his life. By the end of the month, however, he wrote in his diary, 'I arrive at the idea that the highest and most ideal aim of Life and Being is *Love* and the joy that Love brings. This may afford some renewed interest again'. A fortnight later, he had a long talk with 'Pater' Arkell (Henry Arkell), minister of Trinity Congregational Church, and decided to become a member.

Six months after reading *Resurrection*, Cadoux bought and read Tolstoy's *The Kingdom of God is Within You*, a book which called for the unconditional renunciation of violence in every form. Both books had a deep influence on him, and confirmed him in his own conclusions about the teaching of the Synoptic Gospels. They led him to carry on a lengthy correspondence with Arthur about civilisation and the proper conduct of civilised societies. In November 1904 he finished a long letter to Arthur thus:

> I would not be taking so keen an interest in the matter, if it did not touch me personally so closely. The way in which it does so I have confided to very few; and I will now – with your leave – tell you in black and white some of the thoughts that are in my mind and of whose existence you may have already guessed.
>
> I want my life to be in accord with the laws of life laid down by Christ.
>
> Christ forbade violence – even in self-defence – teaching that

[1] See Martin Ceadel *Pacifism in Britain 1914-45* (1980) chapter 1 for an interesting discussion of this.

earthly injuries are really not injuries at all. Mt v 38–45, x 28–31, Lk xii 4, Mt xxvi 51–52, Lk xxii 49–51. This sentiment is corroborated by the actual practice of Jesus himself, of the Apostles, and of the Christian martyrs.

Therefore war is forbidden by Christ and is wrong. Therefore the maintenance of armaments is wrong. I am spending my labour in maintaining an armament which I hold to be inconsistent with my conscience as a Xtian. Why don't I chuck it up? Because to do so would provoke too much bitterness of feeling (and reasonable bitterness too from one pt of view) in those to whom I am under the greatest obligations for kindness shown towards me in the past. My question is – Is this sufficient reason to warrant a compromise between my conscience and circumstances?

This commitment to non-violence as the way of life demanded by obedience to the Gospels was one from which he never wavered throughout his life, though in later years he realised that the direct application of Jesus' teaching to contemporary ethical problems presented serious difficulties. From this time until the end of his life he spent a good deal of time, energy and thought in grappling with these difficulties. He was now beginning to call in question the morality of his daily work, though for the time being he continued with it.

Arthur never accepted his brother's arguments on this subject, and he wrote a long letter on New Year's Day 1905 putting the contrary point of view. The subject frequently recurred in their correspondence. Despite this disagreement, Arthur was the brother closest to Cadoux in friendship and interest. He had been in South Africa since 1898, first of all in business, but since the end of 1903 preparing to enter the Congregational ministry. He was a great support to Jack, and the two brothers were able to conduct an argument and to disagree without any rift or ill-feeling.

Cadoux's relationships with his two other brothers were not so easy. Herbert as head of the family was continuing to take his responsibilities seriously. Several times he asked his brother to regard him as a 'chum adviser and confidant' but it is not clear that the invitation was ever accepted. As Cadoux himself began to formulate and declare those strong convictions which in future always characterised him, he wanted to influence his younger brother and sister for what he believed to be their good. Not surprisingly, they resisted the attempt. Whatever theories of harmonious relationships Cadoux was working out with his intellect, he was finding very difficult to put into practice. In September 1903 he wrote in his diary, 'The question of living peaceably with Connie, Maud and Bernard is becoming daily more and more of a puzzle to me'. As the year progressed, there were more and more references to quarrels at home. A month or two later, he wrote in his diary, 'I feel a strange dissatisfaction about everything'.

Early in 1904, Herbert wrote to his brother about his attitude towards the family:

> I have watched with interest amd pleasure the growth of your mind and character the last five years and admire the perseverance and application which has obtained you a good position.
>
> It has also been not unpleasant to note the development of certain religious and moral qualities which must ever give vigour and strength to a man's character.
>
> Alongside these I have watched, I must confess with a little apprehension, the growth of just a little narrowness of view, a desire to mould everyone's ideas into your own, even a slight contempt, shall I say, for the opinions of those who have seen you pass from boyhood to youth and from youth to manhood.

This led to a lengthy, difficult correspondence. Herbert persuaded his brother to promise not to try to influence Bernard's and Maud's religious ideas and practices – a promise from which he soon asked leave to be released. On Christmas Day, 1904, Herbert wrote to him from Elisavetpol:

> . . . on religious subjects, I think your better self or rather your kindlier self is blinded not seldom by bursts of zeal, which make the attainment of the immediate object you have in view, of such supreme importance in your eyes that other people's feelings are apt to be entirely neglected.

Bernard was quite able to resist Jack's attempts to influence him. He replied to one of his brother's letters about their difficulty in getting on happily:

> As you say, we perhaps don't get on together as well as we might, but I don't see that the fact that we are all stokers, stoking away, and we don't see the results but we simply stoke, helps us. I think the main reason is that I cannot stand it when you try to 'dominere' over me. So if you would stop that we should be alright.

There were no hard feelings in their relationship, and they got on well enough to enjoy walking tours together. Maud was equally able to hold her own.

Connie was married in July 1904 to Adam Brown Kelly, who was a consultant surgeon in Glasgow. He was the brother of Herbert's fiancée, and it seems that it was through this connection that they first met. They were married in what Jack called in his diary 'an impressive ceremony' at St John's Presbyterian Church, Forest Hill; Herbert gave Connie away, and Jack acted as usher. Jack wrote in his diary: 'The most important day! Severed from CON.' Connie had been a calming and caring influence in the household and her departure did not improve matters. Later that summer, Cadoux's diary records more quarrels and rows. On 3 August: 'Long and violent stormy talk with Herbert. His bitter blaming of me: cruel injustice, what have I done to deserve it!' On 22 August: 'I dash the latchkey down in a rage: it breaks the glass door!' The day before this entry, Herbert had left home again for the East; he was now working in Iraq, where MacAndrews and Forbes were planning to open another liquorice factory. The family home, which was kept up for another seventeen months, now consisted of Jack, Maud and Bernard (who had left school and was working for MacAndrews and Forbes) along with Katie Eppstein who kept house for them.

Cadoux was now 21. He was almost six feet tall, well-built, handsome with dark closely curled hair, a good forehead and clear features. He had had to wear glasses from quite an early age, but was not severely short-sighted. He cultivated what he described to his sons as 'a good soldierly bearing' almost to the end of his life.

The end of 1904 was a time of low spirits – 'in many ways the most unhappy year I have ever spent', he confided to his diary. He then stated his New Year resolutions:

> As I pause here at the beginning of the year, I mean to go forward with the following aims in view, which with God's help I shall attain:
> 1. To renounce a flesh diet.
> 2. To improve in music.
> 3. To serve the boys faithfully.
> 4. To find work which shall not grate upon conscience as the Admiralty does.
> 5. To master the 'old man' within me.
> 6. To learn and know more of Jesus, so as to become a better son of God and a better citizen of His kingdom.

Since the beginning of 1903 he had been taking a regular Sunday School class (of boys only – girls were taught separately) and a Boys' Brigade Bible class each week. Both these classes were based at Trinity Congregational Church. In addition, as a Boys' Brigade officer he attended at least one weekday evening meeting. In many ways these classes formed the focus of his life. The best weeks of each year throughout this period were the weeks of the Boys' Brigade camp in the Isle of Wight and the Sunday School camp at Minster in Kent. In the summer of 1904 (otherwise a year of depression), he had written in his diary on the day of his return home after the camp outing to Porchester, 'I could write pages of this day's delight but space fails . . . I have been on Mt Olumpos (of Transfiguration) 3 days. Now I have descended'. He used to act as quartermaster of the Boys' Brigade camps and enjoyed applying his Admiralty victualling experience to this smaller sphere.

The Boys' Brigade movement was founded in 1883 by William A. Smith, a member of the Scottish Free Church in Glasgow; it spread to England, where it was popular in the 1890s. The boys were usually from working class homes, and the officers middle class. The members wore uniform, with pill-box hats, and were taught marching and drilling, but without weapons. The Catford company was the 76th London: its captain was Roger Peacock. A survivor of that company remembers with pleasure

> many a Saturday afternoon or Bank Holiday spent on Hayles Common with a group of boys and young men playing Giants and Pigmies with a picnic tea at 'Mother Swathons', a café on the common. Cadoux had a fund of anecdotes which delighted his hearers. [1]

The Sunday School class, distinct from the Boys' Brigade class, was part of a network of boys' classes in south east London which owed its inspiration to Sydney Milledge. Milledge began organising Sunday classes for boys when he was in business in the city of London. When he began training for the Congregational ministry, he handed over the running of the group to one of his former pupils; from this class there developed a number of others, taken by boys themselves as they grew up. Several of these young leaders entered the ministry, and the friendships of the group were long-lasting. This circle, including Sydney Milledge himself (21 years older than Cadoux), Stanley Shrubsole and Charlton Short, offered Cadoux great support and encouragement at a critical time of his life.

Cadoux made many lifelong friends among the boys he taught; one of them, Horace Fuller, later wrote, 'I was told that Trinity had a Bible class leader who was different – and he was'. What was different? In the first place, his intellect and his accumulation of knowledge were formidable. Like all good teachers, he was himself excited by learning, to which he devoted so much of his spare time. Second was his concern that 'his boys' should be brought into contact with, and follow, the best ideals in life. In his boys' classes this passionate desire

[1] H. W. Fuller, letter to author, March 1982.

to persuade others to recognize the truth as he had discovered it did not produce conflict as in his own family, but in the long run earned him respect and gratitude. The boys did not always follow his guidance, and they were not let off lightly when they chose and followed a different path (that is, they would have to face long discussion and argument) but they did not fail to recognise Cadoux's honesty, dedication and genuine warmth of friendship. He sent birthday and Christmas cards to all members of his class, and for those who responded to his friendship the practice was continued for the rest of his life.

Some years later, when he had begun full-time theological training at Mansfield College, he wrote a long letter[1] to some of his former class members and colleagues who were continuing the boys' classes at Catford, encouraging them and offering them 'a measure of impulse and inspiration' for the new season's work. It throws much light on the way in which he had viewed his own work with these classes.

Though he recognised that each boy was different, and that one had to be sensitive to the individual, and though each teacher was also different, Cadoux thought that helpful guidelines could be drawn up. He listed four stages in leading boys towards an understanding, and if possible, acceptance of the Christian faith. First, there was 'the stage of friendship pure and simple', exemplified for the boys from Catford in the hikes, outings, games, camps and general fun as well as informal talks and kindness. Simultaneously there would be specific teaching – 'the simple and vivid narratives of the Old Testament are well in keeping with the general method of treatment necessary at this stage'. After this phase, which should include 'the encouragement – by precept and example – of the elementary Christian virtues (like truthfulness, generosity, sportsmanship, kindness, loyalty) and the habits of Bible reading and prayer', there would be a year devoted to lessons on the life of Jesus:

> Explain as you go along just so much of Jesus' ethical and religious teaching as seems to you to be clear and useful to the Boy's mind. Above all, give the story of the Betrayal, Trial and Crucifixion in the fullest possible detail. I speak thus strongly because it is my firm conviction, that the contemplation of the Passion of Jesus, by means of pictures or verbal descriptions, is the first solemn introduction of the human soul to that great event which God uses to convince man of His amazing love.

The later stage should involve working through 'the substance of what Christian Discipleship means for a boy, under present and probable

[1] 15 October 1912, in *The Cadoux Papers*.

future conditions', and bringing a boy to accept that discipleship. This needed 'very delicate handling', but could not be avoided. In this memo of 1912, Cadoux stated that he now regarded it 'as more important than I used to, that Boys should be taught to attend service somewhere regularly at least once every Sunday'.

There is of course no ideal scheme for introducing young people to spiritual ideals and the Christian faith and way of life, and each generation, if not each decade, has to work through to its own solution. But sincerity, honesty and devotion can be detected with unerring accuracy by the young, and these, as well as any particular method, will make their own appeal to a new generation. When these qualities are united with a formidable intellect which can formulate ideas and principles simply and clearly, then there is opened up the possibility of an influential and inspiring ministry to young people. This is what Cadoux could offer to his classes, and they responded to it eagerly. As another member of his class, Harold Bligh, wrote after Cadoux's death, '. . . more than any other man he shaped my ideals in youth'. Others could have said the same.

The natural high spirits of the boys meant that the work was never plain sailing; some of them found Cadoux too dogmatic, or too pressing in his attempts to influence them. Cadoux's growing conviction that physical violence and more especially war could not be reconciled with the Christian faith led him into long arguments, not only with the boys, but also with his fellow officers. But he found the work immensely enjoyable and satisfying, and never spared himself over the preparation of lessons and talks. In the process, he was furthering his own theological education.

At this stage of his life, it was probably true that he found emotional as well as intellectual satisfaction in his work with boys. His closest friendships were with his colleagues there – especially Charlton Short, whose father was the secretary of Sydenham Congregational Church – and he cared for the boys in his charge as he would like to have been able to care for his own younger brother.

The year 1905 was not much happier than the previous one. He continued to feel unsettled in his work at the Admiralty, and at one time thought of joining the Salvation Army. After one or two visits to Salvation Army meetings, he wrote in his diary:

> These people do a splendid social work, and are earnest and sincere in the theology they preach; but it is a theology admirably adapted and suited to them only; others must needs state what truth they know in other terms.[1]

[1] 16 September 1905.

Then he began to think about fruit farming in Canada, and wrote to a friend who had recently emigrated there. The friend discouraged him, saying that fruit farming might 'satisfy the dictates of your conscience' but would require a good deal of capital whose yield would be uncertain. In any case, though Cadoux was a competent gardener, he had no great love for working outdoors. It was an attractive idea in theory for one influenced by the ideas of Tolstoy ('is it my duty to throw up wealth and become a poor worker?' he confided to his diary on 23 June), but hardly appropriate for one of his temperament and ability.

In July, his superior at the Admiralty gave him the task of requisitioning some glassware for the use of the Prince and Princess of Wales. 'My conscience won't let me do it', he wrote in his diary; 'awaiting the thunderbolt of his wrath to fall'. Nothing happened, and he was left to nurse his socialist conscience alone.

After Connie's marriage and departure, the family was less happy; Jack's arguments with Herbert by letter continued in the spring of 1905. The two brothers were still arguing about Jack's attempted influence over Maud and Bernard, and some hard words had been exchanged in correspondence between them. Herbert was back in Smyrna in the early part of 1905, but returned for his wedding to Anna Kelly in September. Jack hesitated at first about accepting Herbert's invitation to the wedding, but a letter[1] from Ida in Tonbridge finally persuaded him to go. 'He has given up some of the best years of his life for you all and has known so little home life of late years, and I think it is surely the least one can do to show our sympathy in his long-delayed happiness'. He was persuaded by this, and on 6 October caught the over-night train to Glasgow in order to attend the wedding the following day. Herbert was duly married to Anna Kelly, the sister of Connie's husband; the Cadoux family were reunited for the occasion, and as it turned out, this was the last time that Herbert and his brothers and sisters were all together.

Towards the end of 1905 family relationships grew even worse. Herbert, indignant at Jack's wish to be released from his promise (not to try to impose his views on Maud and Bernard), had ceased to write to him. Maud, much to Jack's disapproval, was earning a little money doing fashion drawings for ladies' magazines. Bernard was working at MacAndrews and Forbes' London office. The three did not get on, and eventually it was decided that the family home should be given up; and Maud and Bernard, with Herbert's knowledge and approval, decided to seek lodgings separately from Jack. Apart from the

[1] 21 September 1905.

quarrels, Herbert may have decided that the house was too large for three unmarried people, and that after his own marriage he could no longer afford to contribute to the rent. The family home was given up in December – a traumatic experience for Jack. At the end of his diary for the year he wrote that he had 'suffered acutely from my attitude at home; feeling myself and being regarded as an unimportant nonentity soon to be discarded'; and in a letter to Arthur in February 1906 he reviewed the whole development thus:

> During the last year or so, I have been unhappily drifting deeper and deeper into an unfortunate misunderstanding with Bert – the origin and progress of which I must not describe in detail now. The sum of the matter was this – Bert got the idea (perhaps partly well-founded) that my keenness on religious matters was getting dangerous, that what he called my intolerance was making life unhappy for the rest of the household, and that my influence if successful would be pernicious in its results. In October 1904, before going abroad, he got me to give him a promise which (tho' given and accepted in good faith) I found I could not keep, and was obliged to tell him I must be released from. I am afraid that this vexed him deeply, and he has since shewn a noticeable aloofness towards me, even in personal intercourse when he has been at home. He has not written to me since he wrote a year ago to signify his disgust at my breach of faith. The outcome was that when the home was dissolved in December, I was left to conclude that I was to find lodgings separate from M and B. They have both gone to board with two rich old maids at Lordship Lane (near Dulwich) – a place too expensive and too far away from the SS and the BB for me to have gone too. I am at present digging over a bookseller's shop and find myself settling down comfortably.

He went on to express his concern about Bernard, who was spending all his spare time learning shorthand, and whose 'regard for Bert has somehow produced in his mind a deification of business obligations'.

For the next five years he lived in 'digs' in the Forest Hill area. He felt lonely at first, but as time went on he would spend part of each Sunday with Bernard and Maud, going to church and then for walks with them.

He found relief from his depression in purposeful activity and study. Apart from the Admiralty and his boys' classes, he was taking piano lessons from his cousin Wynnie Hill (a kind and supportive friend to him in all his moods), and he was attending Boys' Brigade ambulance lectures, arranging family papers and preparing a life of his father, and reading as much as possible. He described his life as 'full to overflowing'.

The summer camps, with their companionship, fun and open-air life, were some of the happiest days of Cadoux's life. His enjoyment of puns, limericks and simple humour were given ample rein in the camp newspaper, *The Chaffinch*, which he produced at the Boys' Brigade camps.

The issue for 28 July 1905 included the following notice:

GRAND CONCERT

Tonight   All are welcome

The Komikle Kooks will give an Exhibition of Punimosity.
Mr Shrubberdike will oblige with stale stuff.
Mr Peacockadouxdaldoux will sing sweet sonorous *symphonies*.

Ten days later the following appeared:

The Wesleyans of Sandown were anxious to have some patches for their trousers and consequently showed the company into sticky seats, which removed portions of our trousers.

In the early summer of 1906 Herbert died suddenly of an aortic aneurism at Elisavetpol in the Caucasus. The previous winter had been hard for him. He had been alone in Elisavetpol, for Anna, his new wife, did not join him there until the late spring of 1906, and he was living in the context of recurrent disputes, if not civil war, between Russians and Armenians; he endured a good deal of nervous strain and anxiety, which his family believed contributed to his death. He was almost 35 and had been married for only eight months; for most of those months he and his wife had been apart. He had worked very hard for his family, had had to wait a long time for the possibility of marriage, and had never been able to concentrate for long on his real interest – midle eastern languages, history and geography. It was a hard blow for his brothers and sisters and his widow when he died so suddenly, and Jack felt that their unsettled differences made acceptance of this tragedy even more difficult. In spite of the differences he had a great admiration and respect for his brother, and recognised that he had made great sacrifices for them all. Herbert's body was brought back to England; he was buried in Norwood cemetery after a funeral at Forest Hill. Jack borrowed something appropriate to wear for the occasion after Ida and Bernard had pleaded with him to wear 'orthodox funeral clothing' so as not to upset other members of the family. This tragedy did bring the family closer together again – Jack even interested Bernard in joining him in the fruit farming idea in Canada, but the idea came to nothing. A few months later, Bernard was sent out by MacAndrews and Forbes to Smyrna, where he remained for three years, 'thus separating me', Cadoux wrote in his diary, 'from a life in whose welfare I am deeply and anxiously interested'.

It took time for these wounds to heal, but by the end of 1907, Cadoux could write in his diary, 'Time is healing the past. I have exchanged visits and loving letters with each and all of my kith and kin from time to time during the year'.

Meanwhile he was setting himself new objectives. On 21 February 1907 he recorded in his diary, 'I go to Library to see Inter-Arts syllabus – having provisionally decided to work up leisurely for degree'. For some time he had been planning and carrying out a systematic study of the Bible (reading three pages a day), of ancient history and of critical theology, together with careful preparation for his Sunday classes. What he thought of initially as a leisurely activity soon gathered momentum, and the more he studied the more he wanted to learn. It took him three years of part-time study as an external student, but eventually he achieved a first class in the London University Bachelor of Arts Pass examinations in Latin, Greek, Philosophy and History.

He continued to take his Sunday classes, preparing detailed schedules for study, and himself training the new generation of teachers. He also prepared for and took the civil service examinations (clerkships class 1) in the summer of 1909, in the hope of qualifying for a department other than the Admiralty. His position of 88th in those examinations was not good enough, and he had to come to terms with remaining in the Admiralty for the time being. A few days after receiving the result of the examination, he wrote in his diary:

> I come to feel that I can continue to serve in the Admiralty Victualling Dept without being inconsistent with my peace views. The Navy – right or wrong – is there – and, right or wrong, it may justly be given food and clothing. For this purpose an organised Dept is necessary, and therefore right.

His anti-war views were instead given a strong airing within the Boys' Brigade, and were a sore trial to Roger Peacock, the captain of the company. He wrote letters to Peacock protesting about 'militarising tendencies' in the Brigade, and he refused to read out notices about visits to military tournaments; he was banned from playing hymns because he would not also play the national anthem. Peacock complained that 'it is extremely unpleasant for me to live in the atmosphere of your strong and constant displeasure and to feel that I can hardly open my mouth without violating your susceptibilities and bringing down your wrath upon my head'. And then he underlined the paradox of the peacemakers: 'Is it any use pleading for peace and goodwill from one so warlike as yourself?' The disputes did not sever their relationship or respect for each other, however, and their friendship lasted a lifetime.

Thoughts of the ministry as his vocation were beginning to surface, especially after Arthur's return home. Arthur returned to England from South Africa in June 1908; he was already an ordained minister, but undertook further study in England before being called as minister to Belvedere Congregational Church near Erith in Kent. The two brothers enjoyed each other's company and found stimulus and inspiration in their discussions and sharing of ideas and problems. Arthur opened his home to Jack after his marriage to Bessie Asplin at the beginning of 1910.

Cadoux was also helped by the young minister of the Church in the Grove, Sydenham, the church he attended after the departure of Henry Arkell from Trinity Congregational Church, Catford, in 1907. George Darlaston was seven years older than Cadoux. After taking an English degree and lecturing for a year in Birmingham, he had trained for the Congregational ministry at Mansfield College, Oxford under Andrew Martin Fairbairn. He then won a travelling scholarship and went to Marburg, and to Berlin, where he listened to both Adolf Harnack and Otto Pfleiderer. He came to Sydenham, where he was ordained, in 1903. Henry Arkell had been something of a father figure; George Darlaston was more like another encouraging older brother to Cadoux, and his acute mind and experience of the frontiers of theology in Germany were immensely stimulating.

Study was continuing. On the day (3 December 1909) that he heard that he had passed the London University's BA degree he began working for the MA, by thesis and examination – taking as his subject the history of Smyrna. Arthur suggested this subject to him, and he had no hesitation in accepting it. 'Smyrna possessed the dual advantage of having been both an important city in ancient times and our common birthplace', he wrote later. It took him nearly eighteen months to complete; 'the essay filled 167 typed foolscap pages, and narrated the story of the city down to 180 AD'.[1] It was a study to which he returned from time to time, and eventually it formed the basis of his *Ancient Smyrna* (1938). It was his first opportunity to develop and cultivate the meticulous, scholarly, systematic methods of study for

[1] *Ancient Smyrna* (1938) p.vii.

which his teachers at St Dunstan's had laid the foundation. It was the basis of his future life of scholarship.

The same careful systematisation went into his collection and collation of family papers which he was pursuing at the same time. He seems never to have thrown a letter away, and often kept drafts of letters sent to others. His daily life was similarly ordered, with every available half hour allotted to purposeful study or activity.

At the beginning of 1910 he wrote in his diary a list of 'Irons in the fire': a page of the New Testament in English daily and the week's readings in Greek on Sundays, Geikie's *Life of Christ*, a harmony of the gospels, Rollin's *Ancient History*, Ruskin's *Elements of Drawing*, the thesis on Smyrna, the life of his father, the Boys' Brigade ambulance class, the Sunday School class, historical reading for the MA examinations, and the monthly *Review of Reviews*.

In September 1910 Cadoux recorded for the first time discussing with someone else – his friend Charlton Short – the possibility of entering the Christian ministry. The next month he talked it over with Darlaston, with Ida and with Arthur. He also wrote to his cousin Wynnie Hill about it, for in December she was offering words of encouragement: 'You know far better than I whether you will succeed as a pastor . . . With regard to your getting on with others – deacons for instance – personally I think that would be no difficulty – you are much more tolerant than formerly . . .'.

The idea had probably been in his subconscious mind for a long time. There was a family tradition of serving in the ministry. He had entered the Admiralty out of necessity rather than choice, appeared not to find it particularly interesting or fulfilling, and disliked and disapproved of the policy he was serving. He cannot have been ignorant of the naval arms race with Germany signified by the building of the Dreadnoughts. A good deal of his energy was going into resisting the ideals of patriotism and militarism which he felt he was serving. The work itself presented him with little intellectual challenge, and did not call upon his enormous reserves of ability and energy which were instead being channelled into other activities. For it was in his academic study and in his work for boys, closely connected with the church, that he found fulfilment. This must have suggested to him that his future lay in pastoral and academic work.

He was now – in the autumn of 1910 – aged 27. He had no family commitments, he was still in lodgings, and he was feeling generally dissatisfied and unsettled. There are hints that he was thinking about marriage in general, but he had not formed any particular friendships with girls. He was therefore free to respond to this challenge, a challenge which came not as a sudden strong and irresistible urge, but as a gradual realisation. There were practical problems in that he was not financially independent, and would need to win a scholarship to support himself; fortunately appropriate scholarships were available.

The next problem was where to apply. There were then eight colleges in England, as well as others in Wales and Scotland, which trained students for the Congregational ministry. Two of these – Hackney College and New College – were in London. The Principal of the first, P. T. Forsyth, was a great and creative theologian; but Cadoux does not seem to have considered application there. New College, under A. E. Garvie, might have seemed an obvious choice, especially as his friend Stanley Shrubsole was studying there. However, George Darlaston urged Cadoux to consider his old college, Mansfield, realising that Oxford could offer him a wide and stimulating company and range of thought.

In April 1911 Cadoux travelled with Darlaston, and two of Darlaston's friends, to Oxford. Darlaston showed him round some of the colleges before taking him for a short interview with W. B. Selbie, the Principal of Mansfield. He then went home to think it over. Stanley Shrubsole tried to press the claims of New College without success. He decided to apply to Mansfield.

Prior to this he had been formally recommended for ministerial training by the minister and members of the Church in the Grove, Sydenham. He had also prepared and attached to his application a statement of his 'principal articles of faith' – such a statement was required from all candidates. He drafted this statement four times, revising it in form, though not in basic content, according to Darlaston's suggestions. His final statement was as follows:

1. That the supreme good for man, involving his full development as a moral and spiritual being and promoting his greatest and everlasting happiness, is to know and to obey the will of God.

2. That God has revealed Himself to man by becoming incarnate in Jesus Christ His Son.

3. That the essential attribute of God as revealed in Jesus Christ is His Holy love for men, and that it is His will that men should love Him and should love one another.

4. That sin consists in the free choice of that which the chooser believes to be contrary to God's will, and that the life and death of Jesus Christ reveal the heart of God in relation to human sin, displaying the essential antagonism of sin to God, the Divine suffering which involves the Divine mercy by which it is forgiven, and the personal power which comes to man through

forgiveness and through the sense of God's continued trust.

5. That the chief aids to the knowledge of, and to compliance with, the will of God, are to be found in the habit of prayer, in the effort to understand the application of the teaching of Jesus to modern life, and in the personal union and spiritual friendship between the human soul and Christ.

6. That every member of the Christian church ought to be in some way 'a fisher of men' i.e. that he ought to use any powers he may possess, such as example, friendship, intercessory prayer, teaching and preaching, to induce others to become disciples of Christ.

7. That there is a future life continuing eternally after the death of the body, and that among the conditions of that life will be the active service of God and the liability to reward and punishment.

Cadoux was already, what he remained, a theological liberal. He had read, thought long about, and discussed R.J.Campbell's *The New Theology*, published in 1906 – the best-seller which gave in a clear and systematic form the core of the teaching Campbell had been giving from the pulpit of the City Temple in London. Campbell was an omnivorous reader with 'a gift for assimilating new ideas and then popularising them';[1] he had read Harnack, Sabatier and Réville, and shared their excitement in opening up a new understanding of the Christian faith acceptable to 'modern man'. In its emphasis on the individual Christian vocation, and in its lack of emphasis on the Church and the sacraments, Cadoux's statement shows the influence of 'the new theology'. His vocation, then and always, was to search for the truth about God through the use of his mind. He wrote, many years later, that 'the theologian best displays his loyalty to the Christian religion by giving the first place in all things to truth'.[2] To that search for truth, particularly through a study of the gospels, and through prayer, he was committed throughout his life.

In the letter of 1912, written to the leaders of the boys' classes in Catford, and already referred to, Cadoux pointed to the need for 'a new doctrine of Christian salvation' – 'a teaching that will do the work of the old evangelicalism'. The inspiration behind the vocation to be a Christian came, he argued, from 'the energising Grace of the Great Lord of the Harvest . . . mediated to us through Jesus Christ'.

And where does all this bring us? It ought to bring us within view of a better method of self-culture for the sake of the Kingdom of God. This Grace of God, of which we have been speaking, has no

---

[1] See A.R. Vidler *20th Century Defenders of the Faith* (1965) chapter 1.
[2] C.J.Cadoux *The Case for Evangelical Modernism* (1938) p.11.

limits but those which we ourselves impose. It can work only by our co-operating with it: and the reason why we do not succeed better in our work, why we do not in fact become 'levers to uplift the world, and roll it in another course', is because we have not risen more above our own limitations. Our part then must be to apprehend more consciously in our own hearts the loving Grace of God, and to see how best we can keep our end of the channel of His Grace well dredged, how best we can render ourselves efficient as tools for the use of the Great Artificer.

No one could have complained that Cadoux did not work hard to render himself efficient for his vocation.

In June 1911, he went again to Oxford for the academic examination and interview for admission to Mansfield. On the 16th he presented himself for examination in the college hall. He took papers in Old Testament, New Testament, translation of Greek and Latin patristic texts, and a general paper. On the 19th he and four other candidates were questioned by the Board, and in the afternoon he heard that he had been awarded a full scholarship of £60 per annum. On the same day he chose lodgings with Mrs Mansell at 109 Southmoor Road. The next phase of his life was now taking shape.

Arthur wrote to congratulate him and offered practical help:

> I hope you will consider this your home during vacations. We are as nearly vegetarians as you will probably find, and although our accommodation is not of the greatest, you have philosophy enough not to mind that.

The Principal of Mansfield wrote to send him a reading list, particularly recommending him to read Peake's *Critical Introduction to the New Testament*, Gwatkin's *Knowledge of God* and Sanday's *Ancient and Modern Christologies*. Three weeks after receiving these letters he heard that he had passed the London degree of Master of Arts, with distinction.

It remained for him to bring his existing activities to a conclusion. He sent in his resignation to the Admiralty and finished there on 25 August. He prepared to leave both his Sunday classes at Catford; at least one of the former members of his Sunday School class, now a leader – Alfred Bunker – wrote to thank him for his friendship and influence:

> It now seems strange, that however much I have misconstrued your apparent propensity for sticking your grand old nose into my business, most of the spurned advice has, consciously or unconsciously, been eventually followed.

After finishing at the Admiralty, he went to his regular Sunday

School camp at the end of August, and then some days later to Swanwick, to a Conference of Free Churchmen at which Darlaston was one of the speakers.

Later in September he spent three days in Oxford taking Responsions, the preliminary examination which all university undergraduates had to take (technically Cadoux's two London University degrees were not recognized by Oxford). Finally, he left his lodgings in Forest Hill on 9 October and took up residence in Southmoor Road. His Oxford career had begun.

III

Mansfield
1911–1914

MANSFIELD COLLEGE was entering its twenty-sixth year in Oxford when Cadoux joined it in October 1911. The college derived its name from its original benefactors, George Storer Mansfield and his two sisters Elizabeth Mansfield and Sarah Glover, who had vested the Spring Hill Estate, Birmingham, in the hands of trustees who were to be responsible for the establishment of a college for the training of Nonconformist ministers. Until its move to Oxford, the college, opened in 1838, was known as Spring Hill College, and as such prepared many young men for the ministry of Congregational and other Nonconformist churches, in affiliation with London University.

The suggestion of a move to Oxford was first made in 1876, five years after the universities of Oxford and Cambridge were fully opened to Dissenters. R. W. Dale, minister of the Congregational Church at Carr's Lane, Birmingham, and one of the greatest and most influential of Birmingham's citizens, was the main exponent of the idea, though it did not originate with him. A few years after the suggestion was first made (probably in 1880), Dale received a letter from T. H. Green, Whyte's Professor of Moral Philosophy at Oxford, pressing the case for a Nonconformist academic 'presence' in Oxford:

> The opening of the national universities to Nonconformists has been, in my judgment, an injury rather than a help to Nonconformity. You are sending up here, year by year, the sons of some of your best and wealthiest families; they are often altogether uninfluenced by the services of the church which they find here, and they not only drift away from Nonconformity – they drift away and lose all faith; and you are bound, as soon as you have secured the opening of the universities for your sons, to follow them when you send them here, in order to defend and maintain their religious life and faith.

These and other arguments eventually prevailed, and the college moved to Oxford in 1886, changing its name from Spring Hill College to Mansfield College. At first, the college premises consisted simply of two rooms at 90 High Street, but within three years an impressive new building, designed by Basil Champneys in Gothic style, was opened in what is now Mansfield Road, only a few minutes' walk from the Bodleian Library, Broad Street and the long-established colleges of the university. The chapel and library were particularly fine. The chapel included statues and stained glass windows representing Christian leaders of many different traditions; when Friedrich Heiler visited it in the 1920s, he called it the most Catholic place he had seen in Oxford.[1]

A new principal joined the college when it moved to Oxford – Andrew Martin Fairbairn,[2] a Scot who had most recently been principal of Airedale Congregational College in Bradford. Fairbairn was essentially the founder and creator of the Mansfield tradition, and did as much as anyone to gain the respect of the Oxford Board of Theology for the Nonconformist contribution to theological scholarship and to ensure that Nonconformity had a place in Oxford. He set very high academic standards and gathered round him a remarkable group of teachers who ensured the continuance of those high standards.

Fairbairn was 47 when he came to Oxford and spent the rest of his career at Mansfield, resigning only two years before Cadoux joined the college in 1911. He was by then living in retirement, visiting each of his children in turn, and died during Cadoux's second term. His influence was still strong. His theology was 'liberal evangelical', wrought through hard struggle and study, a struggle which had involved first abandoning the inherited forms of his faith, and then gradually building up new ones in the course of a period of study and reflection in Germany. It was his aim to produce scholars who could interpret the Christian faith in terms appropriate and meaningful for a generation being brought up in a time of intellectual ferment and challenge.

No one was allowed to train for the ministry at Mansfield unless already holding a first degree (usually in an 'arts' subject) whether of Oxford or another university; though Oxford undergraduates who intended to come on to Mansfield might be admitted to the Junior Common Room. As Mansfield was not a constituent college of the university, those who came there with first degrees from other universities were required by Mansfield to matriculate as a condition of joining the college; they usually registered as members of the Non-

[1] C. J. Cadoux 'The doctrine of the Church in the light of Christian history' in *The Congregational Quarterly* July 1934 p.293.
[2] See W. B. Selbie *Andrew Martin Fairbairn* (1914).

Collegiate Society (later St Catherine's Society), in order to do so; and at the end of their three years' course they were required to sit and pass the university's degree of BA in Theology. Mansfield was deliberately non-residential, so as to avoid what many deplored as the 'seminary spirit'; but the Junior Common Room, Dining Hall and Chapel, on the Oxford model, ensured a basic communal life and that interchange of ideas and interplay of personalities which are an important element in higher education. The students found lodgings mainly in the area off Walton Street round Southmoor Road, where Cadoux lived, about a quarter of an hour's walk, or five minutes' cycle ride, from Mansfield or the centre of Oxford.

Fairbairn's successor as Principal was W. B. Selbie, a great admirer of Fairbairn and one of his ablest students. Educated at Manchester Grammar School and Brasenose College, Oxford, he had been amongst the first group of Mansfield students, and after a year as a tutor had been minister of the churches at Highgate and Emmanuel, Cambridge, successively, before returning to Oxford in 1909 as Principal of Mansfield. Cadoux revered him greatly and later summed up his character and achievement – 'a brilliant and effective preacher and a prolific writer, he was withal a simple and humble Christian and an unfailing friend'. He was small in stature but could be intimidating in person, and his ideas and convictions were clear. His aim as principal was to educate men to become preachers; one of his successors (Nathaniel Micklem) described how 'the pulpit was his throne'. A historian of Mansfield has recounted how in sermon class 'his most sweeping condemnation of a feeble effort was "That wouldn't save the soul of a tomtit"', and how 'he aimed at helping to fashion a new world not by forging ideas but by making men, and this made him a superb educationist'.[1] The themes of his preaching were the central doctrines of the Christian faith, delivered with the note of authority.

Selbie taught dogmatic and pastoral theology to the Mansfield ordinands. His three senior colleagues on the staff, known within the college as professors, were Vernon Bartlet, George Buchanan Gray and (from 1912) James Moffatt. Vernon Bartlet was Mackennal Professor of Church History, a title Cadoux was to inherit 22 years later; He was 'tall and spare, with a piquantly Spanish appearance and an amusingly oracular and erudite manner of utterance'.[2] He was known amongst his students as 'the elongated saint' or 'the last of the early Fathers'. It came naturally to him to choose the longer and more

[1] W. T. Pennar Davies *History of Mansfield College 1886-1947* (1947) p.34.
[2] *Ibid.* p.27.

complicated way of expressing an idea; hence as a lecturer he had deficiencies, which some of his students used to overcome by occupying themselves with pressing correspondence of a different nature. Nevertheless, he was greatly respected and loved by them all, to many of whom he was 'a father in God'.

Like Selbie, Bartlet had been one of Fairbairn's earliest students; he had remained at Mansfield, first as tutor and then as professor, ever since. His academic background was not unlike Selbie's – Highgate School and Exeter College, Oxford – but his family background was narrower and stricter; Cadoux himself gave this account in a biographical memoir attached to Bartlet's last, posthumously published work:

> It was as a pupil of Dr Fairbairn that he gradually and happily emerged, through what must have been painful as well as long-drawn-out struggles, and (it must be added) to the lasting regret of both his parents, from the grim obscurantism in which he had been trained, into a serene and open-eyed faith. Firmly grounded in a devout and filial trust in God as Father through the revelation of Him given to us in Jesus Christ, his religion no longer stood in need of evading or defying the clamorous demands of history and of reason. [1]

He was a sensitive, sympathetic friend and scholar of complete integrity; one of his favourite words was 'eirenic'. The death of his first wife and second son in 1904, his acceptance and coming to terms with it, deepened and strengthened his faith, so that Pennar Davies, historian of Mansfield, could write that 'his life was a perpetual inspiration'.

His chosen field of specialisation was early church history, though William Sanday regarded him as one of the most valuable members of his New Testament seminar, and regretted that he did not concentrate on New Testament studies. His major contribution to church history was *The Apostolic Age* (1899), but other important books followed. In theology he described himself as 'a liberal of the Harnack or right-wing Ritschlian type', adding 'I have my own way of harmonizing Harnack with Luther and Calvin . . .'. He was a prominent member of the Oxford Society of Historical Theology, a society which included Anglicans and Roman Catholics as well as Nonconformists, and later exercised what Cadoux described as 'a quasi-paternal control' over it. He was both a convinced upholder and expounder of Congregational principles and a searcher after church unity who was proud to number

---

[1] J. V. Bartlet *Church Life and Church Order during the First Four Centuries* ed. C. J. Cadoux (1943) p.xvii.

such Anglicans as Sanday and Gore as his friends. Cadoux was fortunate to have Bartlet as his teacher and friend.

George Buchanan Gray taught Hebrew and Old Testament Studies. He had begun his theological training at New College, London, where his teacher had recognized his ability and promise, and recommended him to come to Oxford to study Semitic languages under S. R. Driver, a great Old Testament scholar and Semitic philologist. He came to Mansfield as a student a year after Bartlet, took a first in the Honours School of Semitic Languages, collected most of the available prizes and scholarships, and then went to Marburg to study Arabic and other Semitic languages and related studies. He returned to Mansfield as Professor of Hebrew and Old Testament Exegesis and later was also appointed Grinfield Lecturer in the Septuagint in the University. He published distinguished work in the field of Old Testament textual studies, including several critical commentaries, and made an important contribution to Old Testament studies with his posthumous *Sacrifice in the Old Testament* (1925). His scholarship was recognized in his election to the University Boards of Theology and Oriental Studies. He introduced his students, at Mansfield and at other colleges, to the most rigorous standards of scholarship, and his energy and enthusiasm for study and for social reform were stimulating and encouraging to others. Altogether he was one of the most respected Old Testament scholars and teachers of his generation. In addition, he and his wife were generous in their hospitality to students, and Cadoux found support and friendship from them during his first years at Mansfield.

The Yates Chair of New Testament Greek and Exegesis was vacated by Alexander Souter just before Cadoux came up to Oxford; the new professor was James Moffatt, who came south from Scotland for three years. His *Introduction to the Literature of the New Testament* (1912) was published in the year in which he came to Mansfield, and his notable translation of the New Testament was published while he was teaching there. A cultured and versatile scholar, he added further distinction to the Mansfield staff.

Though Mansfield was not officially a part of the University,[1] it had sufficient connections with it (the staff were almost all Oxford graduates and the students all took Oxford degrees) to ensure good academic standards. Indeed, as the University gradually recognized, Mansfield made a lively and substantial contribution to the development of theological studies in Oxford. During Cadoux's last year as a student, Selbie was co-opted as a member of the Board of Theology,

[1] Mansfield became a Permanent Private Hall in 1955.

and some of his lectures, along with some of Bartlet's and Gray's, were placed on the Board's lecture list. Mansfield performed, as was originally intended, another function as well, in providing a centre for worship and friendship for Nonconformist undergraduates in the University reading subjects other than theology. In no sense was it meant to be a place of retreat, but rather a place where those brought up as Nonconformists could be helped to use the critical understanding they were acquiring through study to deepen their religious life and faith, and bring it towards maturity.

When Cadoux arrived at Mansfield, it was in the company of four other new students; two of them, Nathaniel Micklem and Eric Muncaster, were preparing for the Congregational ministry, Bernard Macalpine for the Baptist and Ronald Rees for the Wesleyan. Three other men, A. J. Haile and the Lawson brothers (A. C. and E. J.), who had already been members of the college whilst taking their first degrees, now joined the new group as first-year theological students. Cadoux was the only one without an Oxford or Cambridge degree; he was also older than the others.

Their three year curriculum covered six main subjects – Hebrew language and literature, history and thought; New Testament text and textual criticism; church history (the first four and a half centuries of Christianity, Congregational history since the Reformation, and church institutions); philosophical theology, systematic theology and pastoral theology (this course included the sermon class, in which each member in turn had to preach a sermon, after which the tutor and the rest of the class would offer criticism). It was a rigorous and demanding course, and at the end of the second or third year each student was expected to sit for a degree in the Oxford Honours School of Theology.

Cadoux spent the first week visiting his tutors and planning his course of study. On the first Monday of term, 16 October 1911, he had to appear before the members of the Senior Common Room, and announced his plan, already agreed in June with Selbie, to sit for the London BD examination the following summer. He met with some opposition to the plan, for he noted in his diary, 'Dr Bartlet criticises the plan as rather precipitate'. The following day he persuaded Selbie to let him study Hebrew on his own, without attending the regular class, so that he could go to Bartlet's seminar on 'Primitive Christianity' instead. Dr Bartlet however had as little enthusiasm for this plan as for the previous one; Cadoux's diary noted, 'he warned gravely against studying too hard and falling into a barren intellectuality'. A day later he wrote again in his diary, 'Selbie gives a speech warning us against aiming at anything other than being preachers'.

Cadoux certainly did study hard. His life was ordered as in the past, with regular hours for study and preparation of essays, addresses and sermons. From Tuesday to Friday mornings were filled with Mansfield lectures, sermon classes took place in late afternoons, and some evenings were taken up with formal talks and discussions. But there were other facets to life as well. He usually took some form of exercise in the afternoon – this became a lifelong habit. At first it was rowing, but that activity did not survive more than one season. In the summer it was tennis. Apart from these sports, he enjoyed cycling, running or walking, which he loved, preferably with congenial company. His favourite way of spending an afternoon was to go for a walk with an interesting companion and then return to the home of one of them for tea together. His lodgings were conveniently near Port Meadow, the Thames and Binsey, with an ample variety of walks.

He loved talking and could not have too much discussion of theological and ethical problems. He made new friends in Oxford but also kept up his old friendships, corresponding regularly with his 'boys', his former colleagues in the Sunday School and the Boys' Brigade. He returned to Catford to visit them whenever he could. His correspondence with Arthur also was regular and extensive.

He managed to remain solvent by dint of careful management, and with the help of the friends and relatives who offered him hospitality during the vacations. The Mansfield 'Information for intending candidates' for 1911 lists the expenses which a student could expect to incur each year. Board and lodging for 25 weeks together with dinner in hall amounted to £43 15s; university and delegacy dues and examination fees came to £9 4s 6d. Cadoux's scholarship of £60 per annum just covered this with some money left over for books. For anything else, he was dependent on gifts, modest savings, fees for preaching, and any further prizes or scholarships he could win.

All the students were expected to accept preaching engagements on some weekends, and for certain periods to undertake student pastorates. During his first year Cadoux was invited to be student pastor at Witney Congregational Church, a task he agreed to accept, though the long vacation away from Oxford necessarily limited the nature of the commitment. During that first year he preached in several churches, including Summertown (North Oxford), Hungerford, Colchester and Paxford. If the place were within range he would cycle, and often spent the night with a church family. He became expert at avoiding a chill after cycling through a downpour; the skill of lining his trousers with carefully folded newspapers, learned at camp, proved invaluable. He also made great efforts to start a boys' club in Summer-town, and persuaded eleven boys to commit themselves to regular attendance, but it was difficult for him to maintain the interest and enthusiasm amidst his many other commitments.

Academic success came easily and quickly. At the beginning of his third term, in April 1912, he gained the Mill Hill prize, awarded to the student who had done best in the college examinations. Later in the year he was awarded the Henry Rogers Essay prize for an essay on the subject, 'The eschatological teaching of Jesus in the Synoptic Gospels' (a theme which recurred several times in his later writings). Together the two prizes were worth just over £25, a welcome supplement to his funds. In addition to these honours, he heard in July that he had passed the London BD examination.

The long vacation at Oxford lasted sixteen weeks. It was intended for private study as well as recreation and Cadoux put in a good deal of hard work as well as visiting friends and relatives. He returned more than once during the long vacation of 1912 to Catford to stay with Alfred and Harold Bunker, and also visited Ida in Tonbridge. In late July and early August he went to the Boys' Brigade camp on the Isle of Wight, and in early September to the Sunday School camp at Minster. He had been encouraged to try for the Dr Williams' Trust Divinity Scholarship, for which he was eligible as a candidate for the ministry among Dissenters, and spent three weeks at Arthur's home in Kent studying hard for it; he took the examination in late September, and heard within a short time that the scholarship had been awarded to him.

The high point of the vacation, however, was the conference of Free Churchmen at Swanwick in the last week of August, the second in the series which had begun twelve months previously. Those who were present at these conferences have spoken of the sense of worship, the inspiration and the fellowship of these meetings, which in this year, 1912, were formalised as the 'Free Church Fellowship'. Cadoux himself shared in these feelings, and in the biographical memoir of Bartlet wrote about the experience in these words:

> Time would fail me to tell of the leaders of that and subsequent gatherings, or to describe the tone of the fellowship, the character of the proceedings, the thrill of the awakened vision, the buzz and hum of questing minds, the tense atmosphere of the devotions.[1]

Amongst the other members were Darlaston, Richard Roberts, W. E. Orchard and Nathaniel Micklem, who had been deputed to draw up

[1] *Op.cit.* p.xxvi.

35

the statement of aims of the Fellowship. This statement included the following:

> We are determined . . . to gather from all ages and all churches all that may be known of Christ in his familiar dealings with his people . . . [We hope for] a Free Church of England so steeped in the spirit and traditions of the entire Church Catholic as to be ready in due time for the reunion of Christendom.[1]

On 30 August the members of the conference adopted this Covenant of the Fellowship.

Richard Roberts' words about the beginnings of the Fellowship, written a month after that second conference, were echoed by many others: 'Many of us had prayed, and had eaten our hearts out in a dreary isolation, but that week we walked into a new world and things have never since been quite the same to any of us'. It was in the wake of this conference that Cadoux wrote the letter to his former colleagues in the boys' classes at Catford to which reference was made in the last chapter. To many of its members, the Fellowship was a life-long inspiration.

Cadoux returned to Oxford early in October. On the Friday before full term began, as was customary, he called on the Principal to discuss his plans for academic work. It was agreed that he should work for the University Junior Greek Testament prize examination in the following March, for the London BD Honours examination in the summer of 1913, and for the Oxford Theology Schools at the end of his course in the summer of 1914. He loved to have clear objectives to work for and this plan gave him a steady framework for study.

He was now 29. He already had considerable academic achievement to his credit, had shown much promise for the future, had proved that he could become a convincing preacher, and had earned the respect of his teachers and fellow students. But he had no settled home, and though Arthur had promised him hospitality whenever he needed it, and Ida was happy to entertain him at times, and though the families of his colleagues and former class members welcomed him to their homes, he felt something of a wanderer and was longing for the support and stability of a home of his own. He knew he could not marry and settle down until he had finished his course, but he wanted the prospect to look forward to. The lack of any such prospect contributed to periods of depression, and it was his work which kept him going.

It was in this frame of mind that he encountered the sister of an acquaintance amongst his contemporaries, herself an undergraduate

[1] Quoted in J. W. Grant *Free Churchmanship in England 1870-1940* (n.d.) p.218.

who attended Mansfield chapel. The chapel was one of the few places where the undergraduate members of both sexes could meet; early in 1912 Cadoux wrote in his diary, 'I force a brief convers[n] with A— outside after service and then settle down to 40 years in wild[ss]'. He had to enlist the help and support of the wives of one or other of the Mansfield professors in order to arrange any further meeting, for the chaperon rules were strictly adhered to. After two river expeditions in the summer, organised by others on his behalf, he himself issued a further invitation to another river trip, an invitation which was firmly refused; a succeeding letter 'telling her of my love' was further rejected. Given the context, a university society which was essentially male and self-contained, in which girls were strictly protected and in which few opportunities were provided for meeting members of the opposite sex, it was hardly surprising that he had no success. No doubt it was all to the good that the girl concerned rejected Cadoux's advances, for he had idealised her and wanted to leap into a commitment without sufficient preparation or understanding. But it caused him a great deal of unhappiness at the time. He confided in several people about it, amongst them his cousin, Wynnie Hill. She wrote back to him:

> You asked me whether I would advise you to think no more of A— and look for someone else? . . . But if you felt you could put another woman in the place A— has in your love at present, I hardly think she is *the* one for you.

These were wise words, but at the time brought little consolation.

This personal unhappiness had no adverse effect on Cadoux's academic progress. The J.C.R. notes of the *Mansfield College Magazine* for December 1912 included the following:

> Let us now praise famous men. C. J. Cadoux (incurably erudite and desperately encyclopaedic) gained a Dr Williams' Scholarship and a London BD. With a view to his programme next year he hopes that the DD Oxford will be opened to Nonconformists.

He duly won the Hall-Houghton Junior Greek Testament prize, a university award, in the spring of 1913, and a place in the first class of the London BD Honours examination in the summer. ('But what is the good of that without A—?' he wrote in his diary). His fellow students summed up his style in the following verse, one of a series on each member of the college, written for the college 'smoking concert':

> Next beams the cheery punster, old Cadoux,
> Winner of pots and prizes not a few;
> Encyclopaedias he devours with ease
> And plans a schedule while you pass the cheese.

The smoking concert ('smoker') was an important Mansfield institution. Each term, members of the Junior Common Room invited friends from other colleges to an entertainment, provided by themselves, at which ample provision was made, in the form of long clay-pipes, tobacco and cigarettes, for an evening's relaxation, according to the then Oxford ritual. There was plenty of opportunity for the display of the wit and humour with which potential ministers are frequently well endowed.

Cadoux spent the long vacation of 1913 in a similar way to the previous year – except that he paid his first visit abroad (since he left Smyrna) in early July, to Sy in Belgium for an informal conference with some of his old Sunday School friends. He also attended two conferences at Swanwick, one arranged by the Student Christian Movement, the other by the Free Church Fellowship. He attended the regular camps, visited Connie in Glasgow, and Arthur in East Boldon, near Sunderland, where he had moved with Bessie to take over another church earlier in the year. Towards the end of the vacation he took part in a Mansfield student missionary campaign in Bradford.

In the midst of all this travelling, conferring, preaching and studying, he was thinking seriously about his future. In a year's time he would finish his course, his scholarships would come to an end, and he would need to support himself. W. A. Davies, the Hebrew tutor at Mansfield, had just left Oxford to join the staff of Hackney College in London, and his post was vacant. Should he apply for it? Was his vocation to teaching and scholarship, or to a pastoral and preaching ministry? While staying with Edward Yuill, one of his former Sunday School pupils in Chingford, he went over to consult W. E. Orchard, the Presbyterian minister in Enfield whom he had met and admired at the Free Church Fellowship conferences, about it; his diary does not record what Orchard said. He also wrote to Arthur, who replied:

> As to the work itself, I should think it would offer less opportunity for actual Christian activity than a pastorate.
>
> . . . As to preaching, you will no doubt get many opportunities but I find that preaching to practically unknown people is a very different thing from preaching to those of whom one has peculiar knowledge and for whom one has peculiar responsibility. . . . On the other hand of course it would give an excellent opportunity of prosecuting one's study.

Though Arthur did on one occasion consider applying for an academic post, in the end he decided to remain in pastoral charge of a church, where he found he was able not only to sustain a pastoral and preaching ministry, but also, in due course, to write books which stood comparison with his brother's. Jack, however, finally settled on the other course, and decided to let his name go forward for the Mansfield post. He visited Selbie at the end of July, between visits to Arthur at East Boldon and Ida at Tonbridge, and told him he would apply for the Hebrew position. Though he was prepared to work thoroughly and conscientiously at whatever subject he was required to do, his own preferred subjects were New Testament and early church history. He took the opportunity while he was in Bradford to visit the United College, a college similar to Mansfield, in order to discuss with A. J. Grieve the possibility of his taking up the New Testament professorship there. This idea came to nothing, but the Mansfield application proved successful, though the appointment was not to be confirmed until the following summer.

During that summer of 1913 Bernard had announced his engagement. Maud too was engaged, to James Brown of Glasgow, and they were married by Arthur in Glasgow on 29 November. Jack Cadoux went up to Glasgow for the wedding. Connie and Ida were there as well as Arthur and Bessie, and after the wedding the family party went to the theatre together. The experience of seeing his younger brother and sister settled or about to be settled in marriage depressed Cadoux more about his own situation. He wrote in his diary the day after Maud's wedding: 'I cannot go on in this miserable loneliness – but how to get out of it I know not. Domine, dirige nos'.

There was nothing to be done but to return to work and the routine of lectures, study, friendship and discussion at Mansfield, with visits to members of the family in the vacations. Early in 1914 he won two more awards: the Junior Hall-Houghton Septuagint prize, which he shared with Alfred Guillaume, and the Nathan Whitley travelling scholarship, which he shared with Clifford Lawson. The former was a university prize, the latter a Mansfield award.

The travelling scholarship meant that he could go abroad again and enlarge his intellectual and social horizons. In 1914 the scholarship was awarded for travel in Italy. On the last Friday of the Hilary term Cadoux and Lawson left Oxford to catch the overnight boat from Southampton to Le Havre from whence they travelled to Paris. Here they were met and given lunch by a friend of Lawson's and were joined by another friend, H. F. Angus of Balliol, who travelled with them for part of the time. They then travelled by train to Genoa and began their sight-seeing. From Genoa, the party travelled to Pisa where they stayed a night and spent the following morning sight-seeing, before making their way to Rome, where the party temporarily broke up. Lawson and his friend stayed in Rome, while Cadoux went on to Naples, where he spent two complete days, visiting the churches and cathedrals of the city, and most important, Vesuvius and Pompeii.

Cadoux then rejoined his travelling companions for a week of sight-seeing in Rome. It was on the second day there that he heard from Selbie that he had won the Septuagint prize. Angus went off elsewhere, and Lawson and Cadoux were left to carry out an energetic and thorough sight-seeing programme. Cadoux's diary lists all the places visited but gives none of his thoughts and feelings on seeing this centre of western Christianity and western culture. The ancient historian in him must surely have been excited by seeing so much remaining of the city which had been the focal point of the Roman empire and the Roman civilisation; while the theologian of Nonconformist training and formation will have had mixed feelings about the splendour of St Peter's and the Vatican. His appreciation of the magnificent Renaissance architecture and art, however, was blunted by his enthusiasm for Ruskin's doctrines. Altogether he was too prone, in responding to works of art, to be persuaded by arguments (such as Ruskin's), instead of allowing an artist's creation to make its own impact.

Clifford Lawson left him at the end of the week to go on to Greece, and Cadoux was now left to travel on his own to Assisi, Florence, where he stayed for almost a week, Venice and finally Lugano. In Venice he was in the midst of that Gothic architecture which he had learnt from Ruskin to admire, and the latter's *Stones of Venice* was his constant companion. Altogether he was away for a whole month, encompassing on his tour most of the important classical, religious and artistic treasures which Italy had to offer. At Lugano at last he even seems to have taken a rest, walking round the lake and enjoying the Italian sun. He reached England again on Good Friday and travelled up to Arthur's home for Easter.

At the end of April he came back to Oxford for his last term as a student. He was still working hard, preaching, and taking his place in college life. In May he took part in an important discussion about the position of women at Mansfield, which shows the future Congregational ministers to have been more enlightened on the subject of the participation by women in the life of the church than most of their fellow ordinands in other churches. Constance Todd had joined Mansfield as an ordinand in October 1913 and had in general been made welcome by the Junior Common Room. Problems arose, however, when student activities open only to male undergraduates and graduates were held in Mansfield. At its discussion, the common room agreed that

> This House desires to place on record its approval of the admission of women to the College, and its belief that women as being by right of Christian principle members of the Christian church on full equality with men, should be accorded full facilities for the study of theology, and as far as practicable full enjoyment of the advantages afforded by theological colleges.[1]

There followed a complicated debate in which Cadoux opposed an amendment to this resolution. In principle the resolution was passed. Constance Todd completed her training, became the first woman to be ordained[2] to the Christian ministry in the United Kingdom the day before she married a fellow student of Mansfield, Claud Coltman. She remained a friend of Cadoux and became a friend of his wife, and later stayed with them while working for the Oxford BD examinations.

A week later Cadoux took part in another debate, this time a formal debate with Manchester College Discussion Society. He supported the motion, 'That this house upholds the right of the individual to rebel against constituted authority'. The motion was lost by a small margin.

It was now time to prepare for his last examinations as a student – the Oxford Honours School of Theology papers. He kept up his regular exercise, running every morning and playing tennis most afternoons, but working for the rest of the day. On 24 May he went to Mansfield Chapel as usual, to hear W. E. Orchard preach. As he was cycling towards Mansfield he passed the girl who had rejected his advances the previous summer; she bowed and smiled at him. A week later his 'urgent love letter' received a curt refusal. It did not make it easy for him to join in the celebration of Stanley Shrubsole's wedding in London a few days later; nor to face the final examinations on 11 June.

In the Oxford manner the examinations were intensive, for the eleven papers were fitted into five and a half days. The night before the last paper he noted in his diary: 'Selbie's dinner – I am faint and don't go in'. Next day he finished the last paper at lunch time and by way of celebration spent the afternoon going for a drive to Benson with Bernard Macalpine and C. H. Dodd (at that time minister of Warwick Congregational Church but a frequent visitor to Mansfield).

He soon recovered his energy and took part in the formal end of term celebrations – the valedictory service, the garden party and

[1] Mansfield College J. C. R. Minute book 6 May 1914.
[2] At the King's Weigh House Church, London on 17 September 1917.

college dinner. By Friday 19 June he was writing in his diary: '5 – 6.45 with Dr Gray – discuss a thesis for DD and go thro' Theol papers with him & Hughes and Brenni. Gray tells me I am appointed Hebrew tutor if Schools are all right'. The subject he chose initially for his DD (which had to be a London degree since Nonconformists were excluded from Divinity degrees at Oxford till 1920) was the chronology of the Hebrew prophetic writings.

So his immediate professional future was almost assured. Confirmation came on 9 July when he heard that he had been awarded first class honours in the Theology Schools. His appointment as Tutor in Hebrew for five years from 1 October (at a salary of £200 per annum with rooms) was confirmed. In addition, he was now an accredited minister of the Congregational Union. He could look forward with some confidence to a fully occupied summer, with several camps included in his plans: first the Swanwick SCM camp, then the Boys' Brigade camp on the Isle of Wight, to be followed immediately by the Free Church camp for schoolboys at Matlock, and finally the Catford Sunday School camp to be held at Eynsford in Kent. In between he was to visit Arthur and Bessie at East Boldon, Connie in Glasgow and Ida in Tonbridge.

Three years previously he had entered Mansfield a largely self-taught, intelligent, hard-working, methodical, aspiring scholar. Since then he had achieved academic distinction in an ancient university, and had been taught by men with first class minds who challenged their pupils to ask deeper, more searching questions than before, and to regard the study of the Scriptures as a life-long task; he had at least to some extent met men from wealthier social backgrounds than his own; and he had begun to find his voice as a preacher. He was still conscientious and methodical, but he had gained more confidence as a scholar, and a clearer grasp of the grounds of his faith. He was now prepared to work out, painstakingly, the implications of this faith for the living of the Christian life, and to pass on to others the results of this careful, thoughtful and thorough enquiry.

From Selbie he had learned what preaching should be and what it could achieve. From Gray he had learned how meticulous textual study could lead to a deeper conception of religion, of God's working in and through history, and how an understanding of the Old Testament was essential to a full understanding of the New. From Bartlet he had learned to practise more thoroughly that 'historic method' which he attempted to define in the memoir of his former teacher:

> In essence it means the effort to discover first what the extant
> records have to tell us of the thoughts of those who first penned

them, without regard to any preferences we investigators may have touching what they ought to have meant, and before attempting to assess their religious meaning and value for later generations. [1]

He had also learnt to understand Paul from Bartlet, for he described Bartlet as 'one of the very few men I have met who could give a convincing interpretation of the great Apostle's central teaching'. [2]

Cadoux retained a veneration for these teachers, who were about to become his colleagues, and kept a photograph of each of them in his study until the end of his life. Beyond their undoubted academic competence, these men had demonstrated the effect a living and lively faith could have, and inspired Cadoux, as other students, in his 'high calling' as a minister, and as what Eric Gill called 'a dispenser of truth'.

[1] *Op.cit.* p.xl.
[2] *Op.cit.* p.xlii.

IV

Mansfield, war and marriage
1914–1915

NONE OF THOSE leaving the college for the summer vacation at the end of June 1914 had any conception of the change that was to come over their lives, and over their country and the whole of Europe and beyond, before they re-assembled for the Michaelmas Term in October. The conflict which was sparked off by the assassination of the Archduke Franz Ferdinand and his wife in Sarajevo challenged the theology, the social conscience, the ethics and the faith which was shared by the members of Mansfield with the whole Christian Church, and Cadoux was to meet that challenge with all the energy and ability at his command.

He had already visited Arthur and Connie, had returned to Oxford for the viva for his degree, heard that he had been awarded a first, and had formally received his degree in the Sheldonian Theatre; and he had attended the Swanwick SCM camp and Boys' Brigade camp on the Isle of Wight, before travelling straight to Matlock for the Free Church camp for schoolboys – an annual event for which Mansfield always provided some of the leaders. His diary for 5 August, the day they heard that war had been declared, recorded simply: 'Matlock camp. Britain declares war on Germany. Aftn. Scouting game'. For the time being, little was changed in his life, except that when he went to Swanwick from Matlock, he found that the St Andrews League conference he was due to attend there was cancelled, and he had to change his plans and travel straight back to Oxford.

The war did not affect the Catford Sunday School camp, which took place as usual, though at Eynsford instead of at Minster; this was an opportunity to keep his long-standing friendships in good repair, though his diary suggests a rather gloomy, flat atmosphere.

He was due to spend most of September in East Boldon again, with Arthur and Bessie. Just before he set off north, he received a letter from Arthur with a kind of apology:

Marguerite Asplin has come rather suddenly (hospital vacations being upset owing to the war) to give us a long promised visit and will be here part of the time that you are with us. But please do not let this make any difference to your coming, as we have plenty of room. Also if she and Bess go out on the spree there will be company for me.

Marguerite was Bessie's half-sister, 19 years younger and a nurse at Paddington Infirmary.

By the same post Cadoux received a letter from Cowley Road Congregational Church, Oxford, asking him to take charge of their services for the next three months. This invitation he agreed to accept.

On 9 September he travelled up to East Boldon, and found Marguerite Asplin already with Arthur and Bessie. It may not have been the first time he had met her, but the acquaintance was only superficial. According to his diary, he spent the following twelve days working in the mornings on his DD thesis, finally coming to the conclusion that 'my thesis for London DD on chronology of Hebrew proph'l wtgs is too large to be practicable'; the afternoons he spent walking with Marguerite and Bessie, Marguerite and Arthur, or Arthur alone; and worked at his thesis again in the evenings. On 21 September he took the train to Newcastle with Marguerite, and saw her off on the London train. That evening he wrote in his diary: 'Feel very unhappy now she is gone . . . come suddenly to the conclusion that Maggie is the right girl for me'. Arthur and Bessie had not guessed what was going on in his mind.

Two days later, after feeling 'very low spirited and sleepy all day', he wrote to Marguerite to ask her to meet him in London on 3 October, ten days ahead, when he would be passing through Paddington on his way to undertake a preaching engagement at Kingston. He waited for the reply in an agony of suspense; on 24 September he was 'very miserable all day'. On 25 September he was 'very, very miserable, intolerable in fact', though it was quite impossible for a reply to have come by then. The next day his mood was transformed: 'A letter from dear Maggie at last: she will meet me. I rejoice with trembling'.

He returned to Oxford at the end of the month in order to prepare for the new term. He must have known that there would be difficult and painful conflicts to face over his attitude to the war, and his first interview with Selbie, the following day, apparently brought the issue straight out into the open. 'Call on Selbie', he wrote in his diary, 'he warns me agst preaching agst militarism'.

Personal affairs were also in the forefront of his mind. The day after his interview with Selbie, he took the one o'clock train to Paddington, and met Marguerite Asplin 'under the clock' at the station, conveniently near the hospital where she worked. It was on the surface a prosaic meeting. 'Walk with her in Park and chat abt trifles. Cup of tea in Lyons'. They met again, after the same fashion, on his way back to Oxford on the Monday. '2.30 Meet MA at Padd[n]. Very pleasant walk and chat in Park. Cup of tea tog'r in Lyons. See her off to Inf'y abt 4'. In between the two meetings, he had preached at Kingston, taking 'Christianity and War' as his theme in the evening; he felt impelled to speak on this theme, even though he felt depressed afterwards, 'by thinking of oppos[n] (probable) to war sermon'.

His mind was now quite clear on both the public and the private issue. He never wavered from his belief that the waging of war was incompatible with Christian faith and practice; and he was quite sure, then and always, that Marguerite Asplin was the right choice for him as his life's companion.

For her part, Marguerite Asplin had not had very much opportunity to get to know the man who was about to propose marriage to her. There was, of course, a family connexion, going at least as far back as Arthur's engagement to Bessie Asplin in 1898. The Asplin family lived in Perry Hill, on the edge of Forest Hill, within a mile or so of the Cadouxs, and some of their children attended the Sunday School at Trinity Congregational Church, Catford, with which Jack Cadoux was connected from 1901. On the other hand, the link was weakened by Arthur's long absence in South Africa, and though Jack Cadoux continued to live in the area after the break-up of the Cadoux family home, his diaries contained no reference to any member of the Asplin family except in connection with Arthur's long-delayed marriage in 1910. After that, however, Marguerite Asplin must have heard occasional, if second-hand, news of her sister's brother-in-law's activities, ideas and achievements.

Marguerite's father, Thomas Asplin, was a city merchant who imported silks. His household was comfortable, with servants and ample material provision. The family had both Anglican and Non-conformist connections. Thomas Asplin and his first wife had two daughters, one of them Bessie, and four sons; after his first wife's death, he married Florence Wright, a piano teacher, and he and Florence had two daughters, Marguerite and Dorothy. When Jack met Marguerite, he was 31 and she was 25. She had been educated at Lewisham High School, and after a short period of looking after an elderly invalid had trained and qualified as a nurse at Paddington Infirmary.

She was a lively person with a happy temperament, not incapable of firm and quick reproof when occasion demanded it, but equable and realistic in outlook, with a strong sense of humour, which was to stand her in good stead in the future. She was capable and practical, kind and considerate. In appearance, she was a little under average height, well-made, with dark brown wavy hair, a fresh complexion and an attractive smile.

Cadoux's third meeting with her was two and a half weeks later, on 23 October. She must have had some idea what was to come, for they arranged to visit her home in Perry Hill. They met as before at Paddington, had a cup of tea together, and then travelled to south London. He went 'in great fear and trembling'. After tea – 'we talk over our relationships, views and prospects, and agree to take one another for better or worse. Happiest moments of my life hitherto'. The following day his diary simply records 'Indescribable feelings'.

In spite of such a brief acquaintance, the engagement was the prelude to a lasting and satisfying marriage. The two had a similar background, and a common brother- and sister-in-law. Some things they did not share. Marguerite was neither a Congregationalist, nor a pacifist nor a vegetarian, and it must have meant some sacrifice for her to stand by her husband in all these convictions (which she did willingly and unswervingly). Her interest was in caring for people, in making a home and in enabling others more intellectual than herself to 'dispense truth', though she had her own way of arriving at it for herself. Above all, she was able to provide the security and warmth of a home which he had lacked for so many years. Perhaps it did not take her long to realise intuitively that this could bring her, too, happiness and security.

Three days after the engagement Jack met Marguerite again and took her to Mappin and Webb to buy an engagement ring. He wrote to Arthur, who had just been awarded the DD degree, to offer congratulations, and to give his own news. Arthur replied by return of post:

> The letter from you which we found awaiting our return from Sunderland last night was a great surprise. Please accept our heartiest congratulations and best wishes for your united happiness. I hope you will be as happy as we have been, which is saying a great deal. I wish I knew Marguerite better. I must confess that I have liked her considerably more each time I have met her during the last four years, but of course the brief glimpses we have had have not given one a chance of knowing her thoroughly.

Cadoux now visited Selbie to tell him about the engagement, and his future plans – 'I propose to leave Mansfield, get a church and get married at the end of the summer term 1916'. That was not a wholly realistic plan, for as a Congregational minister seeking a church he must receive an invitation from a church meeting, at which all members could vote; and since he had resolved to preach pacifism while war was being fought, such an invitation might be hard to find. He soon discovered that Congregational churches were not necessarily receptive to pacifist preaching when on 17 November he took services in Highbury Congregational Church, Cheltenham, for his old friend Stanley Shrubsole. In the evening, as at Kingston, he preached a sermon on non-resistance to evil, provoking strong resentment amongst some members of the congregation, who conveyed their feelings to Shrubsole in no uncertain terms. A few days later Cadoux received a letter from his old friend, written in some embarrassment:

> Some of my officials are furious, first because they say the putting forward of your personal views was out of place at the present _juncture, as such an attitude weakens the nation in the struggle, which once embarked on, can only be carried on to a conclusion . . . and second, because they think you had no right to take advantage of another man's pulpit to put forward views which you knew were contrary to him.

Shrubsole dissociated himself from these feelings, but made it clear that he was placed in an awkward position, and thought Cadoux should consider whether or not he really was furthering his own cause. There followed a lengthy correspondence, for Cadoux was convinced that he was expounding the authentic Christian message about war, while Shrubsole felt that such teaching could not be offered in isolation, but must be set within a careful exposition of Christian ethics and theology. Shrubsole finished one of his letters with the following comment:

> . . . I ought perhaps to add that there is something characteristically aggressive about you that makes it harder for you to win the hearts and minds of hearers to doctrines that are distasteful to them.

Cadoux did not always succeed in convincing others that he could hold in balance the desire and indeed duty to proclaim what he believed, through experience and study, to be the highest Christian ethical teaching on a particular issue (in this case war), and the duty to respect the views of those who had reached a different conclusion. It required a combination, not easy to achieve, of courage, sensitivity and indeed humility to proclaim pacifist views from the pulpit amidst the atmosphere of patriotic fervour and enthusiasm which pervaded the first months of the war, and to congregations whose sons had volunteered without hesitation to go off to fight in France. Perhaps it was only in the context of regular preaching to the same congregation that a pacifist preacher could expect to touch his hearers.

One of the famous Congregational pulpits in London, that of the King's Weigh House, was now occupied by an equally fearless pacifist preacher, W. E. Orchard. Orchard had more skill and perhaps more grace in his preaching, and, though he encountered opposition from those who heard reports of what he had said, he usually reduced to silence any critics who actually came to hear him. He was in the unique position of attracting politicians and soldiers on leave to hear him preach against the war in which they were involved. It must be said however that Cadoux could put on paper an intellectually more rigorous defence of the pacifist position than could Orchard. Cadoux, like others, was drawn to the Weigh House for inspiration and support in his views, and he and Marguerite often went to hear Orchard preach when they were able to meet on Sundays during the winter of 1914–1915. Whenever possible, they also had a talk with him afterwards.

Cadoux's professional life was still centred at Mansfield. He was now given rooms in the college (in the tower), and no longer had to walk or cycle from Southmoor Road two or three times a day. His official title was Isherwood Fellow and Tutor in Hebrew, and he became a member of the Senior Common Room along with his former teachers. His teaching responsibilities left him ample time for research and writing. He had now chosen another subject for his thesis for the London DD – 'The Christian's response to the claims of the state and society'; it was finally changed to 'A history of the Christian attitude to pagan society and the state, down to the time of Constantine'. It proved a fruitful subject, for he was able to offer a synthesis of the available evidence, as well as original comment, in a form which was not previously available in English, and which had not been presented so clearly in any language. In addition, the work involved a study of the early Christian attitude to war, and provided an underlying unity to his scholarly activities and his current, practical ethical concerns. His research enabled him to offer something constructive to the debate on the most important issue of his generation.

He did not find support for his pacifist views in the Senior Common Room at Mansfield. Selbie was definitely opposed to them, but did at times offer Cadoux the opportunity to discuss them with him. By November there was a recognized pacifists' group in the college, consisting of at least four of the students and Cadoux. When they met in hall one evening they earned the Principal's strong disapproval: 'Selbie comes in and pitches into us for wanting to preach agst war etc', he wrote in his diary. Vernon Bartlet was not a pacifist, but showed more sympathy for and understanding of the pacifist position. Cadoux wrote in his biographical memoir of Bartlet that 'his personal charity . . . coupled with a sense of the real complexity of the problem and a very characteristic reverence for conscience, gave him more sympathy with conscientious pacifists than was felt by many who agreed with him on the practical issue'.[1]

At the end of 1914, Cadoux had the opportunity to meet and enjoy fellowship with ministers and lay Christians who shared his opinions on war. After spending Christmas at Mansfield House, Canning Town, the East End Settlement where Mansfield students were encouraged to experience life amongst the urban poor, and after going with Marguerite to the Weigh House to hear Orchard, he went straight on to a conference at Trinity Hall, Cambridge. The aim of the conference was to discover, formulate and publish 'a mutually acceptable Christian pacifist philosophy'; it was organized by Henry Hodgkin and Richard Roberts.

Henry Hodgkin, a Quaker, had been attending an international conference (the founding conference of the World Alliance for Promoting International Friendship through the Churches) in Constance when war threatened. As he left Cologne station on 3 August, his German fellow delegate, Friedrich Siegmund-Schultze, Lutheran pastor at Potsdam, parted from him saying, 'Whatever happens, nothing is changed between us'. This strengthened Hodgkin's conviction that no war could be right, let alone one in which Christians in the countries at war were required to kill each other. Richard Roberts, Presbyterian minister of Crouch Hill in north London, was also attending a conference when war broke out, the first conference of the Presbyterian Fellowship at Swanwick. He returned home to preach on the following Sunday, 9 August, but never gave his prepared address:

> As I started up the pulpit that morning, I observed something that seemed to make my heart stand still. For many months previously, the first thing that I saw as I went up those stairs was a group of young Germans – business men who had rooms in the neighbourhood. And that morning, they were not there. My mind became a tumult – I had a momentary vision of those lads and other lads who called that church their own, killing each other on some continental battlefield. I knew I could not preach the sermon I had prepared. What I actually did say, I cannot now recall. All I remember is that I called the attention of

[1] J. V. Bartlet *Church Life and Church Order during the First Four Centuries*, ed. C. J. Cadoux (1943) p.xxviii.

the congregation to the empty seats of the young Germans and what the circumstance implied – Christians engaged in mutual fratricide. Anyway, whatever I said, it created a considerable scandal.[1]

These two men, Henry Hodgkin and Richard Roberts, soon gathered round them a group of like-minded clergy, including Orchard and G. K. A. Bell, and discussed the possibility of publishing a series of papers. As the discussions continued, it became apparent that not all the members of the group were prepared to commit themselves to a pacifist position. This was hardly surprising, since it was the first time that Christians in England had really had to face the challenge presented by full-scale war of this kind. Roberts at first believed that the war could be justified politically; but 'to have it spoken of as being a Christian enterprise seems to me to be going beyond fact and reason'. Soon, a small group, led by Roberts and Hodgkin, began meeting separately in the home of Lucy Gardner, another Friend, in an endeavour to work out a basis of agreement on fundamental principles. They then organised the Cambridge conference.

There were about 150 people present. The speakers included Orchard, Richard Roberts, Henry Hodgkin, Fearon Halliday and Maude Royden. The outcome was the formation of the Fellowship of Reconciliation,[2] an organisation which still exists at the present day. As its name suggests, it was a society which recognised the call of Christians to a 'ministry of reconciliation', and to a way other than violence of defeating evil.

As time went on, Cadoux came to play an important role in the Fellowship – that of providing an intellectual formulation of its aims and principles. Apart from the writings of Tolstoy, there was no such formulation, and in fact it was only through the dialogue with those who assumed different principles and convictions that such a defence could really take shape. A Peace Society had been in existence in London since 1816, founded under Quaker auspices; Cadoux seems to have had some minor connection with a South London branch when he was living in Catford. The secretary of the Society at the outbreak of war was Evans Darby, a Congregational minister. But as Keith Robbins writes, the Peace Society had 'no elaborate theological framework for its convictions, simply a reiteration that Christians

[1] Quoted in H. G. Wood *Henry T. Hodgkin: A Memoir* (1937) pp.151-2.
[2] See Vera Brittain *The Rebel Passion: a History of the Fellowship of Reconciliation* (1964).

held out the hand to all men of goodwill'.[1] When war actually came, the London Peace Society had little positive to offer, and did not take a prominent part in anti-war activities. The focus, or foci, of war resistance moved elsewhere.

The members of the Fellowship of Reconciliation wanted to offer a positive rather than a negative contribution to social and political policy and to Christian ethics. Members and sympathisers now had to make individual decisions about their degree of participation in the conflict in which so many of the nation were now involved. A group of Quakers had responded to the challenge within one month of the declaration of war. Philip Baker (later Lord Noel-Baker) issued an appeal in *The Friend* for 21 August 1914, asking for volunteers to form an ambulance unit. About 80 young men, mostly undergraduates at Oxford or Cambridge, responded to the appeal and met for training at Jordans, in Buckinghamshire. The first detachment of eight surgeons and 46 men arrived in France at the end of October, establishing their headquarters at the Hotel du Kursaal, in a suburb of Dunkirk. They set up a hospital at the Villa St Pierre in Dunkirk, then another at Poperinghe, near Ypres; these were followed by others.[2] This group became known as the Friends' Ambulance Unit. The possibility of asking to join it had already begun to formulate in Cadoux's mind before Christmas 1914, when he wrote a preliminary letter of enquiry to Sir George Newman, chairman of the Friends' Ambulance Unit Appeal. He already had some basic first aid and ambulance training, acquired in the Boys' Brigade. He would have to face danger without being involved in the killing of others, satisfying his pacifist principles but countering a charge, from others or within his own mind, of cowardice. He was never an absolute pacifist, that is one who refused to undertake any task at all connected with the war.

Towards the end of Hilary term, during which he had continued his regular routine of morning and evening study and afternoon exercise, with plenty of discussion in between, he approached Sir George Newman again about his eligibility for membership of the Friends' Ambulance Unit. Newman replied that with his ambulance certificates he was acceptable without further training. He then approached Selbie with a view to taking a term's leave from Mansfield, and was happy with Selbie's suggestion that Theodore H. Robinson, Professor of Hebrew at Serampore College, Bengal, should take over his teach-

---

[1] Keith Robbins *The Abolition of War: the Peace Movement in Britain 1914-1919* (1976) p.13.
[2] See M. Tatham and J. E. Miles *The Friends' Ambulance Unit 1914-1919* (1920).

ing while he was on sabbatical leave. He wrote to J.R. Little, honorary Secretary of the FAU, offered his services on a temporary basis, was accepted and received a list of kit to be collected. He then wrote to tell Orchard, who replied:

I cannot say I am sorry you are going . . . you will have more power as a pacifist after what you will have seen.

Come back and help me. Come back with Newman's resolve: 'We have a work to do in England'.

His brothers and sisters did not share his pacifist views, though they respected them as utterly sincere. Connie wrote – 'We both think it a splendid idea and I am sure you will be awfully glad when the war is over that you did this'. His brother Bernard was already serving in the army. Marguerite was prepared to support him in his decision, and as a nurse had some conception of the sort of work he would have to face.

The date fixed for crossing the Channel was 5 April, but, when the small party with whom Cadoux travelled reached Dover, the sea was too rough to enable a boat to land at Dunkirk. They had to return and spend the night in London again. Next day the storm had abated and they were able to cross to Boulogne, though Cadoux was seasick en route. They drove in an ambulance car to Dunkirk and spent the night at the administrative centre at the Hotel du Kursaal. After a day getting to know the town he began his work as an orderly, looking after wounded French soldiers. He had to overcome a natural squeamishness; the first time he watched a dressing being removed from a wound, he felt sure he would be sick when the wound was laid bare – but wasn't.

His duties were to act as an orderly every afternoon and evening at the Villa St Pierre. The mornings were free, if the area was not being shelled, for walking, talking and writing. He had taken some books out with him, and records in his diary reading Scott, Byron, Coleridge, Shelley and Keats. The routine continued reasonably uneventfully for the first two weeks. Then on 22 April, he noted in his diary: 'on leaving work, we hear that Germans have broken British line at Boesinghe and threaten to surround Ypres: and may be here tomorrow aftn'. The second, bitter battle of Ypres had begun: it was to last for five weeks. The Germans now used gas for the first time. Three days after the battle began, on 25 April, Cadoux and two colleagues were told they must go to the FAU station 20 miles inland at Poperinghe, closer to Ypres, where the Unit was working in a number of centres. There followed three days of hectic and frightening activity, moving patients from one hospital to another amidst heavy shelling.

These were his diary entries for Monday and Tuesday, 26 and 27 April:

MONDAY

Poperinghe

6.30 Rise – go to bkfast at Pop B (Hotel du Cercle Catholique). After bkfast wash everyth'g up and cart everyth'g to Pop E.[1] After lunch, talk on journalism with Geoff Young, buy bread, then visit Pop D (29 Rue d'Ypres) and talk to Drs Rees and Thompson. Then return to Pop D and try to go to sleep. Germans begin to shell Poperinghe with heavy shells. 8 shells. 1 every 10 minutes – abt 5–6. Can't sleep. 6 Grub alone 7 pm try to sleep and finally do so soundly, abt 11 three more shells sent into town – rise – Pop E rapidly evacuated by Unit. I collect some things, and clear out of bldg last of all. Go to Pop D (hosp) arr abt 11.45. Find evac^n of patients going on: help.

TUESDAY

A terrible n't at Poperinghe. Evac. Pop D and remove all patients to Pop C (Eliz Chateau). Help Dr Thompson move his effects and others'. Go to Pop C. Help Terrell in Ward Albert. Attend patients. Carry corpse to mortuary. Carry nearly all patients out and send them off by motors. 5.30 Scrap up bkfast. More ward work. Wash in ward. 8.30 Bkfast – come off to Pop E and glad to find it re-inhabited. Write to Maggie.

11.30 am try to sleep – but sleep only till abt 3 pm. After that, stroll round and then lie and try to sleep till 6.45. Then come 3 or 4 shells, 2nd breaks windows of our bedroom: I, Stopford and Priestman clear out hastily: and go at once to Chateau. After dinner, return and remove kit from Pop E. Then go to bed in a motor car outside Chateau.

The next day, after more clearing out, he was sent back to Dunkirk along with other recent arrivals, while many of the original members of the Unit stayed in Poperinghe. The shelling caught up with them in Dunkirk, and on 29 April one shell landed every five minutes in the middle of the day, and the shells came again in the evening. 'Everyone has nerves about more shells. Go to bed in fear and trembling', he wrote in his diary.[2]

On the whole life returned to the previous routine for the rest of Cadoux's stay; he remained in Dunkirk, which was shelled heavily on

[1] Either a theatre or concert hall in the town.

[2] See T. Corder Catchpool *On two fronts* (1918) pp.75-84, for another account of FAU activity during those few days, and also papers of George Barbour, Geoffrey Winthrop Young and R. D. Rees in the Imperial War Museum.

two more occasions. All the time he was helping to look after wounded French soldiers, and civilians hurt in the shelling; as the weather grew hotter, there were opportunities to bathe and walk by the sea in the mornings. He received regular post, including parcels of vegetarian food from Charlton Short.

Cadoux did not record the effect this experience of war at first hand had on him. His mind was already made up about the horror and wrongness of war; his attitude had been reached on rational and ethical grounds and experience of war did not apparently alter the way in which he defended that view. He was fully committed to the work of the Fellowship of Reconciliation, and to preparing for the work which would need to be done when the war was finished in building a 'peace movement'.

On 29 June he returned to England at the end of his term of duty, tired and weary, and went straight to Tonbridge. Ida told him that she strongly disapproved of his engagement to Marguerite. Why she should have done so is not clear. But one can understand that Cadoux left Tonbridge 'feeling flat'. However his spirits were restored when he had 'a very joyous meeting' with Marguerite two days later.

He then returned to Oxford to tidy up his affairs before preparing for the summer conferences at Swanwick – the FOR conference in July and the Free Church Fellowship conference in August. In between, he visited East Boldon; Marguerite was there for part of the time, enabling him to write in his diary, 'These days are the happiest I have spent since I was born'.

He and Marguerite had decided to marry before the end of the year. He had a reasonably secure job with sufficient income to maintain a household, and there was no reason for any further delay. At the beginning of October, Marguerite came to Oxford for the day, and the two of them spent all day looking at houses. They finally decided to rent 204 Divinity Road, a well built semi-detached late Victorian house about a mile from the centre of Oxford. It was an easy cycle ride to Mansfield, and not too far from good walking country. The wedding was planned for December.

The Michaelmas term was busy, back to teaching Hebrew, work on the thesis, and lecturing and writing for the FOR. The FOR had not gained in popularity amongst the Mansfield Senior Common Room during his absence. When Cadoux visited Selbie on 18 October, he noted in his diary, 'He breaks out violently about FOR'; one does not know what may have sparked off this outburst, but a week later Selbie went for a walk with him, listened to his point of view, and took him home to tea. There was a new member of the Senior Common Room,

C. H. Dodd, who was sympathetic to Cadoux's views, though he expressed his own in a much quieter key. Both men were fond of walking, and they often spent the afternoons together in this way.

Sundays were usually spent preaching somewhere in or near Oxford. At the beginning of November he undertook a short lecture tour to Friends' meetings in the Newcastle and Sunderland area, talking about the attitude of the early Christians to the State.

He also kept up with his former Sunday School boys, now scattered over England and France. Both the Bunker brothers were in the army, Harold at the front in France, Alfred a second lieutenant still in England. Some of the others were prepared to take a pacifist stand, which they were free to do so long as conscription was delayed.

When the term ended, he and Marguerite went to Maple's store in London and spent £110 on furniture. On 22 December he returned to London, and spent the night with the Shorts.

Next morning he and Marguerite were married at the Church in the Grove, Sydenham. George Darlaston and David Nicholas conducted the marriage ceremony and Charlton Short was best man. Of Cadoux's five surviving brothers and sisters, only one was able to come – Ida (in spite of her disapproval) with her husband. Their cousin, Wynnie Hill, was also present. Some members of the Asplin family came too, but altogether it was a small wedding.

There was no honeymoon. They prepared for a quiet but happy Christmas, and Jack tried to teach Marguerite to cycle. His diary has few details for the last days of 1915; simply 'Record lost. Housework, study, Bikelesson'. A greater happiness entered his life than he had known before. Bernard wrote from Salonika: 'If you don't give Marguerite too much nut butter or read Grote at the breakfast table, I'm sure your married life will be one of great happiness'.

V

War and peace; the founding of a
family and the making of a scholar
1916–1919

BY THE BEGINNING of 1916, Mansfield was much depleted of students. Some were serving in the army, some were working with the YMCA, and two were with the Friends' Ambulance Unit. Nine were still in residence, which meant only a small teaching load for the members of the Senior Common Room. The college premises were shared with others; two classrooms were handed over to the Serbian Relief Committee for teaching Serbian boys, and the gardens were used each afternoon by the wounded soldiers' garden club.

It was inevitable that sooner or later Mansfield would feel the effect of the war in a personal way. It came in the summer of 1916; within a month two members of the college community were killed; the Principal's son, Robert Joseph Selbie, at Ypres on 13 June, and P.G. Simmonds, an ordinand, on 1 July on the Somme. Cadoux knew them both; Joe Selbie, although nine years younger, had been quite a friend, and P.G. Simmonds had been a pupil. The Principal did not allow his grief to interrupt the end of term formalities, but all knew that the suffering of the war had now reached the heart of the college.

P.G. Simmonds' letters from the front to his friends were later published privately (with a foreword by Selbie), and Cadoux wrote a review of the volume in *The Venturer* (May 1918). After writing of 'the patent beauty and utter unselfishness of PG's character', he continued:

> The reader of pacifist sympathies will naturally hope to find in the book some account of the reasons which led a man of this truly Christian mould to feel it to be his duty to participate in the carnage of Flanders . . .
>
> I for one refuse to believe that actions done under so solemn and earnest a conviction that, in the circumstances, it was God's will that one should do them, can lose their reward, or be without their value for the kingdom of God.

Cadoux's solution to this dilemma was to develop a concept of 'the relative justification of war'. He first gave public expression to the idea at the FOR conference in July 1916, when, according to his diary (4 July), he 'raised a storm' by suggesting that participation in war might have to be regarded as right for some people. He developed the idea further in an article on 'The Implications of Mutual Tolerance' published in *The Venturer* in January 1917. The article began with a brief description of the chief ways

> in which we can try to find out what is the right course of action in any given circumstance. Either we can ask what is the right thing as a matter of principle, or we can seek to discover what course is likely to produce the best results.

Actions done from the right motives, he went on to say, must lead to the best ('relatively, not absolutely') results. For that reason, different points of view must be tolerated. This in turn implied that those who took opposite sides of the argument about the validity of war must recognise

> that, though great evil may result from every man doing that which is right in his own eyes, yet that evil is, so to speak, the minimum possible in the circumstances, i.e. it is less than what would result from a man doing anything else . . .

This point of view was not anarchy, but it did place a very high value on the conscience of the individual, within a general framework of civil government. It was a view he maintained for the rest of his life, and one which he expounded more fully in *Christian Pacifism Reexamined*, written during the first months of the second world war.

For himself, conscience required that he continued to speak and write in opposition to the war. He wrote letters to *The Oxford Chronicle* explaining and supporting the pacifist viewpoint, and contributed several articles to the FOR-sponsored magazine *The Venturer*.

Conscription had become law on 2 March 1916. As an accredited minister, Cadoux himself was exempt, but he was closely associated with others who were not. Early in February, he attended a meeting of representatives of the FOR, the Society of Friends and the No-Conscription Fellowship in Oxford; they constituted themselves the Oxford Joint Advisory Committee to those who had conscientious reasons for refusing to join the forces.

While recognising a man's own conscience as supreme, they recommended the members of their societies to go before the new Military Service Tribunals:

> By appearing before the Tribunal, you do not necessarily agree to accept its judgment as final; on the contrary, you are there for the express purpose of saying that you are bound by no decision save

that of conscience, and there should be no more hesitation in placing your testimony before a Tribunal than before the nation. It will, in fact, give you an exceptional opportunity of stating your belief in the sovereignty of conscience and the wrongness of war. [1]

A refusal to appear, the committee suggested, would be a refusal even to discuss an alternative service to the community, and 'service to humanity' was after all one of the bases of their unwillingness to fight. In addition, 'a cause is always prejudiced by a refusal to come forward and state it, particularly when there is a prevalent suspicion that its upholders are insincere'. The committee were not in unison on acceptable forms of alternative service, but nevertheless were able to offer some helpful guidance. Cadoux's fellow signatories for the FOR were Vernon Herford, V. E. Blott and Frank C. Bryan. For the Society of Friends the signatories were Margaret Gillett, Richard Graham and Edmund New, and for the No-Conscription Fellowship D. H. Blelloch, J. Allan Kaye and H. R. Runacres.

When the tribunals began their sittings in March, Cadoux spent a good deal of time at the hearings, giving moral and where necessary vocal support to those whose cases were heard. On 16 March he travelled out in the morning to Chipping Norton to support the appeal of four young men. Ten days later, while Cadoux was attending a conference at Woodbrooke Settlement, Birmingham, on training for peace work after the war, there appeared a report of this sitting in *The Oxford Chronicle*:

> During this appeal and the three subsequent ones there was present a Mr C. John Cadoux, of Mansfield College, Oxford, who, it was gathered, attended to assist these four applicants . . . Mr Cadoux, with the consent of the Tribunal, spoke in support of the Appeal. His main point was that under the Military Service Act, a man was entitled to exemption from combatant service on conscientious grounds, if the sincerity of the appeal is accepted.

Selbie happened to read this during a railway journey; he wasted no time in putting pen to paper on Rugby station:

> I was greatly troubled to see in the paper that 'a Mr Cadoux of Mansfield College' had been appearing before the tribunal on behalf of some conscientious objectors. I suppose nothing that I can say will persuade you of the extreme unwisdom of such action but I must beg you to keep the name of the college out of it. Give your private address and do not compromise us.

[1] Recommendations of the Oxford Joint Advisory Committee, 11 February 1916, in *The Cadoux Papers*.

There followed an awkward interview. Cadoux did not record in his diary whether or not he agreed to Selbie's request, but it appears that in practice there was no more trouble on this particular account. It should be said that this strong disagreement in no way affected Cadoux's respect for his former teacher as a theologian or educator of preachers, neither did it alter Selbie's willingness to talk with Cadoux or to help him to pursue his vocation.

Cadoux's Catford friends still kept in touch with him, and he with them. Horace Fuller's appeal to the local tribunal was turned down, his firm dismissed him and by June he was serving a sentence of hard labour in Wormwood Scrubs. He spent the rest of the war in and out of prison; when out of prison he spent his time in work camps. He managed somehow to smuggle letters out of prison to Cadoux, in minute writing on the only paper available. Wilfred Bligh was granted a non-combatant certificate and spent a good deal of time road-making in Newhaven. Edward Beck was allowed to work on farms in Norfolk and Cadoux was able to visit him once or twice. Edward Yuill, on the other hand, like the Bunker brothers, was in the army; he went out to the Middle East, was sent copies of W. E. Orchard's articles and sermons by Cadoux and others, and discussed them at length in his correspondence with Cadoux.

In the summer of 1916, Cadoux and his wife were able to take a holiday together – the first since their marriage. After Cadoux had attended the FOR conference at Swanwick, they went to Inkpen, a few miles south of the vale of the Kennett in Berkshire, and spent ten happy days, reading and walking in the peaceful countryside. Cadoux always felt very strongly the healing power of nature, and gathered strength, emotionally and physically, for his work. He and Marguerite were expecting their first child in December, and had much to look forward to. They had friends in Hungerford – the Congregational church secretary and his wife – near enough to visit from Inkpen once or twice. There was one preaching engagement on the last day of the holiday, at Hungerford, when Cadoux preached what must have been one of his favourite sermons (since he delivered it so many times in different places) – on failure and perseverance.

The most important event of the year for Cadoux and his wife in their personal lives, was the birth of a son, Theodore John, on 6 December at home. Both parents were thrilled, and Cadoux immediately (within hours) wrote postcards 'to everyone' and called on 'dozens of people'. A letter of congratulation came by return from Arthur – 'A long and good life to him. But do not start him on Hebrew too soon'. Another letter came from H. H. Rowley – 'Doubtless you have already taught Baby to live according to schedule, and have demonstrated the incontrovertible logical basis of Pacifism'. A fortnight later, Jack and Marguerite celebrated their first wedding anniversary. He gave her Basil Mathews' *Paul the Dauntless;* she gave him Grote's *History of Greece.* One cannot help suspecting that both presents were the choice of one partner. Their marriage was now cemented, their happiness deepened; Jack had a family to work for, and Marguerite had a family to look after.

By the beginning of 1917 theological students were liable to be called up, and there were even fewer students at Mansfield and less teaching to be done. By the autumn there were only two students left. Cadoux was given charge of the library and did a good deal of reorganisation. Apart from a little teaching and preaching in country churches at weekends, he was otherwise working at his thesis. The thesis itself was finally completed early in August, just before the family set off on another holiday at Inkpen, which provided a short, but necessary break. Cadoux then went off on his own to the FOR and Free Church Fellowship conferences. When he came back, he settled down to typing and checking the thesis. The purposeful routine was broken at the end of September when he heard 'the dreadful knews [sic] of dear Harold Bunker's death in action on 20th'; the shock had even disturbed his spelling. That very day he had written to Bunker, re-affirming their 'long and great friendship' which could not be severed even by their strong differences on the war, and expressing the hope that Harold would come and visit him on his next leave 'despite my being a dragon on certain subjects'. The letter was returned unopened. When Jack and Marguerite had another son, they named him Harold after the friend they had lost.

The typing of the thesis was completed by the last week of November, and on the 23rd Cadoux noted in his diary: 'Aftn M and I take thesis to binders in triumph. Evg. Draw up plans for study'. He was able to take it up to London early in December and hand it in to the university; that same day he visited the headquarters of the Friends' Ambulance Unit to see if they would be prepared to allow him to go out to France again for another term of four months. Selbie favoured this idea and thought that the college would be able to keep him for another year after his return. Ida, whose son Ronald was about to join the Honourable Artillery Company, wrote that she was '*delighted* to hear you think of taking Ambulance work. Had long been wishing and hoping you would do that or chaplain's work'. But when the FAU committee came to consider his offer, they were not able to arrange for him to go abroad for a short period, for the Unit now consisted solely of those who had committed themselves for the duration of the war. When there were rumours of the possible calling up of clergy and ministers in the spring of 1918 he contemplated offering his services for the rest of the war, and was given Selbie's blessing in this idea. Leyton Richards (now general secretary of the FOR) advised otherwise:

> If you can find a pulpit willing to accept you, take it! Nothing is more needed just at present than to bear a positive witness for Peace, and though less dramatic I feel it is far more worth doing than trotting off to Dunkirk or elsewhere under the FAU.

In the end that particular form of conscription never came into force. For the time being he was occupied with his academic work, the library, a little teaching, preaching each weekend at Hungerford, and membership of the FOR Council. He had also joined the Oxford Society of Historical Theology, and enjoyed the papers and discussion greatly. But he had not taken a really substantial break from work for years, and in the spring of 1918 he was forced to take a month's leave because of pleurisy. On his first day in bed, the notice came from London University stating that he had been awarded the degree of Doctor of Divinity. The relief and satisfaction made it easier for him to let go a little and relax, in so far as he ever did relax, and allow his body to draw on its own healing powers, in its own time. Arthur wrote immediately, 'I have always felt there was something wrong about my having the degree when you had not; now I shall feel more comfortable about it'.

He was now beginning to publish articles and to lay the foundations of his work as a scholar. There was one dominant theme of all his writing during this period: the Christian response to evil. Three articles dealt with the place and functions of the state under the Christian dispensation. The first, published in *The Expositor* (August 1916), dealt with 'St Paul's conception of the state'; the second, published in *The Expositor* two months later (October 1916), dealt with 'Our Lord's conception of the state'. 'The Christianisation of the world . . . does not mean the removal of restraints on wrong-doing, but the substitution of a better method of restraint for a worse'. The process would inevitably be slow; but the fact that society as a whole could not practise this 'better' method ('the Cross of Christ, as preached and lived out by Christ's Church' was 'the one true and radical solvent of human sin') should not prevent a minority from trying to follow it. And a Christian was able to undertake many of the State's tasks without any disloyalty to his faith so long as the use of force was not involved. A third article, published in *The Expositor* in April 1917, on 'The attitude of Jesus to the Jewish administration of justice' dealt with a similar theme.

A more significant piece of work was a chapter on 'The witness of the Church' in a volume entitled *The Ministry of Reconciliation* edited by Hugh Martin (1916). The volume was produced by members of the Fellowship of Reconciliation and included chapters by W. E. Orchard, Richard Roberts and Henry Hodgkin, amongst others. Cadoux's contribution was a concise survey of the attitude of the Church towards participation in war throughout its history; much of the material in the essay was derived from his current research on the attitude of the early Church towards the world. History, he argued, could not answer directly the question whether or not Christians should fight, but it could throw light on the problem. While demonstrating that there was no consistent teaching on the subject, he claimed that the Church had always stood for peace (even if war were not explicitly forbidden), and that in every age some voices had been raise᠎ ᠎᠎ condemnation of war.

> ᠎᠎ time rolls on, the Christian conscience is ever gradually awakening, now to this, now to that, new problem of applied Christianity.[1]

The existing situation required those who wished to awaken or re-awaken this conscience to

> . . . think out and present to their fellow Christians a system of ethical conduct, in which due account shall be taken of the divergence of Christians' views on this matter, due justice done to all honest convictions, due provision made for the authority of a priori Christian principles, the relations between the Christian individual and the partially Christianised society in which he lives adequately worked out, and the respective provinces of the Christian and sub-Christian standards properly adjusted.[2]

This was one of the major themes he tried to develop in his later writings.

His most important work at this period was his first book, *The Early Christian Attitude to War*, written early in 1918 and published the following year. It drew largely on material in his thesis, illuminated by his personal response to Christian teaching and to the war being fought while the book was being written.

It is one of his best books and one of his most enduring (it was reissued in 1940 and again in 1982). It contained the essence of much

[1] P.32.
[2] *Ibid.* p.49.

of his later thought: an insistence that Jesus left behind a body of teaching which contained specific requirements, that this teaching had political implications, and that the Church had compromised this teaching by the concordat with Constantine. In addition, there was Cadoux's oft-repeated emphasis on the positive aspects of non-resistance, and a discussion of the relative justification of differing moral standards.

The book contains a careful, detailed, systematic study of the teaching of Jesus about war, and of the writings and teaching of early Christian leaders before the conversion of Constantine and consequent alliance between church and state. As Cadoux explained in the introduction, his thesis had involved working through 'virtually the whole of pre-Constantinian Christian literature', and while doing this he had taken the opportunity 'to collect practically all the available material in the original authorities'. The subject had not been covered adequately in any work in English. Adolf Harnack's recent comprehensive work, *Militia Christi (The Soldiery of Christ: The Christian Religion and the Military Profession in the First Three Centuries)*, published in 1905, was only available in German. Cadoux believed that there was a place for a fresh work in English, for despite Harnack's 'thoroughness, the extent of his learning, and his general saneness and impartiality of judgment, the arrangement of the material, and, in some cases, the conclusions arrived at, leave something to be desired'.[1]

The whole work was written in the form of a debate, with arguments on both sides of the question discussed. Thus the first section, on the teaching of Jesus, presented both the statements of Jesus inconsistent with the lawfulness of war for Christians, and those apparently legitimizing warfare for Christians. But to this exposition he prefixed a discussion of the range of Jesus' teaching:

> There is a sense in which it is true to say that Jesus gave his disciples no explicit teaching on the subject of war. The application of his ethical principles to the concrete affairs of life was not something which could be seen and taught in its entirety from the very first, but was bound to involve a long series of more or less complex problems; and the short lapse and other special conditions of his earthly life rendered it impossible for him to pronounce decisions on more than a very few of these.[2]

---

[1] P. 11. The material in the book was later incorporated in a somewhat different form into another work, *The Early Church and the World* (1925). See below, pp. 100-101.

[2] C. J. Cadoux *The Early Christian Attitude to War* (1919) p. 19.

Much of the teaching in the gospels specifically condemns killing: there is the reiteration, in *Matthew* 5. 21, of the Mosaic commandment, 'Thou shalt not kill', and the precept of non-resistance later in the same chapter (38–44). Behind this specific teaching is the way in which Jesus interpreted his mission; he refused to advance his ideals by coercive means, and finally offered no resistance to those who brought him to death.

On the other hand, there were Christians who argued that 'obedience to the non-resistance teaching of Jesus is so obviously inconsistent with the peace and well-being of society that he could not have meant this teaching to be taken literally'.[1] Cadoux rejected this argument; such teaching may not be appropriate for 'the whole of unredeemed humanity' but it is 'strictly relative to the status of discipleship' – 'essentially a law for the Christian community'. Similarly he rejected the idea that Jesus' teaching was intended as 'an interim ethic' and therefore no longer appropriate for modern Christians who did not live in daily expectation of the break-up of the existing world order. Such an argument, said Cadoux, was 'the last fortress of militarism on Christian soil'; it could not be justified by critical study of the New Testament, which did not prove that the gospel ethics could be entirely explained by reference to Jesus' expectation of the approaching end of the world.[2]

The second and third parts of the book discussed the forms of the early Christian disapproval of war, and the forms of its acceptance, with detailed reference to the teachers of the early Church. Cadoux examined both the teaching and the social setting in which it was given. Military service was not at first an issue for Christians, for the emperor was able to man his army with volunteers, and very few Christians were also soldiers during the first two centuries of the Christian era. Thus

> the mind of the Church, while in full possession of the pertinent teaching of Jesus, had for a long time no occasion to make a definite application of it to this particular question or to lay down a definite ruling in regard to it. There was thus a certain unguardedness, a certain immaturity of reflection, which, besides accounting for the silence of early Christian authors on the point, helped to make room for various compromises and commitments.[3]

Origen, 'the prince of early Christian thinkers', was the most

[1] *Ibid.* p.42.
[2] *Ibid.* pp.44-47.
[3] *Ibid.* p.247.

important writer on the subject in the early church; 'his defence of the early Christian refusal to participate in war is the only one that faces at all thoroughly or completely the ultimate problems involved'.[1] Cadoux devoted a number of pages to a careful discussion of Origen's views, defending him against those critics who regarded him as short-sighted and unrealistic.

Cadoux admitted that the whole question was complicated. But he believed that Constantine's conversion had caught the Church off her guard:

> She found herself compelled by the eagerness with which she welcomed him, and by her own immaturity of thought and inconsistency of practice, to make his standards of righteousness in certain respects her own.[2]

His final challenge to the reader was this:

> . . . is there anything in our modern conditions which really invalidates the testimony against war as the early Christians bore it, and as Origen defended it?[3]

On the whole the book was welcomed by critics. H. T. Andrews, writing in the *Mansfield College Magazine* (July 1919) asserted that 'Cadoux has won his spurs in the lists, and proved his title to an accredited place in the foremost rank of modern scholars'. He, like some other reviewers, wished that Cadoux had dealt with a longer period of history by taking the discussion on past Constantine to the time of Augustine, but recognised the investigation of Origen's position as one of the most valuable parts of the book, and acknowledged the value of a clear and forcible statement of the Christian ideal in the face of war. J. F. Bethune-Baker, Anglican editor of *The Journal of Theological Studies*, who had himself written a monograph on Christianity and war for a university prize essay at Cambridge, wrote a review (April 1921) in which he regretted that the book 'is a good deal coloured by his own conviction that approval of war is incompatible with the profession of Christianity' but recognised the value of the work in general. To be fair to Cadoux, it was hardly possible for a Christian minister writing in 1919 to approach such a subject from a neutral standpoint. His pacifism preceded his historical study, but his examination of those early sources enabled him to give a more scholarly defence of his ethical position.

The book remains today one of the most thorough expositions of the subject, though a work by Jean-Michel Hornus, *Evangile et*

[1] *Ibid*. p.129.
[2] *Ibid*. p.262.
[3] *Ibid*. p.263.

labarum: Etude sur l'attitude du christianisme devant les problèmes de l'Etat, de la guerre et de la violence[1] (1960), which began as an attempt at a revision of Cadoux's work, has covered the same ground (and continued the study into the post-Constantinian era) while setting it within a more recent understanding of the eschatological background.

The end of the war in November 1918 found Cadoux and his wife celebrating not only the armistice, in common with everyone else, but also their personal joy in the birth of their second son, Harold John, three weeks earlier.

During the next few months Cadoux took pastoral oversight of the small Free Church in Benson, about 14 miles from Oxford. Every Sunday he cycled over to take the morning and evening services, and in between would visit members of the congregation. The church was regularly served by Mansfield students and staff, and what it lost in the brevity of its ministries must have been amply compensated for by their quality; C.H. Dodd was an earlier pastor, and now, for several months, Cadoux. Cadoux, in his turn, was able to experience the rewards and satisfaction of a more continuous ministry to a settled community. In succeeding years he corresponded with some of the friends he made there; one of them told him how much they later missed his 'cheery visits'.

His appointment at Mansfield was due to expire in the summer of 1919, and with a growing family to support, he must find a new position with, if possible, a larger salary.

In March 1919 he heard from Selbie that the Yorkshire United Independent College in Bradford, one of the other institutions for training Congregational ministers, was seeking a professor in New Testament Studies (the post's official designation was 'the Chair of New Testament Criticism, Exegesis and Theology as applied to Modern Thought and Life'); the vacancy, unfilled for the previous eighteen months, had been created by the appointment of A. J. Grieve to the Principalship of the Congregational College in Edinburgh. Selbie was prepared to recommend him, and his academic achievements to date were such that he could not fail to be regarded as a strong contestant. Within a few days his mind was made up. He would apply. He set about collecting testimonials from Selbie (who wrote of him as 'one of the most able and industrious students I have ever known'), James Moffatt, Darlaston ('Dr Cadoux is a clear-minded man, with great mental tenacity and an unwearying capacity for

---

[1] Published in English in 1980 under the title *It is not lawful for me to fight*.

work'), A. J. Carlyle, E. W. Watson and William Sanday. Sanday, Lady Margaret Professor of Divinity at Christ Church and an Anglican New Testament scholar, wrote of him:

> I was struck at once by his gift of simple, lucid, clear and exact expression. . . . I should predict for Mr Cadoux in that capacity a career of exceptional distinction and success.

Their encounters would have been chiefly at Sanday's seminars on New Testament studies.

Cadoux did not have to wait long to hear the result of his application. He was summoned to Bradford within a fortnight and interviewed along with two other candidates on 15 April; when he was asked whether he would feel it his duty, if appointed, to continue to express his pacifist views as occasion arose, he replied that he certainly would. He feared that this declaration had cost him the appointment, so it was with some surprise that he was told later that afternoon that the College's Board of Education had unanimously appointed him to the New Testament Chair.

His appointment was welcomed by his friends, by the students at the college, and by the Congregational ministers in the area. Herbert Morgan wrote that the Bradford governors had 'done themselves a good turn'; Darlaston predicted accurately that he would be happy in Yorkshire and would like the people. The students' secretary wrote of their 'great hopes for our future work in New Testament', and 'the great good that will accrue to us'; and a group of Yorkshire ministers elected him to a circle at work on 'Church ideals'.

Practical problems now came to the fore; there was a house to find in Bradford, and affairs at Mansfield to be put in order for handing over to a successor. At the end of Trinity term, Cadoux went up to Bradford for the college commemoration day and took the opportunity to do some house-hunting. After looking at two or three other houses, he chose 8 Sleningford Road, Shipley, and with help from the college and a building society was able to put down a deposit for it. Marguerite did not see it before the decision was made, but was given a careful description of it. She, meanwhile, had been talking in Oxford to Margaret Gaunt (whose brother-in-law was a Congregational minister in Yorkshire), after which she wrote to her husband that she had learned that the Bradfordians 'class the No Hat Brigade and Veg as cranks! I can see we are in for a high old time'.

In between the practical tasks Cadoux was working on a draft manifesto from the FOR to the churches, which was published later in the year as *An Appeal to the People of the Christian Church*. It was an appeal to Christians to think out their attitude to any future war. The manifesto was not produced without a good deal of discussion and re-drafting. The new general secretary of the FOR, Oliver Dryer, felt that Cadoux had not really dealt with the central point at issue in the pacifist argument, that of the position of a Christian within a community which is not yet fully Christian, but had treated it as one among several equally important difficulties. He put this point in a letter to Cadoux in July; Cadoux went up to London for a long discussion. The manifesto was drafted yet again, and the final version dealt more thoroughly with the problem which Dryer had raised.

In August both Jack and Marguerite were very tired. She was finding herself irritable, and he was feeling weary and depressed. He did have one bright interlude when he visited Harpenden to preach in the middle of the month. He wrote in his diary: '. . . a wonderfully inspiring weekend in a most beautiful house [designed by Frank Salisbury] w charming host, hostess and family'. It was like a shaft of sunlight in an otherwise cloudy summer.

The move to Bradford took place in the middle of September, just a few days before the college term was due to start. This was the beginning of a new stage of life for the family, in a setting very different from Oxford.

VI

Bradford: teaching
1919–1920

BRADFORD WAS a proud Yorkshire industrial city, a centre of the wool and worsted industry. It had a long Puritan tradition, going back to the sixteenth century, and Nonconformity was still strong. The hill-top villages surrounding the city centre had large, thriving, wealthy chapels, where the virtues of hard work, cleanliness and a sober life were extolled. The climate could be harsh, and the smoky, dirty atmosphere of the city and the mill villages contrasted sharply with the beauty of Wharfedale and the further dales. It was a vigorous, wealthy but in many ways hard place in which to live; certainly a great contrast to Oxford.

Sleningford Road, where the Cadoux family established their new home, was in Shipley, about four miles to the north of the centre of Bradford, in the Aire valley and on the edge of the open countryside. It was a short, steep, unmade road, turning downhill to the north off the main Bradford-Bingley road. The back gardens of the houses on the west side – of which the Cadouxs' was one – gave direct access across stone stiles to a wood of oak trees, scattered with boulders of millstone grit; this wood extended to the bottom of the Aire valley. Along the valley ran not only the river, but also the railway and the Leeds-Liverpool canal; not far away to the west, the canal was carried over the river by a spectacular seven-arched bridge. To the east, river, railway and canal followed parallel courses, reaching Saltaire within a mile of the Cadoux home. Saltaire had been built by Sir Titus Salt (1803–76) as a model town for the employees in his alpaca factory. Salt had been a Congregationalist and the finest building in the town was the Italianate Congregational church, which the Cadoux family attended regularly.

The Cadouxs' home, number 8, was half-way down Sleningford Road; it was semi-detached, single-fronted, about a dozen years old, and like the other houses of the same area and date, was solidly built of buff-coloured sandstone. There was a good-sized garden to the front as well as at the back. It was of four storeys, including a basement and attics. The basement, owing to the inclined site, was level with the ground to the north and west. The floor above contained the dining room at the front, and to the rear, Cadoux's study, which also served as a drawing room, and the kitchen. The study had a fine view over the woods and up the valley. With all four storeys in use (the basement for washing and storage) the house was hardly labour-saving, but the employment of a living-in maid did something to lighten the load for Marguerite. For the children, the gardens and surroundings were ideal, and for Cadoux the area offered exceptional variety and attraction for walking. From Saltaire one could strike northwards up Shipley Glen, with its little funicular tramway, to open moorland and the rounded top of Hope Hill (927 feet), on the edge of the uplands that continued unbroken to Ilkley Moor and Wharfedale. Here Cadoux found what he later called 'expansion of the spirit', and when alone, the opportunity for prayer and meditation, which fortified him to meet the stresses which his sensitive nature encountered in daily life.

The people were friendly, direct and down-to-earth. The Yorkshire mind is not by nature speculative or philosophical, but rather pragmatic and practical. Where appreciation is offered, it is genuine and spontaneous. When Cadoux visited one local village church to preach, soon after arriving in Bradford, he received this letter of thanks from a member of the congregation:

> Many thanks for your sermon Sun even, it was splendid in every way. We could follow every word and take it all in, and it will be a long time before the lesson of Barnabas will be forgotten. My immediate companions said what a pity we could not show our appreciation by giving you a right good clap.

The other side of the coin was a readiness to criticise, a suspicion of anything too academic, and in some quarters a singular reluctance to put a fair value, in monetary terms, on preaching and pastoral ministry.

This is not to deny the existence of a broader, more educated, more cultured atmosphere as well. There were two excellent grammar schools, one for boys and one for girls, in Bradford, which had always enjoyed a high standing; the City Council, too, was ahead of the national achievement in the provision of local authority education. And it was a Bradford MP, W. E. Forster, who had been chiefly responsible for the Education Act of 1870, the first piece of legislation to attempt to give at least an elementary education to every child in the country.

The cultural life of the city owed much to the German and other European merchants who settled in the Manningham area of Bradford in the late nineteenth century. Two doctors of European background added great distinction to Bradford life in the early years of the twentieth century, and both became friends of Cadoux. Dr Andrea Rabagliati (known among the local community as "im wi' t' name'), born of an Italian father in Edinburgh, had worked in Bradford as a physician for many years, and held unconventional ideas on diet. He believed that the chief cause of disease was an excess of food – 'plugging and blocking and choking up the body with nourishment', he told a journalist of the *Bradford Weekly Telegraph* (16 December 1910); though few of his colleagues agreed with him, he was held in much respect in Bradford and elsewhere. Dr F. W. Eurich,[1] another highly respected consultant physician, was a pioneer in conquering anthrax. Both these men began to attend the Bradford Friends' Meeting, with which Cadoux came to have many associations, and both belonged to the Athenaeum, a small, select intellectual society in Bradford at which each member in turn read a paper, a society of which Cadoux was soon elected a member.

The Yorkshire United Independent College[2] was in Emm Lane, a mile and a half from the centre of Bradford, close to the road to Shipley. This meant either a cycle ride for Cadoux along this busy road (he frequently conserved both time and energy by holding on to a lorry taking the same route, until he was threatened with prosecution for doing it), or a walk over the top of Moorhead Lane and across a golf course. The college was pleasantly situated near Manningham Park and the Cartwright Memorial Hall, the municipal art gallery.

The buildings of the college dated from 1877, when the then Airedale College (directly descended from a Dissenting Academy) moved from an earlier home on the other side of Bradford, acquiring at the same time a new principal, Andrew Martin Fairbairn, later the architect of Mansfield's theological reputation.[3] At Airedale College he served his apprenticeship as a theological college principal. One of the first changes he made in Bradford was to separate the arts and theology courses; except in special circumstances, a prospective ordinand was in future to have an arts degree before beginning his theological course. He arranged that the students should take their arts degrees at Edinburgh University, a custom which continued as

[1] See Margaret Bligh *Dr Eurich of Bradford* (1960).
[2] For the history of the college, see K. W. Wadsworth *Yorkshire United Independent College* (1954).
[3] See above p.29.

long as the college functioned. When Fairbairn departed to Mansfield, Airedale College was amalgamated with another college at Rotherham to form the Yorkshire United Independent College (1888). After the short principalship of F. J. Falding, and the longer one of D. W. Simon, the college governors appointed Ebenezer Griffith-Jones as Principal in 1907. Griffith-Jones retained that position almost to the end of Cadoux's time in Bradford, and in spite of some sharp differences of theological and ethical opinion (he had no sympathy with pacifism), the two held each other in mutual respect and affection, and remained lifelong friends.

Griffith-Jones was a Welshman, educated at the Presbyterian College, Carmarthen and New College, London. The first half of his career was spent as Congregational minister in churches in both England and Wales, during which time he published *The Ascent through Christ* (1899), his most successful book – an attempt to reconcile modern scientific thought with Christian faith. In 1907, at the age of 47, he came to Bradford as Principal and Professor of Systematic Theology. A vigorous, energetic teacher with a temperament which could erupt with Welsh fire when occasion demanded, he was a respected figure in Yorkshire Congregationalism and beyond. In the year 1918–19 he served as chairman of the Congregational Union of England and Wales. Theology was his life, and the opportunity to discuss it was always more attractive to him than anything else – unless it were driving his well-known elderly motor car; even when driving, theological questions could suddenly seize all his attention, much to the consternation of his passengers. He was an engaging man, whose motto was said to have been, 'we must learn to disagree without being disagreeable'.

Soon after his appointment, Cadoux wrote to Griffith-Jones to ask him to clarify what the governors of the college and appointing committee had had in mind when advertising for a professor to teach 'New Testament Criticism, Exegesis and Theology *as applied to Modern Thought and Life*'. Griffith-Jones' reply, dated 26 May 1919, included the following:

> What I have to complain of as a professor of Homiletics is that students do not use the New Testament as the real text-book of their Faith in a fair way. They choose texts apart from their context, and use them as mottoes for their own little philosophy of life, without any real regard for their meaning as written, and often the text has only a remote and accidental relation to their subject. The New Testament never seems to have gripped them in any vital way . . . The remedy lies in my opinion in the hands of

the man who has the great privilege of dealing with the New Testament in their College life . . . All great preachers are Biblical preachers, and the reason why they are great is that they themselves have been gripped by the Book, and that their teaching is controlled by its power over their own souls.

On receiving Cadoux's reply (unfortunately not extant) Griffith-Jones replied on 5 June:

There is not much divergence between us in regard to the matters you deal with. I am as far as you are from being a Bibliolater . . . I agree that the New Testament is more a record of the working faith of the Primitive Church than an authoritative text-book.

In the event, Cadoux's liberal theology proved something of an embarrassment to Griffith-Jones on some occasions, but not to the extent that it strained their mutual respect and co-operation. On pacifism they never agreed; Griffith-Jones had supported the war and had encouraged the students to enlist. The college was closed for much of the war, enabling the Principal to go on a lecture tour of the United States and Canada under the auspices of the Ministry of Information, while the rest of the staff had looked after vacant churches.

The Old Testament teacher was Archibald Duff, now 75 years of age. Born in Scotland, his family emigrated to Canada when he was eleven, and he was educated at the universities of McGill, Boston, Halle and Göttingen (where one of his teachers was Albrecht Ritschl). He received a thorough grounding in Germany not only in doctrine and philosophy, but also in Semitic languages.[1] He began his career teaching mathematics and Semitics at McGill University. He first came to Airedale College in 1878 at Fairbairn's invitation. A man of great courtesy, learning and devotion, who had inspired many generations of students with his teaching, he was now past his prime as a lecturer, and out of touch with the new generation returning from the war. He was later remembered by the post-war generation of students as 'kindly, friendly and approachable', but more of a talker than a listener. His classes and lectures provided an opportunity for students to pursue other quiet business without being unduly observed or disturbed, and it became more and more of an embarrassment to the college authorities to know how to effect any change in the situation. He proved a loyal and scholarly colleague of Cadoux's, and a personal

[1] See Duff's interesting draft of the first part of his autobiography, published posthumously in *The Congregational Quarterly* (Oct. 1936) pp.302-314, 'A theological professor's training in the 19th century'.

link with that German theological thinking to which Cadoux owed much.

Apologetics and philosophy were in the hands of Ernest Price, a man of similar age to Cadoux. He had joined the college in 1914, and was just getting into his stride as a theological teacher after the disruption of the war. He was a versatile, acute scholar, an informed and balanced exponent of the Reformed tradition, and an excellent historian; a man of equable temperament and a congenial colleague. He had come to the college after training for the ministry at the Lancashire Independent College and a four year ministry at Farnworth.

The last member of the staff was the Arts tutor, Ambrose Pope, the only other member of the college to have been educated at Mansfield. He loved to talk about his time there under Fairbairn in the 1890s and found in Cadoux a willing listener. When Cadoux wrote Pope's obituary in the *Mansfield College Magazine* (July 1928) he described him as 'stiffly conservative in his theological outlook' and as confessing 'to have no appreciation of poetry'; but 'within the limits set to him, the quality of his service was beyond criticism'.

The Cadoux family moved into their new home on 22 September 1919. Four days later, Cadoux met his classes for the first time. That same evening, he recorded in his diary, 'feel very sad'. It is not clear just why he was sad, but presumably it had something to do with the fact that the academic standards of the Yorkshire College could not be set so high as at Mansfield. He realised that he was now launched on a career which would keep him away from Oxford for several years, in a place and amongst a people as yet strange and untested, in a city without a university, and far away from his family and friends. It was only as time went on, and only fully in retrospect, that he came to appreciate the advantages, as well as the drawbacks, of Bradford and the United College: the open and generous comradeship of his colleagues, the liveliness and enthusiasm of his students, the respect accorded to his own scholarship, and the freedom, relatively speaking, which he enjoyed in pursuing 'our common search for truth' (one of his favourite phrases).

The occasion of his inaugural address was not a promising event. He wrote in his diary for 7 October, 'Evg M & I cycle to Coll for my inaugural address but in view of absence of audience it resolved itself into a fireside talk in the Liby with Prin'. The likelihood is that no proper advertisement of the lecture was made. There was a larger attendance at his official induction to the professorial chair, which took the form of a service, held in the presence of the governors, most of them representatives of the local Congregational churches which provided much of the income for the college.

There were twelve students in college for the beginning of term. Others already accepted as students for the ministry were in Edinburgh, working for their arts degrees or diplomas before taking the theological training. The Edinburgh students lived in a hostel specially provided for them, but the Bradford college, like Mansfield, was not residential and the students lived out in digs. They met together for prayers each morning, and staff and students usually had lunch together.

Most of the students had been doing war service of some kind, many of them in the trenches in France. Their meeting with the newly-appointed New Testament professor, an exacting scholar opposed to war and any participation in warlike activity, must have engendered a certain tension. Many years later, Ralph Turner, students' secretary in 1919, writing to congratulate Cadoux on his Edinburgh honorary DD (23 March 1932), took the opportunity to look back on that meeting and on what it came to mean:

> Our meeting was at a difficult time. You came to a body of students who (with one or two exceptions) had all been soldiers. They were fresh back from the war, out of the habits of the study, and with a background such as no generation of students had within living memory. There were sore places in their lives. They had lost years out of their expected span. They were stiff in the joints so far as close application to books was concerned. It took them all their time even to keep awake after being in a room for a couple of hours. They felt this disablement keenly and it seemed to them that those who did not go to the war but who had gone on with their studies had made more out of the war than those who suffered. You came with pronounced pacifist views. You held them sincerely and somehow they kept cropping up in lectures and talks. It seemed to us, using the habit of careless judgment we had acquired in the war, that you thought we were a very poor set of Christians and that you were a little puzzled to know why ex-soldiers were in training for the Ministry at all . . . By the time we had had three years with you we knew a good deal more about you and you about us . . . I think really we have grown. . . . I am sure that as the years have passed by you have found a bigger and bigger place in the hearts of the men you first taught at Bradford.

Cadoux's teaching was based chiefly on the Gospels, with careful study of the Greek text of selected passages, an introductory course on the text and canon of the New Testament, and an emphasis on the historical value of the New Testament record. For each professor's course there was an examination at the end of each of the three years, with external examiners; Cadoux invited C.H. Dodd to act in this capacity for him, and the arrangement continued happily for several years. The best students were allowed to register for the BD examination at the University of Edinburgh, which recognised the teaching at United College for this purpose. As time went on, a larger number of students registered for this degree, but in the immediate post-war years, it was only a minority who were able to reach the required standard. The remaining students worked for an internal college qualification.

Cadoux was an exacting teacher. Inadequate preparation, daydreaming in class, impatience with Greek particles, were all given short shrift. His students had to work hard at the Greek text; the chosen passages of the New Testament were studied in great detail – translation, grammar, exegesis and textual criticism. In his second year at the college, he was able to write in his report that 'All concerned have worked together heartily and happily in the study of the origins of our religion'.

There was a certain pedantic aspect to his teaching which students may have found puzzling and even irritating; for example, he insisted on calling the early Church Fathers and their contemporaries by the original Latin or Greek form of their names, in preference to the familiar English form, where that was different, and expected his students to do the same; thus for him Origen was Origenes and Tertullian Tertullianus. These unfamiliar forms often incurred the criticism of reviewers of his books. 'I beseech you, gentlemen', one of his students remembers him saying, 'get it right once and for all. Not Jerome, but Hieronymus'.

> But one day in class, when listing various authorities who supported a certain viewpoint, he forgot himself and concluded, 'Finally, gentlemen, there's Jerome'. At once I enquired softly whether he meant Hieronymus. He flushed red with sudden anger and growled, 'Yes, I did'. By the end of class his momentary annoyance had vanished, and when I apologised if I had annoyed him, he answered, 'Not at all. You did right. How did I come to make that stupid mistake?'[1]

He loved talking with his students, questioning them and arguing with them. Another student remembers:

[1] Harold Wickings, in a letter to the author 21 April 1982.

It was Cadoux's custom to invite his students to have tea with him at his home near Shipley. I remember well his sparsely furnished study with open bookshelves, stretching from floor to ceiling around three of the walls, with a ladder available to reach the otherwise inaccessible volumes.

Before tea, he would take his visitors for a walk sometimes through neighbouring meadows, sometimes on more distant moorland, the main purpose of which was to inspect the furniture of the student's mind.[1]

On other occasions, he would take students out for tea. Harold Wickings recollects:

It was thrilling and inspiring to walk with the Professor in the countryside because he opened up marvellously on a dozen themes. Moreover he possessed a gift for being able to cajole cups of tea and a plate of scones out of Yorkshire cottagers who at first presented a hard and unyielding exterior. He would begin with an engaging smile and the words, 'My good woman . . .' Even a refusal in West Riding accents, 'Nay, we don't do teas 'ere', did not put him off. He wheedled, 'Do I not perceive the kettle already singing a welcome to us? Come now!' He overcame the opposition every time. Some of his opponents in theological controversy might well have appreciated him better if they too had been privileged to enjoy friendship and kindness on the road and at tea-time.

He always encouraged his students to think for themselves, indeed he seemed to enjoy an argument with one who held a different opinion from his own, while hoping that he might have the satisfaction of seeing his own viewpoint prevail in the end. Indeed he believed that all Christians had the duty to work out their own theology. He wrote once that one of the drawbacks of having a professional ministry was that it encourages people 'to imagine that they need never use their own brains in religious matters, seeing that the parson is paid to do it for them'.[2] For this reason, he was happy to lecture to lay audiences as well as ministers on important religious questions.

He was very soon in demand for such lecturing and teaching in the neighbourhood. Sir Michael Sadler, Vice-Chancellor of Leeds University, invited him to give a series of eight public lectures in the university on 'The life of the historical Jesus', during the winter of 1920. The local branch of the Fellowship of Reconciliation soon drew him into their membership and asked him to speak.

[1] Harry Escott, in a letter to the author 28 February 1982.
[2] *The Guidance of Jesus for Today* (1920) p.106.

In addition he undertook regular preaching engagements, usually in or near Bradford, but sometimes farther afield. His salary of £400 was not a large sum from which to provide for his growing family, whose education was soon to think about and pay for, and the extra £100–£200 he could earn in this way was very welcome.

The small village churches at which he often preached were also frequently served by students. On one occasion, remembered by Harold Wickings, he was given the opportunity to improve the lot of his generally impecunious students:

One Friday the senior student realised that there were more churches needing preachers than there were students available to serve. In college he encountered Dr Cadoux and asked him if he could possibly help. 'Yes, I happen to be free on Sunday', came the cheerful response, 'Where do I go?' Particulars were then given about a train, where to alight and be met, and what the church members expected, namely, to chair an adult Bible class at ten o'clock, lead morning service, address Sunday School children in the afternoon, and conclude with evening service and communion. Cadoux agreed. On his arrival the deacons observed his fresh appearance and curly hair and tacitly assumed that he was a student.

When evening worship had concluded he went to the vestry to put on his coat, and there received from the church treasurer a ten-shilling note. 'What is this?' asked Cadoux. 'That is our usual fee for expenses', answered the treasurer. 'Thank you', came the preacher's response, 'and now will you please call the deacons together for a word?' When all had assembled, Cadoux stood with his back to the door and told them who he was. Naturally they felt embarrassed and assured him that if they had known they would have offered him five guineas. 'That is not the point', he answered sternly, 'I don't want your "fee" for "expenses". I myself draw a salary, but our students have a difficult financial struggle all the time. And *you* have the nerve to offer them *this*!'

We learned afterwards that he had not minced his words in cutting to shreds their pretensions on 'fees' and 'expenses'. In short, Cadoux had unselfishly taken a stand on behalf of hard-up students. His words were not lost, but reverberated around the West Riding churches. Our student gratitude was very real.

Cadoux was beginning to build up a circle of friends in Bradford and the surrounding district. He enjoyed the meetings of the Athenaeum and frequently read a paper there. Two years after he arrived the Bradford Theological Circle was formed, at which again the members read a paper in turn. Amongst the local ministers, his most congenial companion in the first years in Bradford was Vivian T. Pomeroy ('Pom'), the unconventional and charming minister of Greenfield Congregational Church and a fellow member of the FOR who belonged to the Mansfield generation of 1908–11.

He did a good deal of travelling. His preaching and lecturing engagements took him all over the north of England and sometimes to Birmingham. By the beginning of 1921 he had joined the FOR general committee and went up to London regularly for meetings. This gave him the opportunity to keep up with his Catford friends, with whom he frequently stayed. The visits to which he most looked forward were those to Oxford – at least once a year and usually more often – for a part of him regarded that as his true home. But for the time being, Bradford was to be the centre for the Cadoux family life.

The family circle was temporarily enlarged in the autumn of 1920. They gave hospitality to a Hungarian girl, Martha Erdelyi, for a few months; she was one of a group of Austro-Hungarian refugee children on whose behalf Cadoux and others had appealed to people in Bradford. A few days after Martha arrived, Cadoux's sister Maud, with her daughter, arrived in Shipley in flight from her husband. It was Marguerite's readiness to offer a home to Maud and Anna, temporary though it proved to be, which finally won her acceptance by Cadoux's elder sisters, Ida and Connie.

Now that Cadoux was settled in his teaching, and his family accustoming themselves to life in Shipley, he began to build on the foundations he had already laid for the life of a scholar.

VII

The search for truth: writing
1920–1924

CADOUX HAD a profound conviction that the Christian Church had a responsibility to offer moral leadership to a world torn apart by war. 'The crying necessity of today is a re-discovery of God's Will for the conduct of human life', he wrote in *The Guidance of Jesus for Today* (1920).[1] As a teacher of theological students, he had undertaken the task of interpreting the results of theological scholarship to a new generation, of training them in the discipline of scholarship, of encouraging them to ask searching questions and to work out, under guidance, their own answers. As a scholar, he shared the responsibility for discovering, with others, the meaning and implications of God's will, and of explaining by what authority it was to be discovered. And as preacher and lecturer to a wider public, he tried to help all Christians to think seriously about the meaning of their faith, and above all, to apply it in their own lives.

These convictions required his own commitment to disciplined study. For him, this meant a great deal more than microscopic scholarly research. His schedules of study, worked out at least three months in advance, and recorded meticulously in precise detail, involved a continuing broad sweep of general reading in the Scriptures and in English literature: every day a portion of the New Testament in Greek, and a section of the Old Testament in Hebrew, and a play of Shakespeare every month (thus reading every play once every three years, but ignoring the sonnets and other poems). This general reading was to form the broad, humane inspirational background to the many books of New Testament criticism, early Church History, and theology, which were his specialist fields of study.

He believed that historical criticism would yield the key to a true understanding of the New Testament, and therefore of the contemporary relevance of the teaching of Jesus. His Mansfield tutor, Vernon Bartlet, was in sympathy with the 'Ritschlian school', followers of the

[1] P.16.

C. J. Cadoux

German Protestant theologian Albrecht Ritschl (1822–89). From the German school, and from his teachers in Oxford, William Sanday and Edwin Hatch, Bartlet had become a convinced exponent of the 'historic method'; Cadoux, influenced by his tutor and also by his attendance at Sanday's seminars on the problems of the Synoptic Gospels, sought to expound Christian faith and ethics by this method.

Cadoux was also much influenced by the work of Adolf Harnack (1851–1930), one of the most outstanding ecclesiastical historians and theologians of his generation, who was just coming to the end of his term as Professor in Berlin. In the winter of 1899–1900, Harnack had delivered a course of lectures in Berlin, published in England in 1901 under the title *What is Christianity?* Harnack's approach was historical; in the first lecture he stated that his question (the title of the series) would be answered 'solely in its historical sense'. He proceeded to enquire what, according to the Gospels, was the essence of Jesus' teaching; what was unique in the Gospel?

> If . . . we take a general view of Jesus' teaching, we shall see that it may be grouped under three heads. They are each of such a nature as to contain the whole, and hence it can be exhibited in its entirety under any one of them.
>
> Firstly, the Kingdom of God and its coming.
>
> Secondly, God the Father and the infinite value of the human soul.
>
> Thirdly, the higher righteousness and the commandment of love.[1]

Jesus' own unique idea, argued Harnack, was of 'the Kingdom within you'. The Kingdom of God 'is the rule of the holy God in the hearts of individuals; *it is God himself in his power*'.[2]

The eschatological setting, the idea of two kingdoms, of God and the devil, and of a final conflict between them, was, according to Harnack, something which Jesus had inherited and accepted, but was not a part of his own unique teaching. The essential, unique historical gospel of Jesus must be recovered and proclaimed; it must be differentiated from the doctrines, ordinances and ceremonies which will change as the particular historical circumstances which they serve themselves change. And so both Harnack and Ritschl stressed the ethical rather than the eschatological nature of the Kingdom of God, and were concerned with the progressive establishment of the Kingdom in history.

Cadoux greatly admired Harnack's works and studied them care-

[1] Adolf Harnack *What is Christianity?* 2nd edition (1906) p.52.
[2] *Ibid.* p.57.

fully; it is not difficult to trace Harnack's influence on his writings. In the autumn of 1919 he sent Harnack a copy of *The Early Christian Attitude to War*; unfortunately Harnack's letter of acknowledgement has not survived.

One of Harnack's students was Albert Schweitzer, brilliant as both musician and theologian. Schweitzer's challenging book, *Von Reimarus zu Wrede*, published in Germany in 1906, was translated into English as *The Quest of the Historical Jesus* in 1910. His reading of the New Testament had convinced him that Harnack had ignored the importance and significance of the eschatological passages in the Synoptic Gospels; Jesus, he believed, was dominated by the conviction of the imminence of the 'last things', the breaking into history of the supernatural Messianic Kingdom which would bring human history to an end. Schweitzer's originality lay in raising questions rather than in providing answers, but no theologian could afford to ignore the questions in future.

Cadoux took careful note of Schweitzer's arguments, but retained his conviction that the teaching of Jesus, as reported in the Synoptic Gospels, was a reliable and essential guide to Christian conduct. In a work published in 1924, *The Christian Crusade*, Cadoux wrote:

> Because many of Jesus' utterances are concerned with his expectation of a cataclysmic establishment of the Kingdom . . . within the lifetime of his own generation, we must not ignore the fact that much of his teaching is quite independent of any such eschatological scheme, and that the prominence of eschatology in the early records of his teaching varies in inverse proportion to the antiquity (and therefore the trustworthiness) of those records. The recent discovery of the eschatological Jesus has led some to declare that the attractive and reasonable figure formerly portrayed by liberal theologians is a figment, and that the visionary herald of the Kingdom cannot without unreality be modernized into a religious and ethical teacher for today. An honest recognition of the place of eschatology in Jesus' teaching does not, however, involve any such negative conclusion.[1]

Cadoux was acquiring a reputation as an exacting scholar of very liberal views. Sometimes this led him into trouble. In the early months of 1920, he gave a series of weekly open lectures at Leeds University under the title 'The Life of the Historical Jesus'; he did not flinch from facing the consequences of treating the New Testament by the ordinary canons of historical criticism. Some members of his Yorkshire audience found this to be too challenging, and the *Yorkshire*

[1] C. J. Cadoux *The Christian Crusade* (1924) pp. 19-20.

Post reporter understandably wrote his account of the lectures in the conviction that what the lecturer denied was quite as newsworthy as what he asserted. Cadoux was reported, for example, as saying that the birth stories of the Gospels were 'the products of an early Christian devotional fancy' and as rejecting 'miraculous and semi-miraculous features of the story'.

These rather exaggerated and colourful reports did not commend themselves to some of the wealthy Nonconformist subscribers to the United College, and it was not very long before complaints about the new professor were being made to Griffith-Jones. Just before Easter, while on holiday in Wales, Griffith-Jones received a letter from one of the college governors, enclosing another letter which the governor had received from the deacons of a Leeds church:

> The deacons are of opinion that the teaching and opinions expressed in the lectures are very destructive of the authority of the New Testament, and as the Bible is the basis of Christianity they cannot subscribe towards the funds of any college which is giving such teaching.

The governor asked Griffith-Jones 'what steps the authorities propose to take in the matter'. In view of the fact that Griffith-Jones was about to ask local churches to contribute towards the new Edinburgh hostel for students from the college, the question had an embarrassing urgency. Griffith-Jones wrote immediately to Cadoux: 'Of course I shall stand by you in your right to express your views, though I wish it had come later on in your association with the college when your position on central matters wd be assured and well known'. The letter, with copies (longhand) of those Griffith-Jones had received, arrived on Easter Saturday. Over the following weeks Cadoux suffered a good deal of anxiety; his diary several times recorded, 'chat re heresy hunt' with friends. Above all it was to Arthur, now minister of Broomhill Congregational Church, Glasgow, that he turned for consolation; for there was no question of his retracting his views.

Cadoux believed that as a committed Christian scholar and thinker he should grapple with the moral and ethical problems of the society in which he lived. Thus he had readily accepted the invitation to give a series of lectures on 'The guidance of Jesus for today' at the Friends Meeting House in York in the late autumn of 1919, lectures which were published in a revised form in 1920 as *The Guidance of Jesus for Today: An Account of the Teaching of Jesus from the Standpoint of Modern Personal and Social Need*.

The first section of the book dealt with the theological framework of Jesus' teaching. Following Harnack, Cadoux asserted that 'the

Fatherhood of God is the core of Jesus' message and of the Christian Gospel'. Jesus himself claimed to be man's guide and teacher in spiritual and moral affairs; and not only this, but to be the inaugurator of the Kingdom of God. The modern Christian could not share Jesus' sense that the Kingdom would be established through an imminent cataclysmic event, but could nevertheless recognize the truth of Jesus' claim to have established the Kingdom.

> In adapting our Lord's eschatology to the needs of our own minds, we are bound to substitute inward spiritual fellowship with him for his return on the clouds of heaven, the silent operation of God's law for the great Day of Judgment, the future life of the individual after death and the gradual spread of the Kingdom on earth . . . for the sudden erection of the Kingdom by a cataclysmic, Divine intervention.[1]

In studying and applying the teaching of Jesus, one had to ask questions about the nature and authority of the Bible. Cadoux could only deal with these questions in outline in a short book intended for the general reader; but they were not evaded. As a New Testament scholar, he took for granted the duty of subjecting the text to critical analysis. He accorded the most significant attention to the sayings of Jesus recorded in the Synoptic Gospels, since these appeared to go back to 'reliable personal reminiscences and tradition', whereas the Fourth Gospel presented Jesus' teaching with an eye rather to doctrinal interests than to historical truth. Here we meet a recurrent theme in Cadoux's writing – the possibility of distinguishing between the historical truth and the theological interpretation to be found in the Gospels.

The teaching recorded in the Synoptic Gospels was still to be 'both criticised and obeyed, both sifted and reverently observed'. By what authority?

> The truth of the matter is surely this: that Divine guidance is a compound of two elements: firstly, an internal and subjective stimulus and check, the 'testimonium Spiritus Sancti' within us, the 'indwelling Christ' of Paul, the 'Inner Light' of the Quaker, the conscience of the ordinary man, which prompts us to seek God's Will and which, however imperfect may be the use we are able to make of it, is yet our ultimate and most fundamental authority in religious and moral matters, because it is the only point where God and ourselves come into immediate contact and the only means we have of recognizing the Divine Truth and the Divine Will when they are externally presented to us; and

[1] *The Guidance of Jesus for Today* (1920) p.69.

secondly, the external embodiments of the Divine Truth and
Will in nature, reason, human goodness, and in Jesus – embodiments which are subject indeed to the certification and the check
of the Inner Light, but with which the Inner Light, for all its
ultimacy and fundamentality, cannot dispense. [1]

This doctrine of the inner light was to play a crucial part in Cadoux's
thinking, especially during these years of study in Bradford. The
fullest exposition of the theme was to come in his longest book,
Catholicism and Christianity, and a full discussion of this aspect of his
thought must await consideration of this work in a later chapter.

The larger section of the book was devoted to the responsibilities of
a Christian in the world. The first commandment, to love God, will
involve repentance (best understood as a change of heart and mind),
worship, prayer and faith in Christ. The second commandment, to
love our neighbours as ourselves, 'branches out into four important
but derived principles: mercy, wisdom, truthfulness, and humility'.
These in turn find practical application in the recognition of the
sanctity of marriage (Cadoux was always opposed to divorce), in a
Christian's family responsibilities, and in his concern for justice.
Their application to economics was a subject which 'bristles with
subtleties and uncertainties', and one which raised the same question
as did the Christian attitude to war: how was the Christian to act
within a society which had not yet accepted the Christian ideal? For
the application to economics there was no clear guide:

> . . . we are thrown almost entirely on our own resources, and get
> but little help from the words of one who was never faced with the
> problem as it challenges us. It is only the most general economic
> principles that we can gather from him: for the practical applica-
> tion of them we are left to ourselves. [2]

The requirement to live out a philosophy of non-resistance to evil,
however, was clear; in this way evil was to be overcome by good.

> What the adoption of Christian non-resistance involves is the
> going on of two processes pari passu, firstly, the gradual diminu-
> tion in the number of wrongdoers, and secondly, the gradual
> substitution of spiritual for material, of Christian for pagan, of
> more effective for less effective, means of dealing with wrong-
> doers. [3]

It followed from this that the Christian could not identify himself with
the coercive activities of the state: 'The Christian will refuse firmly to

[1] *Ibid.* p.20.
[2] *Ibid.* p.137.
[3] *Ibid.* pp.166-67.

become a soldier, or a maker of shells, or a policeman, or a magistrate: for all these callings stand for the pagan method of handling the wrongdoer.[1]

The book was well received, though most reviewers picked on the last passage quoted as being a point of view not generally shared by Christians. C. H. Dodd, reviewing the book in the *Mansfield College Magazine* (December 1921), took his friend to task for not having taken synoptic criticism far enough, and suggested that Cadoux 'has given us Guidance for Today from early Christian tradition', and 'has not given us any indication how to identify the elements in the tradition which have the best claim to full authenticity'.

Two years later Cadoux wrote another short book for the general reader on a similar theme; it was published as *The Christian Crusade* in 1924 and dedicated to 'the younger Christian generation'. Here we find similar themes worked out. The growth of the Kingdom of God would come about through 'the submission of an ever increasing number of individual lives to the will of God': 'the *present* "Kingdom"', as the inward royal control of God over Jesus and his disciples, was thus the correlative of the future "Kingdom", as the apocalyptic royal control of God over the whole of society'.[2]

The Church had taken a 'wrong turning' after the rapprochement with Constantine in the fourth century, and had fallen short of the ideals of the first Christian centuries. It was true that the Reformation had stirred the Christian conscience to challenge inhumanity, but the social structures of the twentieth century fell far short of any Christian ideal. What was needed, Cadoux said, was a company of Christians with 'vision and courage to break loose from the hampering timidities of the past, and to order their lives according to that Divine standard of values in which he whom they call their Lord had such utter trust'.[3]

Cadoux believed that a Christian society would be built up by the recognition and acceptance by one individual after another of the demands of the Christian ethic. He never lost an appropriate opportunity of challenging individuals to work out a responsible pattern of Christian behaviour. He believed that every Christian bore a political responsibility – 'It is a part of man's daily work as a "political animal" to take the status of his fellow-creatures into consideration and to devise what means he can for "Abating this accursed flood of woe"'.[4] Casuistry should have its place in working out general guidelines for

[1] *Ibid.* p.167.
[2] *The Christian Crusade* (1924) p.19.
[3] *Ibid.* p.51.
[4] *Ibid.* pp.14-15.

'our times of perplexity'; there was no reason why 'the systematic regulation of one's conduct . . . is necessarily an outrage against our filial relation to God', for 'there is no contradiction between a right and wise legalism and salvation by faith'.

His continuing pacifist witness led him to take a part, albeit small, in preparing for the great CO PEC (Conference on Christian Politics, Economics and Citizenship) gathering in 1924, chaired by William Temple, an almost exact contemporary of Cadoux's. Cadoux was a member of the commission appointed to study Christianity and War. Here he met some of his FOR associates, and also, probably for the first time, Charles Raven.

As a New Testament scholar, theologian, student of the early Church, and seeker of truth, Cadoux was closely involved in the debate on the reunion of the churches. On the one hand, he wished to see the mutual acceptance by all Christians of each other as fellow-Christians, both in an individual capacity and as representatives of different communions; he himself greatly valued his contact and friendship with members of other churches. On the other hand, he felt, like Harnack, that Protestantism was under threat, and threw himself into its defence with all the intellectual powers at his command; reunion, he believed, must not be achieved at the cost of surrendering the Protestant witness.

It was his custom throughout the years in Bradford to return to Mansfield in June for the Old Men's meetings. On the first occasion, June 1920, he followed the Mansfield reunion with participation in an important conference on Christian unity.

This was the year of the Lambeth Conference, the agenda of which included a discussion on church reunion. A few church leaders, Anglicans and Nonconformists, had met at Mansfield in January 1919 and in January 1920 (the membership of the two conferences overlapped but was not identical); by discussing the nature of the Church, the ministry and the sacraments, they wished to explore ways in which these different denominations might move towards unity. These two conferences had achieved a remarkable unanimity, in recommending that each church should recognize the others' ministries as a first step towards reciprocal participation in Holy Communion; in agreeing that a reunited Church must include a reformed episcopacy, and in advocating an immediate interchange of pulpits so long as it was 'under proper authority'.

In further preparation for the Lambeth Conference, A. C. Headlam, then Regius Professor of Divinity at Oxford, and Walter Lock,

Lady Margaret Professor of Divinity, summoned a conference of fifty scholars at Christ Church at the end of June, in order to explore the problems of reunion in greater depth. Headlam had just finished his series of Bampton lectures in Oxford; the last one was delivered on 6 June, and the following day they were published as *The Doctrine of the Church and Christian Reunion*. Cadoux was amongst those invited to the conference; others included were C. H. Dodd, John Oman, C. F. Burney and Orchard. Cadoux read a paper at the first session on 'The crux of the problem of Christian reunion'; his article in *The Venturer* in August, under the same title, contained the substance of this paper.

The fundamental question, he argued, 'Who is my fellow Christian?', was usually ignored in the controversy about valid orders and sacraments. Rejecting both a credal test (because 'no set of men is capable of fixing the Christian essentials for others') and a moral test (for 'any practical application of this test involves a decision as to what is the minimum of Christian morality below which a man forfeits his claim to the Christian name' – an impossibility), he concluded that the only possible test was a person's 'simple claim to the Christian name'. And then, in characteristic dialectic style, he continued:

> If it be objected that this means flooding the Church with unsatisfactory and insincere Christians, I reply, tell me which of the existing schemes that perpetuate disunion keeps only satisfactory and sincere people within the Church? If it be asked how, without credal or moral tests, the unity, purity, and true orthodoxy of the Church are to be secured, I reply, by the unifying, purifying and enlightening power of God's Holy Spirit.

He concluded:

> . . . as soon as it is frankly admitted on all hands that the Church can mean for us only the sum-total of all who make public confession of faith in Christ and who desire fellowship with their fellow-believers, the crux of the problem of Christian reunion will have been solved, and we can then turn with profit and with better prospect of success to those important but secondary problems which are but too apt to engross our whole attention.

That view of the Church, held by many Nonconformists, fell far short of what most Anglicans believed to be essential. So too, Cadoux's view of authority: 'the only really fundamental authority is the testimony of God's Holy Spirit within [man's] own breast'. These ideas were to simmer in his mind over the next few years and find detailed and thorough exposition in *Catholicism and Christianity*.

The scholars present at the Christ Church conference did however reach a broad unanimity. There was general agreement that the

Church consisted of all those who 'professed the name of Christ' and who had been baptised; and that the members present would be prepared to recognize each other's orders in the hope that future ordinations would be regularised.[1] Though Cadoux's views were more liberal than the generally agreed consensus, they were not extreme.

The 'Appeal to all Christian People' from the bishops of the Lambeth Conference appeared a month later, a document expressing a new tone of humility, understanding and commitment towards non-Anglicans. The Appeal, like Headlam's Bampton Lectures, proposed that the Nicene creed should provide the doctrinal basis for reunion. Cadoux could not accept this; in an article on 'The proposed credal basis of Christian reunion', which appeared in *The Journal of Religion* in November 1921, he maintained that a required acceptance of the Nicene Creed would exclude some who nevertheless professed their faith in Christ, and as such, should properly be admitted as members of the Church.

However, he welcomed the Appeal for many reasons, and urged a sympathetic and constructive response to it; there was now a much greater opportunity for growth in mutual understanding. In a further, more substantial article (alongside four others on aspects of reunion) in *The Constructive Quarterly* in March 1922 – 'Anglicanism and Reunion – a Freechurchman's Eirenikon' – he urged that 'if the Lambeth Appeal really represents the mind of the Church of England' Anglicans should be able to agree to intercommunion and the interchange of pulpits immediately. Freechurchmen in their turn might reconsider their attitude to episcopacy; it is possible, he said, to accept episcopacy as necessary 'for the good order and regular procedure of the Church' while not believing it to be necessary 'for the existence and ministry of the Church in the abstract'. More than one interpretation could be held of a common practice.

Cadoux had a brief connection with the Society of Free Catholics during the winter of 1920–21, at the invitation of W. E. Orchard. Cadoux had always had a great respect for Orchard and shared his pacifist convictions; although theologically they drew farther and farther apart, their friendship lasted all their lives, and Cadoux invariably defended Orchard's right to introduce Catholic forms and practices at the King's Weigh House in London. The Society of Free Catholics was founded by J. M. Lloyd Thomas, Unitarian minister of Old Meeting, Birmingham, in the belief that unity between Christians would come through sharing the devotional practices (rather than by

[1] See R. C. Jasper *A. C. Headlam* (1960).

trying to agree on common doctrinal propositions) of both Protestants and Roman Catholics. Orchard was the most distinguished member, both in his ability to offer a positive apologia for the movement, and in the cultivated and devout forms of worship which he introduced in his own church. He now invited Cadoux to speak on the modern attitude towards the creeds. 'We want you to take your own line in the way in which I have myself often heard you argue'. Lloyd Thomas followed this up with the information that 'a fairly spiky Anglo-Catholic' would talk on 'The place and use of creeds in the Church'.

When C.H.Dodd wrote a few days later to tell Cadoux that he might be able to have some books from the library of William Sanday, who had recently died, he added:

Herford tells me you are on the programme at the Free Catholic conference. Is that so? And does it mean that you are turning Catholic? I suppose I am a good deal of a Prot, but I always thought that compared to you I was a crusted Papist!

The conference (3–6 January 1921) seems to have been an exhausting and not altogether happy experience for Cadoux. He enjoyed the hospitality of the Quaker theologian H.G.Wood and his family at Bournville and the discussions at night after the meetings were over. But at Old Meeting, where the Free Catholics met, the difference between Cadoux's views and those of Orchard was more apparent than ever before. Cadoux noted in his diary for 4 January: 'Tea w' Orchard and talk after 4–7 re Maud, Higher Crit'm, Person of Jesus, Rome, Nonconformity etc. Come away very depressed and exhausted'. And on the following day: '1¼ hrs sermon from Orchard on Personal and Credal elements in discipleship – a painful experience'. We can assume that Cadoux's contribution to the conference would have covered the same ground as his article on 'The proposed credal basis of Christian reunion'. Orchard, on the other hand, was prepared to defend the acceptance of the Nicene Creed as a basis for reunion; and to defend creeds in general, not because they solved problems, but because they 'shut out some of the rotten attempts at solution that have been made'.

Cadoux's sister, Maud, now living in London and attending the King's Weigh House, heard reports of the discussions. When she wrote to her brother on 17 January, telling him that Orchard was ill and had been forced to rest, she added, 'I hear you and he were 3 hrs going at it and neither budged an inch – no wonder he has collapsed!' Never one to let a subject lie fallow, Cadoux called on Orchard early the following month while in London for an FOR committee meeting, and recorded in his diary: '7.30 Call on Orchard at K.W.House

Parsonage and discuss Nicaea w' him till 9 and leave with a sore throat'. Cadoux enjoyed argument, particularly if he could prove his point. But in this case, there was no concession either way.

'The Cross and non-resistance stand or fall together', wrote Cadoux in *The Message about the Cross: a Fresh Study of the Doctrine of the Atonement* (1924). Christian pacifism rested on an understanding of the central Christian doctrine of the Atonement. Cadoux was invited to lecture to an Easter conference of Yorkshire Friends at Grassington in 1923, and chose to lecture on the theme 'The Gospel of the Cross for the mind of Today'. Requests were made for its publication, and he took the opportunity of reviewing and expanding the material, and published it in the following year.

In the preface, Cadoux acknowledged the influence of two recent writers on the subject – the Quaker, William E. Wilson, and the Dean of Carlisle, Hastings Rashdall. Rashdall's Oxford Bampton Lectures of 1915 were published in 1919 as *The Idea of the Atonement in Christian Theology*. The book surveyed the attempts of the early Church to grapple with the problem of the meaning of Christ's sacrifice, and then looked at mediaeval thought. Of the two great mediaeval exponents of the doctrine of the Atonement, Abelard and Anselm, Rashdall found greater truth in Abelard's exemplarist theory (according to which Christ on the cross was the supreme example of God's love and grace) than in Anselm's penal-substitution theory (according to which Divine justice required sin to be punished, a debt so great that only God could pay it).[1] 'At last', wrote Rashdall about Abelard's theory, 'we have found a theory of the Atonement which thoroughly appeals to reason and to conscience'.[2] Cadoux also found this the most satisfactory starting-point for a modern exposition of the doctrine; 'such havoc has been wrought on the Christian conception of God by the treatment of terms like "propitiation" as literally instead of metaphorically true that it would almost be better if they were banished finally and for ever from the vocabulary of Christian doctrine'.[3]

Cadoux defined his task as that of reconstructing the meaning of the death of Christ 'in the mind of Him who was the central figure in that story'. The traditional language of the Atonement had become 'increasingly difficult, meaningless and unusable for the modern mind',

[1] This brief summary refers more to the way in which these two theories have been presented through history than to the original writing.

[2] Hastings Rashdall *The Idea of Atonement in Christian Theology* (1920) p.360.

[3] *The Message about the Cross* (1924) pp.48-49.

though this was not to deny the truth which that language was attempting to express. It was through the Servant poems of Isaiah that 'we may expect to get . . . considerable light as to the view he took of the meaning of his own death'. But the Synoptic Gospels suggest that Jesus also believed that God shared in the sufferings of the Servant. '. . . it is hardly an exaggeration to say that Jesus regarded all he suffered at men's hands as being suffered also by God'. The cross is thus a revelation of God's love, of human sin and the consequent suffering of God; this revelation 'induces repentance, pardon and moral vigour'.

This led to the mystery of salvation:

> . . . if it be asked, why are the natures of God and man so constituted that, when man sins, that sin always involves God in suffering, and unless that suffering is lovingly and patiently borne, unless God is willing to bear in His own person the enormous and incalculable cost of forgiving sin, the sin cannot be overcome and the man forgiven and reconciled? we can give no answer. Forgiveness is effected only at tremendous cost to God. Why? There lies the final and insoluble mystery.[1]

That mystery may not be explicable, but it reveals the nature of God. 'The Christian who has no use for Calvary, whether in his ethics, his theology, or his devotions, is missing the straightest and plainest path to that ultimate reality which is the heart of God'.[2]

From this point Cadoux proceeded to expound the idea which he had first put forward in an article on 'The fellowship of his sufferings' in *The Interpreter* (October 1921): that the uniqueness of Jesus' suffering and death was rather 'in its primacy and potency than in any vital difference of kind from that of his followers. Jesus does first and does best what others are to do under his inspiration'. Jesus accepted death because he believed that love involved non-resistance; this means that his followers are required to do the same. And as Jesus accepted his martyrdom though it seemed to be leading to failure; so Christians must accept non-resistance (not a negative concept, but 'an active and aggressive goodwill') even though there appears to be no prospect of 'success' – this is 'the fellowship of his sufferings'.

Altogether a great deal of Biblical exposition and theological argument was packed into the book's 92 pages. Of the numerous reviews, all praised the section on the relation between Jesus and the Servant poems of Isaiah. The section of the book which received most

[1] *Ibid.* p.52. G. A. Studdert-Kennedy wrote of 'the vision of the Suffering God' in *The Hardest Part* (1918). A contrary view was expressed by Baron von Hügel in 'Suffering and God' in *Essays and Addresses on the Philosophy of Religion* (1926).
[2] *Ibid.* p.40.

criticism was that which suggested that Jesus was unique only in being the first and greatest martyr; many reviewers found this a deficient view of the Atonement. Most reviewers felt that the section on the ethical implications of the cross, with its plea for non-resistance to evil, was the most challenging.

That was the final message of the book. 'The message about the cross' was 'a complete acceptance of that policy of overcoming evil with good, which was in history the one tangible ground for the death on the Cross'. Faith meant risking apparent failure; it means recognizing

that God's chosen instrument for the achievement of His dearest ends is infinite love, untiring in its endurance of rebuffs, and ceaseless in its personal appeal and in its moral challenge, and that, for the enhancement of this instrument's efficacy, God desires the co-operation of men who will grow to be more and more like Himself by becoming extremists in good-will'.[1]

[1] *Ibid.* p.92.

VIII

Light and shade:
the mid 1920s

IN MAY 1923 Cadoux celebrated his fortieth birthday, an appropriate occasion for taking stock of his situation. He held a permanent teaching position in a theological college of some standing; his published work, while not selling in great quantities, had attracted considerable notice and earned respect for its careful scholarship. He was in considerable demand for preaching and lecturing in the area, and was a leading and valued member of the Fellowship of Reconciliation. He had been married for over seven years, and his two sons, aged six and four, were quick-witted, intelligent active children showing promise for the future.

Nevertheless there were considerable strains in his life, which were becoming more insistent. They were probably largely hidden from the outside world, but found expression in his diary. His comment for 9 July 1923 – 'weather – hot, temper – depressed, family – trying', could be a normal 'end of term' feeling, but this and other comments seemed to indicate a rather more depressed mood than usual. On 18 September, he wrote, during a stay in London for the FOR general committee, 'Confide to L [eyton] Richards about my low estate'.

Shortage of money must have been a contributory factor in these difficulties. £400 a year was not a generous salary even in those days, on which to bring up a family, and buy the books needed to keep up to date with theological scholarship. The need to preach almost every weekend, in order to supplement his income, took him away from home on Sundays, and often for two nights as well, and it meant that he did not have a proper day off every week. This contributed to the irritation at home. Marguerite was tired of being left always at home while her husband went off to conferences. She wrote to him while he was at the FOR conference (August 1923), prior to going to Redmire camp in Wensleydale for another nine days:

I should dearly like to be with you. I don't think I should be bored with the meetings. Perhaps one year you could give up camp and we could both go to the conference. I think next year we ought (if there is no 'little') to try to get a foreign holiday together.

She was exhausted with coping with the boys alone, and her husband's admonitions on how to manage better were not always helpful. 'I am remembering all the injunctions you fill your letters with', she wrote on 16 August, while he was at camp.

It is clear that the strains on their relationship were increasing. She, with her quick temper and forthright manner, was actually able to cope with the strains better than he could. She could 'blow up', then apologize, and feel better; through all the difficulties her real and deep love for him was never in doubt. He could not deal with it in the same way. It always hurt him to have a quarrel with someone in which aggressive feelings were expressed; his preferred way was to try to argue a case rationally on its merits, while maintaining 'good' feelings towards the other person. He found it difficult to cope with a hostile reaction, and equally to cease persisting with his own point of view, once he was convinced he was in the right; and an obstinate streak of pride made it difficult for him to accept that he could be in the wrong. Though he did not lack a sense of humour, it did not come naturally to him to dispel angry and disturbing feelings through enjoying a good laugh.

He took the duties of parenthood very seriously, and set before his sons the same high standards of behaviour he accepted for himself. It may be that he expected too much from them, and felt frustrated when they failed to live up to his standards. Theo's talent for argument, which proved to be quite as good as his father's, could make for exhausting meal-times.

At the same time he was able to relax with the family and they enjoyed his fund of jokes and stories. Among his accomplishments was that of effective reading aloud. Early favourites were J.C. Harris' *Uncle Remus* and *Nights with Uncle Remus*, enlivened by his fair imitation of the American negro's style of speech. Later, they were introduced to *The Adventures of Mr Verdant Green*.

In the summer of 1923 the family enjoyed a holiday together in Oxford, enabling Cadoux to do some work in the Bodleian Library on his Smyrna project. There was also time for bathing with the family, sketching in Iffley, and family tea parties with friends. On one of the Sundays he preached in Benson and visited several old friends there. A few days before returning home, he went to tea at the Selbies, and that evening noted in his diary, 'Pipped by nervousness at Selbie's tea'. This nervousness worried him, especially as it was not an isolated example, and it caused him eventually to seek professional help.

At the Mansfield Old Men's Meetings the previous year, the main speaker had been J. A. Hadfield, lecturing on 'The new psychology and ministry'. Hadfield was the same age as Cadoux, had spent three years training for the ministry at Mansfield (at an earlier date than Cadoux), and had then become so much interested in the inter-relationship between psychology and religion that he had taken a medical training so that he could specialise in psychiatry. In the early 1920s he established his own consulting rooms in Harley Street as a psychiatrist. Probably unbeknown to Cadoux, C. H. Dodd had already sought his help, and was to do so over a number of years.

It was to Hadfield that Cadoux turned for help. He had his first interview with him in May 1924, while attending the Congregational Union's annual 'May meetings'. His diary (9 May) records '12.30–1. Interview w' Dr Hadfield on my attacks of nervousness, perspiring etc. He was very helpful'. Six months later, he wrote to Hadfield to ask him for an analysis; this was arranged for the summer of 1925, on condition that Cadoux would allot a good deal of time to it over a span of at least two months. This could only be in the summer vacation, and so it was arranged for July, August and September 1925.

Meanwhile the family spent the Christmas of 1924 in Purley with their relatives. It was the first time that Jack and Marguerite had spent the Christmas holiday away. Bernard came to collect them in his car and drove them down to Purley. Jack had not seen Bernard at all for the seven years between 1915 and 1922, while Bernard was abroad. Bernard's marriage to Marguerite de Hochepied in 1921 had not been the occasion for a family gathering because it took place in Smyrna. Now that Bernard had established a family home in Purley, he and Jack were able to see more of each other. Bernard and Marguerite now had a daughter two years old, Yolande, and the three of them lived next door to Maud, who with her daughter had now managed to establish a reasonably independent life. Jack and Marguerite stayed with Maud on this occasion. Jack visited the cemetery in Croydon where his father and Herbert were buried, and put wreaths on their graves, and he called on and had a 'happy chat' with Charles Stewart, his former headmaster at St Dunstan's. He met his old school friend, Fred Baggs, now a commercial traveller, and the two reminisced about their schooldays. He and Marguerite visited Ida and her family in Tonbridge, and Marguerite's family, the Asplins, in Perry Hill. All this restoration of relationships from the past was a good preparation for the psycho-analysis which was to follow.

Before that began, there was an important family event. For some time, Jack and Marguerite had been hoping for another baby, and Jack at least hoped it would be a girl. On 17 May, while Jack was away preaching in York, a baby girl, whose names, Ruth Mary, had already been chosen, was born. It was a cause for great happiness and rejoicing. Ida came to stay for five weeks to look after the household.

Cadoux's own personal problems remained. Early in July, he went up to Chingford (Essex) to stay with his old friends, the Yuills, and remained with them for much of that summer of 1925. He still took preaching engagements at the weekend, and if these were in Yorkshire, he was able to spend time at home. During that summer, he paid altogether 29 visits to Hadfield's consulting rooms. In between, he fitted in many hours in the Reading Room of the British Museum, as well as visits to his old friends and relatives in south London.

After the first visit, he wrote in his diary: 'he catechizes me ab't my exper^ces before the Mansfield board in June 1911 – for an hour and suggests that tho' feeling hot & humiliated I was prob. giving the impression of bg absolutely sure of myself'. And the next day, 'he lays me on a couch and pumps me abt my feelings at Mansfield Board in June 1911'. From this point, the discussions gradually moved to earlier phases of his life, to his schooldays and his ineptitude for games. After the fifth visit, he wrote, 'describe early terms at St Dunstan's: bullying etc. Led to suspect that I have been suff'g from swelled head fr a very early age'. He dreaded having to describe his dreams, but on the sixth visit there was no escape: 'I tell him all the history of my sex-life: also my recent dreams. Feel relieved to have got it all off my chest'.

At this point, he went home, had a 'joyful meeting with M', wrote a letter to Harnack to accompany a copy of his new book, and looked at his earliest diaries, for 1903 and 1904, in preparation for the next sessions with Hadfield. During the next few interviews, back in London, he explored his early childhood. 'Confess my infantile misdeeds. Come away feeling humbled but better', he wrote on 23 July. A few days later, he recorded, 'We don't get very much further – but I discover I had an unhappy infancy'. He talked about his father; if they talked about his mother, the subject was not recorded in his diary. His silence on that relationship may have significance.

By September, the series of consultations was coming to an end, and Hadfield was trying to help Cadoux to reach some conclusions. On his 22nd visit, he noted, 'We conclude I have been suffering from a repressed sense of inferiority'. After the 28th visit, his diary records:
. . . he suggests as conclusion that my trouble has arisen thro' trying to suppress an early latent feeling of being less manly than

I ought to be (sense of girlishness bg exaggerated by being put in frocks as punishment when very young).

After this visit Cadoux went straight off to the King's Weigh House to have tea with Orchard and to discuss psychoanalysis. Their conversation would have been fascinating to overhear.

One has the impression that while he was greatly helped by his sessions with Hadfield, and was not so much afflicted by attacks of nervousness afterwards, he did not achieve more than a limited degree of self-understanding.

Ida, whom he saw during that summer, and who had virtually brought him up after his mother died, had little patience with the idea of psychoanalysis. She wrote on 31 August:

> With all due regard to your friend – and I'm sure you quite believe I've not the slightest wish to belittle him or his gifts – I cannot help feeling that in all this delving into the past there is serious danger of a bad attack of self-pity . . .

The following year, 1926, the family holiday was spent at Cullercoats, on the Northumberland coast, with Cadoux going off to preach at Greenock each weekend. A ministerial friend in Newcastle who invited the family to visit him was sorry to note that Saturday or Sunday visits were impossible – 'I suspect you of holiday preaching, a most pernicious practice destructive of body and soul'. The preaching visits did have one positive benefit, however, for they enabled Cadoux to visit Arthur in Glasgow and enjoy some good lengthy conversation with him, partly about the family, partly about theology. It was while he was staying with Arthur that Marguerite wrote a forthright letter to him. Her nerves were obviously near exhaustion point:

> I really think that all my irritability is due to the *constant* friction between the children, and my nerves are simply worn away. If you had it like I do with never a weekend respite I think you would go to pieces quicker than I do . . . I know you think that I nag too much at them, but it is only because neither of them respond to *try a little* to be good mannered and helpful unless under bribes or whippings. I just feel that I cannot go back to a winter of strivings and rows and admonitions.

There was the possibility of sending the boys away to boarding school, for there were several boarding schools established specifically for the education of the sons of Congregational ministers, with generous bursaries. Theo had just won a governors' scholarship to Bradford Grammar School; he was suited to its academic character and tradition, and his short sight meant that he might be better at home. So for the time being he went to the Grammar School. But the possibility of

Harold going away to school came under serious discussion. Finally he was enrolled for Caterham School in Surrey, and started his first term in the autumn of 1928, when he was almost ten.

None of these problems affected Cadoux's work, unless it be that he put even more energy into writing. His academic reputation had been enhanced in 1925 by the publication of his DD thesis as *The Early Church and the World*. Part of it had already been published as *The Early Christian Attitude to War*, but this new work was a far more comprehensive treatise, with the material of the earlier book incorporated in it. It was dedicated to C. H. Dodd. It was not a 'popular' or indeed an easily digested work, rather one to study and consult; as such it is still in use. The text extended to over 700 pages, amply supplied with quotations and footnotes. Large sales could not be expected, and were not achieved. Cadoux had to put down £200 of his own money (equivalent to half his annual salary) as a condition of publication.

The sub-title of the book was 'A history of the Christian attitude to pagan society and the state down to the time of Constantine'. There were six chronological sections in the work, dating from the time of Jesus' ministry to the conversion of Constantine. Within each section, several separate topics were covered; the Church and the world, eschatology, ethical principles and their general application, attitude to the state, war, and family life, property and slavery. It was a meticulous, exhaustive study of an important subject. At the end of the work, Cadoux drew the conclusion that

> . . . in the work of the pre-Constantinian church, whatever else we may or may not have, we certainly have a moral reformative movement on a scale and with a potency unparalleled at any other epoch before or since.[1]
>
> . . .
>
> In the life of the early Church, as in no other phase of history before or since, we see a moralizing movement at work, visibly cleansing human society of its glaring transgressions, and bidding fair to establish the kingdom of God on earth.[2]

Part of his aim was to recall Christians to the principles and ideals of that moralizing movement.

Reviewers unanimously commented on the thoroughness of the work. C. H. Dodd, writing in *The British Weekly* (31 December 1925) remarked that 'a piece of research covering a definite field and worked

[1] C. J. Cadoux *The Early Church and the World* (1925) p.611.
[2] *Ibid.* p.612.

out so thoroughly that it will not need to be done again is a pleasure to contemplate', and gave the following delightful description of the book:

Here we have a sort of 'copec' of the early Church, in which questionnaires upon 'politics, economics and citizenship' have been answered by witnesses from the first three centuries according to their lights – apostles, apologists, theologians, men of affairs, Church Councils, and equally the humble Christians whose evidence was given, at no little cost, before persecuting judges.

In other reviews, there were criticisms of occasional pedantry, and of Cadoux's preoccupation with the problem of war. But there was united admiration for the scholarship, careful indexing and immense range of the work. It was one of his best books.

After the publication of *The Early Church and the World*, Cadoux turned over in his mind the possibility of a book on Catholicism. It would be an ambitious work, a vindication of 'progressive Protestantism'; it would deal with the question with which he was much preoccupied at this time, the question of authority in religion. Just before Christmas 1925, Arthur wrote, 'I was very interested to hear you were incubating a book on "The Catholic challenge"'.

Cadoux's friend, W. E. Orchard, was at the time under attack for introducing ritual (which led a Roman Catholic lady who attended the Weigh House on one occasion to say that she preferred the 'simpler service' at the Jesuit Church in Farm Street) in his church, and for declaring his acceptance of the doctrine of transubstantiation in a recent booklet in his series, *Foundations of Faith*, later published in book form in four volumes. A leading Congregational minister, J. Morgan Gibbon, writing in *The Christian World* on 19 October 1925, accused Orchard of 'living on one communion while living in another'. This generated a good deal of heated correspondence in that paper. Cadoux wrote a letter defending Orchard, published on 19 November:

The Congregationalism we are prepared to work for is not an organisation whereby we ensure our severance from all our fellow-Christians who disagree with us, but a polity so framed as to bring us into fellowship with all who say, 'Jesus is Lord', and who will give us the same recognition and liberty that we give unasked to them.

His objection to Catholicism was not so much because of its ritual, as because of its authoritarian organisation, and its doctrine.

He later wrote to Orchard himself, telling him of the book he was planning. Orchard replied on 22 January 1926:

> . . . you get in Congregationalism infallibility vested in individuals who are just as determined to exclude everybody who does not agree with them . . .

> I am afraid your book will only contend that you are *infallibly* right and that Rome is hopelessly wrong! If you are not infallible, how can you declare there is no infallibility?

Undeterred, Cadoux began his book on 29 March. It was a rather longer work than *The Early Church and the World*, but incredibly it took him less than fourteen months to complete the first draft. This was achieved alongside his teaching, writing of articles, external examining for the London BD examinations, and visits to London for FOR general committee meetings. It took another six months to revise and type it, but by January 1928, it was ready to go to the publishers. One can almost *feel* the relief expressed in the words 'LAUS DEO' in his diary the day the parcels of typescript went off by post, one to Stanley Unwin, the publisher, the other to Vernon Bartlet, his former teacher.

While he was writing *Catholicism and Christianity*, he made his application for the degree of D.Litt. at Oxford. For this, he was required to submit published work, showing original scholarship. He sent his major published work to date, *The Early Church and the World*. It was nine months before he heard the disappointing news that his application had been turned down (in March 1927).[1]

In that spring of 1927, he published a pamphlet and an article, both of some importance. The pamphlet came out in February; it was entitled *The Resurrection and the Second Advent of Jesus*. It was an attempt to grapple with the historical evidence for the resurrection, and to try to explain what Jesus could have meant by saying, after the transfiguration, that he would rise again on the third day. Cadoux gave reasons for believing that the phrase 'on the third day' was to be understood, not literally, but metaphorically, and meant 'after a short indefinite interval' – the interval, that is, between Jesus' death and his return to earth in glory to bring in the Kingdom of God. Only God knew how long the interval would be, but Jesus believed it would be less than a generation. According to this interpretation, the resurrection and the return in glory were to be one and the same.

What then can we make of the resurrection appearances recounted in the Gospels? According to Cadoux – and here he was expounding the 'objective-vision' theory defined by Kirsopp Lake[2] – the view

---

[1] He was eventually awarded this degree in 1939.

[2] In *Historical Evidence for the Resurrection of Jesus Christ* (1907).

which seems to reach the nearest to the truth is that

> Jesus after his death manifested himself to individual disciples and groups of disciples, not with the physical flesh of his body raised out of the tomb, but in the manner obscurely suggested to us by various psychical experiences recorded in later times.

And so

> We seem driven by the data to conclude that Jesus expected his triumph to take a form which in point of fact it was not destined to take. But after all, the central thing was the *fact* of his triumph over persecution and death, not the form of that triumph. Jesus never appeared, and never will appear, riding on the clouds and surrounded by legions of angels: but eternally he appears as the re-awakener and re-inspirer of human life, the one by whose standards all men are judged, and who is persistently at work, breaking the power of cancelled sin, and drawing the bewildered, the doubtful, and the contemptuous in homage to his feet – the same, yesterday, today and for ever.

The views expressed in this pamphlet did not commend themselves to Griffith-Jones, who wrote to Cadoux suggesting that he was in danger of throwing over 'the Evangelical faith'. As we have seen, Griffith-Jones was necessarily more sensitive than Cadoux needed to be to the effect of liberal theological enquiry on those congregations which gave financial support to the college; he also felt that Cadoux's emphasis on historical evidence could leave people with a negative feeling. 'Your *positive* position', Griffith-Jones wrote after a discussion with the local Bible society secretary at the college, 'is so vaguely and unhelpfully put, that the uninstructed believer finds himself hopelessly fogged and spiritually starved, and either loses himself in a wilderness of doubt, or retreats into an uncritical fundamentalism'. This threw up the dilemma of the scholar who needs to be free to ask questions, to challenge traditional formulations of belief, yet who must fulfil the role of theological guide to the layman, who wanted re-assurance as well as questioning. Though Griffith-Jones was critical, Arthur expressed himself in 'hearty agreement' with almost all his brother had written.

Cadoux's article, 'A defence of Christian modernism', appeared in *The Congregational Quarterly* (April 1927). He defined modernism as

> the conviction that drastic restatement of Christian beliefs is necessitated from time to time – and in particular at this time – in order to bring out their compatibility with the best modern scientific and historical knowledge and philosophical thought,

and that such re-statement, though involving discomfort for some, is possible without sacrificing any ultimate religious value. This re-statement, he argued, would involve the rejection, as historical facts, of many of the miracles in the New Testament. Jesus' power was not to be found in 'physical marvels' but in 'the moral and religious grandeur of His life, His ministry of healing, and His proved power to save men from sin and bring them to God'.

The basis of our faith is not weakened by withdrawing it from the external and objective things and locating it in the inner witness of God's Holy Spirit. Nay, we transfer it thus from a perilous site where at any moment some new discovery in science or history may deal it a blow, and we plant it – beyond the reach of all criticism – in that one part of our nature where God comes most immediately into contact with us – in the light of reason, the love of truth, the voice of duty, and the experience of the Divine love.

He had the opportunity to debate some of these issues when he attended the first of a series of Oxford Congregational conferences in July. Robert F. Horton, the brilliant minister of Lyndhurst Road Congregational Church in Hampstead, London, former fellow of New College, Oxford, and skilful and successful communicator of the Christian faith, had first suggested in 1926 that Free Churchmen should organise their own conference, along the lines of that of the Anglican Modern Churchmen's Union, to interpret the Christian faith in the light of modern knowledge. Free Churchmen were after all freer than were Anglicans to attempt such a re-interpretation, to help Christianity to shed 'its outworn garments', to demonstrate 'the old truth, liberated and become new'.

This first conference, which attracted 130 participants, had as its theme 'Christian faith in the light of modern science and criticism'. Amongst the speakers were Selbie, R. S. Franks, C. H. Dodd and Nathaniel Micklem (who was just preparing to go out to Canada to teach theology in Kingston, Ontario). Micklem took as his subject, 'Congregationalism and modernism' and expressed a view different from Cadoux's. He agreed that the faith must be re-interpreted in modern terms, but asserted that 'we are in no small danger of becoming undogmatic'. Dogma in the old sense was to be rejected, but the Christian faith was still based on the facts of history, interpreted by the Church. Dogma in this new sense was definite and objective, and carried authority.

Cadoux enjoyed the discussions, took an active part in them, and was glad to have the opportunity of talking with Arthur, as well as other old friends. He persuaded the conference to take the subject of authority for the theme for their next meeting. On the fifth day of the conference he wrote in his diary: *'Feel well.'* It seems that his spirits were beginning to rise.

IX

'Catholicism and Christianity';
looking to the future
1928–1929

CADOUX SENT the manuscript of *Catholicism and Christianity* to Stanley Unwin (who had published two of his previous books) in January 1928. The following month, Cadoux received a favourable report from the publisher's reader (whose identity was unknown):

> I have no hesitation in saying that this is the most important work on this great and timely subject that we have in English. It will at once take rank as *the* classic from the Liberal Evangelical camp.

The only comparable work, the reviewer said, was Karl von Hase's *Handbook to the Controversy with Rome.* But

> Dr Cadoux's is a far greater book in every way. In fact, I cannot imagine a better. . . . Dr Cadoux treats Rome with great generosity . . . Dr Cadoux's position is on the whole much the same as that of the Bishop of Birmingham.[1] Dean Inge too will sympathise with the work.

Dean Inge was asked his opinion and wrote confirming this:

> I agree with your reader that Dr Cadoux's book is a very remarkable one, and that it would be recognised that the learned world owed a debt of gratitude to any publishing firm that accepted it. I am afraid it would be difficult to shorten it much.[2]

Unwin decided to accept the book for publication, on condition that Cadoux could find guarantors prepared to offer financial support. At least ten wealthy Congregationalists were persuaded to act as such guarantors, including Sir Arthur Haworth, the Manchester cotton merchant who served on the Mansfield College Council.

Considering the length of the book, the detail in the footnotes, and the amount of indexing to be done, it was remarkable that it came out within six months of being accepted. It was actually published on 23 October 1928. 1750 copies were printed.

The sub-title was 'A vindication of progressive Protestantism'; the

[1] E. W. Barnes.
[2] 27 February 1928.

extensive criticism of Roman claims was accompanied by a vigorous
defence of the Liberal Protestant position. Nevertheless, the book did
contain an appreciation of what Cadoux called 'the advantages and
merits of Catholicism': its superb organisation and world-wide
membership, the unbroken continuity of its life and tradition, its
cultivation of mysticism and its strenuous loyalty to Jesus' ethical
teaching. (Cadoux accorded warm approval to the Catholic attitude to
divorce). This, and the generally courteous tone of the book, led
Wilfred Knox to write in his review of the book in *Theology* (February
1930) that

> In Dr Cadoux's book there is a spirit of conciliation which
> Anglo-Catholics will do well to acknowledge. How far he speaks
> of Free Churchmen in general we cannot say. But if they on their
> side will learn to meet us in the spirit which he shows, and if we
> on our side are prepared to think out the meaning of our faith and
> practice in a spirit as liberal as his, the time of reunion will be
> nearer . . .

The remarkable nature of the book was in its examination of Roman
Catholic claims from three very different standpoints, philosophical,
historical and moral. The argument was supported by a painstaking
marshalling of evidence, all carefully documented, from both Catholic
and Protestant sources.

The first major section, 'The answer of Christian philosophy',
centred on the problem of authority. 'The problem of authority . . . is
the question, What is the truth in regard to the Nature and Will of
God', and, he might have added, *how* do we find it, and *where* do we
find it. Underlying the whole book and indeed all his writing was the
assumption that truth could be found through reason, argument and
debate, for reason is 'the light of God Himself within the intellect of
man'. He opened the section with an anecdote about a conversation he
remembered at a Swanwick conference. 'I never mind being beaten in
an argument', an Anglo-Catholic friend had said, 'so long as I know I
am on the right side'. This would not do for Cadoux.

> To what purpose should we ever take the trouble of arguing
> anything, if success in the argument is not going to produce belief
> in the conclusion which it establishes? Debate is robbed of all its
> zest and interest, unless the debaters can be supposed to have,
> not only a real desire for truth, but also a trust in honest debate
> itself as a method of arriving at truth. [1]

Since Rome used argument, she should abide by the verdict of the
argument:

[1] C. J. Cadoux *Catholicism and Christianity* (1928) p.87.

We intend to argue our case against her: we shall show that her claim to infallibility is philosophically untenable, that the acceptance of it involves a shutting of one's eyes to the truths of history, and that her claim to be a unique and Divinely-maintained moral guide for mankind is – despite the many virtues of many Catholics – stultified over and over again by facts in her record.[1]

Using the method of argument, he examined all those authorities which Christians had in fact regarded as the mediators of truth about God. He wished to discover which above all was more authoritative than any of the others; which should be followed in cases of conflict. Of seven possible authorities, four could be described as objective: the natural world, which most Christians would recognise as 'furnishing a very valuable supplement to what is believed about God on other grounds'; the Christian Church, with the tradition which it guards and interprets; the Bible; and the historical Jesus. The other three authorities could be described as subjective, in the sense that they are known to the Christian directly without mediation: the indwelling Christ (not necessarily clearly distinguished from the Holy Spirit); conscience; and reason. The relation between these seven different 'authorities' could be described as 'the problem of authority'.

This was the heart of Cadoux's argument. The chapter in which he pressed the claim for 'the ultimacy of the Inner Light' was the one which he regarded as the most important in the book: while writing he referred to it as 'the nutcracker chapter'. The point which he hoped to demonstrate to the reader was 'that, in all experience of authority in religion, the Inner Light is logically and therefore really prior to – and ultimate by comparison with – all objective authorities whatever'. By the term 'Inner Light' he meant 'the whole of those internal powers and endowments which enable the individual to appropriate Divine reality' – conscience, moral sense, the indwelling Christ and man's response to the Divine in a general sense. It was not 'private judgment' in the sense that some Roman Catholics used the term, an independent decision taken by an individual acting on his own initiative, but the 'light of God, the presence of His Holy Spirit'; so that 'Newman's strictures on what *he* calls private judgment do not touch *our* doctrine of the Inner Light'.[2]

This doctrine of the inner light does not dispense with objective authorities; it does enable us to recognise the truth when we find it. It is

[1] *Ibid.* p. 101.
[2] *Ibid.* p. 117 with n. 1.

perfectly consistent with our need of and our trust in many external and objective authorities. It claims, however, that in all our learning from these authorities, in all our search for the witness God has left of Himself, in sifting the data of science, in interpreting the message of history, and in appraising the religious and moral teaching of others – the ultimacy of the inward test is visible in our necessary choice of whom to follow, our right to check and criticize and on occasion to dissent, our potential ability to verify what we take on trust, and finally our monopoly of the right to say when and where we have found the truth.[1]

And so Cadoux took each of the so-called 'objective authorities' in turn, showing how each one was dependent upon the authority of the inner light. In doing so, he discussed at length the arguments which had been given against this contention, by Newman and many others, showing that each argument could be effectively countered. Not that Cadoux claimed that the inner light was infallible; there was no infallible authority, for 'Divine guidance is always conditioned by the human subject on which it acts'; and 'the ever-present margin of uncertainty . . . constitutes no ground for assuming that there must be somewhere an infallible objective interpreter of God . . .'.[2]

This doctrine of the ultimacy of the inner light had appeared in earlier writings of Cadoux's, in *The Guidance of Jesus for Today* and in several of his articles. It played a major role in his thinking. He found the roots of this doctrine in Scripture and in Greek thought; in later thinking it was amongst some Anglican and Quaker scholars, as well as in the writings of the Unitarian James Martineau, that he found stimulation. Martineau had set out to expound the thesis 'that the foundations of religious knowledge are laid by God in the reason, the conscience and the heart of man'; his *The Seat of Authority* (first published in 1890, and re-edited several times) was the result of a life-time's reflection. Since then, many non-Roman Catholic theologians had dealt with the subject.

Of the Anglican writers, V. H. Stanton, whose *The Place of Authority in Religious Belief* appeared in 1891, was the first, and Cadoux drew a good deal from that work. A. E. J. Rawlinson and W. R. Inge were a generation later. Dean Inge had given an important lecture in Liverpool in 1912 on 'Authority and the Inner Light' (published in 1913), which Cadoux also quoted. Inge had claimed that 'the will of God is never and nowhere revealed to us in such a way as to release us from

[1] *Ibid.* p.167.
[2] *Ibid.* p.175.

the responsibility of forming judgments'. [1] The Johannine doctrine of the Logos enables us to reconcile the claims of authority and of the inner light, for 'it safeguards both the transcendence and the immanence of God'. [2] Cadoux found further stimulus in the writings of A. E. J. Rawlinson – in his article on 'The principle of authority' in *Foundations: a Statement of Christian Belief in Terms of Modern Thought* (1912), *Authority and Freedom* (1924), and his contribution on 'Authority and Belief' in *Essays Catholic and Critical* (1926), edited by E. G. Selwyn. Three Quaker writers who provided Cadoux with material were Rufus M. Jones in the Nature of *Authority and Conscience* (1920), Edward Grubb in *Authority in Religion* (1924), and G. K. Hibbert in *The Inner Light and Modern Thought* (1924). Cadoux quoted from and referred extensively to all these writers in building up his argument.

The central and largest section of the book was devoted to 'The answer of historical evidence'. This was largely an attack, supported by historical evidence, on the Roman Catholic attitude to Scripture, to the origins of the Church, to the institution of the sacraments, and to the cult of saints. There was a good deal to attack, as Roman Catholics themselves have realised since that time, and as the modernists within the Roman Catholic Church were already saying. One can recognise Cadoux's debt to his old teacher Bartlet in this section; indeed he had sought Bartlet's guidance in revising the text, and invited him to write the foreword. 'The historical spirit', wrote Bartlet in his foreword, 'which dissolves dogmatisms, is an eirenic influence, and can bring us closer on a basis of large comprehension. May such be the final effect of this book'.

It is doubtful whether that was the effect on any reader of Catholic sympathies, scrupulously fair though Cadoux always was in argument. His wide-ranging criticism of much of Catholic teaching and practice, while not lacking sympathetic understanding, is not eirenic in tone; rather, Cadoux is an advocate who presents his case in great detail and believes it to be unanswerable.

He defended resolutely and absolutely his conviction that truth must be pursued, wherever it may lead:

. . . the fearless love and eager quest of truth is a religious obligation, the discovery and possession of it a religious experience, the impartation of it to others a religious ministry, and the general dissemination of it a religious value and advantage. This unquestioned majesty of truth predisposes us to regard

[1] W. R. Inge *Authority and the Inner Light* (1913) p.7.
[2] *Ibid.* p.30.

the obligation of loyalty to it as absolute, that is, as exempt from the liability . . . to be intercepted or overriden by a higher loyalty.[1]

But there was a difference between Catholic and Protestant perceptions of truth:

> To the Catholic a thing is true because the Church teaches it, and God has made the Church infallible: to the Protestant it is true because specific record or specific experience or specific reasoning substantiates it.[2]

The greatest charge he brought against Catholic truthfulness was 'the declaration of 1870 that the infallibility of the Pope had always been an item in the faith of the Church'.

That doctrine of infallibility held that the Church was infallible in matters not only of faith, but also of morals. Cadoux therefore went on to examine the Catholic Church's record in morals, especially in relation to persecution. In great detail he pressed his case that that Church had been guilty of horrifying persecution in past ages (Arthur later commented that he wondered 'the writing of the chapter on persecution did not affect your health'); and claimed that though she had now ceased to be a persecuting church, 'we are still without any unequivocal and authoritative repudiation of the principle of religious persecution'.

The final section of the book, 'The future of the Christian Church', dealt with the movement for reunion. Reunion with the Roman Catholic Church 'as things stand' was out of the question, and union with the Church of England was unlikely while episcopal ordination remained a condition of mutual acceptance. Free Churchmen must remain loyal to the fundamental values of their inheritance, offering

> a view of church membership which, being based on a really defensible theory of religious authority, avoids the palpable anomalies inherent in the exclusive systems of the Church of Rome and the Church of England, without sacrificing that high and exacting standard of righteousness in life and truthfulness in creed which is incumbent on the Christian as such.[3]

The Congregational basis of the Church 'is in essence the one truly Catholic basis for the constitution of the Church', for this basis alone makes it possible to include within it all who have a just claim, through public profession of faith, to be included. The teaching office of the Church, and the guidance of the Holy Spirit, would ensure that truth and righteousness would not be sacrificed.

[1] *Catholicism and Christianity* p.499.   [2] *Ibid.* p.518.
[3] *Ibid.* p.681.

Congregationalism . . . is a polity so framed as to bring its members *into* fellowship with all who say: 'Jesus is Lord', and who will give Congregationalists the same Christian recognition and liberty which these give unasked to them.[1]

Cadoux quoted A. E. J. Rawlinson, who, though an Anglican, had Congregational forbears, and who had written in his essay on 'The principle of authority' in *Foundations* that there was a sense in which Catholicism and Congregationalism were closely related, in that they shared a transcendental view of the Church. As Rawlinson put it, 'Both are at one in conceiving the Church as primarily a mystical and religious entity, eternal in the heavens, a spiritual communion of the elect people of God which is of a higher order than space and time; and both agree in conceiving the assemblage of Christian people for worship as a manifestation visibly upon earth of this invisible or ideal Church – ubi tres, ibi ecclesia'.[2] Congregationalism could thus be regarded as the true Catholicism, the only basis on which a reunited Church could be built; a magisterial argument, of which we have here only given a very brief outline.

The book was dedicated to the governors, staff and students of the Bradford college. At Cadoux's first meeting with the senior class after the publication of the book, the students rose to their feet spontaneously and congratulated him; on the same day, a portrait of him appeared in *The Christian World*, alongside a heading, 'Professor Cadoux's Great Book', and quoting Dean Inge's commendation of it.

The book was widely reviewed in the presses of all denominations and several other weekly and daily papers. On the whole it was welcomed and praised in the non-Catholic press. Reviewers found points to criticise – an optimism about the power and importance of reason and argument, an undue emphasis on criticising superstitious practices of which Catholic authorities themselves did not approve – and the fact that there were more references in footnotes to *The Hibbert Journal* than to the New Testament! But all praised the enormous erudition, the interest and readability of the text, and the charitable spirit in which the argument was conducted. 'Theological disputation has never produced a book so completely free from *odium theologicum*,' wrote the reviewer in *The New Statesman* (15 December 1928) 'and Dr Cadoux displays a most admirable and Christian temper throughout'. R. S. Franks wrote in the *Mansfield Magazine* that Cadoux had taken up (successfully, though with some reservations)

[1] *Ibid.* p.682.
[2] Quoted in *Catholicism and Christianity* p.682.

the challenge of Newman's statement that 'to be deep in history is to cease to be a Protestant'. J. S. Whale wrote in *The Christian World* that 'the discussion on Reunion, its conditions and implications, is the best the present writer has seen' (6 December 1928).

The Roman Catholic weekly *The Tablet* took a different attitude. Its editor, Ernest Oldmeadow, was a convert from Nonconformity, and hardly likely to feel sympathetic to the suggestion conveyed by the title that Christianity and Catholicism were not necessarily one and the same thing, let alone to be convinced by the arguments of the book itself. The heading of the review (19 January 1929) was 'Pride of Intellect', and after conceding that the book formed 'much the ablest defence of Protestantism that we have seen', the reviewer went on to say of the author that 'one tenth of his learning and his labours, accompanied by humility and prayer, would have made him a happier and a wiser man'. This stung Cadoux, who wrote to complain that 'the reviewer knows nothing of my devotional habits'. It marked the beginning of an unhappy and acrimonious relationship with *The Tablet*. In fact, his correspondence with that journal was one of the few occasions on which Cadoux really let his aggressive instincts have their full fling.

C. H. Dodd was more cautious than some other Congregationalists in his appreciation; he wrote just before Christmas, having read the reviews, though not the book:

> To controversy no doubt some have a vocation, others not. It certainly has its value and is sometimes vehemently necessary. But in the rapidly changing thought-world of our time Catholic and Protestant are almost equally faced with the need for re-adjustment and I suppose that if this is being positively met on each side we may find that some of the old questions upon which we reached a deadlock take on a fresh form in which we can possibly hope to co-operate a little more in their solution. And don't the affirmations of a Catholic like (say) von Hügel encourage such a hope?

When the third edition of *Essays Catholic and Critical* (first published in 1926) appeared in 1929, the editor, E. G. Selwyn, felt it necessary to deal with Cadoux's claims in a new preface; *Catholicism and Christianity* was 'a very weighty and thorough criticism of Catholicism', and 'it is a great thing to have the case thus presented within the covers of one volume'. Selwyn regretted that Cadoux had not concentrated on the *relationship between* the inner light and the objective elements in religious authority 'instead of trying to drive these off the field'. *Essays Catholic and Critical* offered an alternative to

Cadoux's 'radical' Protestantism, but one which had to take account of Cadoux's challenge.

In effect, *Catholicism and Christianity* presented one of the clearest and most comprehensive expositions to date of the Liberal Protestant viewpoint. The reviewer of *The New Statesman* admitted that 'the case for Liberal Protestantism . . . could hardly be better put', but he felt that 'the book will achieve nothing towards reunion, and little towards mutual understanding'. This was a hard but on the whole fair judgment. The book's sub-title, 'A vindication of progressive Protestantism' suggested that Cadoux was trying to prove that the future lay with one particular form of churchmanship (one for which he claimed true catholicity) as much as to improve *mutual* understanding. Just as in conversation he loved to argue, and if possible to win the argument, so in this book he hoped to trounce his ecclesiastical opponents. That said, however, we must acknowledge that Cadoux's pleas for greater efforts for the reunion of the Church were generous and sincere. The book was marked throughout by an eager, energetic, insistent search for truth. On the last page he wrote:

> If truth has been reached, others will see it and accept it: if it has been missed, the missing of it here may perchance subserve the finding of it by another. Of two things at least there can be no doubt. God must and will bless a sincere love and search for Truth; and secondly, inasmuch as God inspires and answers prayer, it is by exploring further the life of prayer in all our doing and thinking that we shall best fulfil His will.

Here we do see marks of that spirit which could truly lead to a deeper understanding.

Cadoux was beginning to feel restless in Bradford. He had been teaching there for nearly ten years, and could justly feel that he had made a significant contribution to the college and to Yorkshire Congregationalism generally. With three children to educate he needed a larger income if at all possible. He could only expect to earn this from another academic position with a higher salary, not from his writing. (In the first twelve years after the publication of *Catholicism and Christianity*, he earned from sales a total of £25, after paying back his guarantors).

His heart's desire was to return to Oxford. His days at Mansfield had been amongst the happiest of his life, and his natural inclination to venerate his old teachers, Selbie, Bartlet and Buchanan Gray, drew him constantly towards the college to which they belonged. *Catholicism and Christianity* had confirmed his reputation as a scholar, and he might reasonably hope that a place could be found for him in his old college. It is possible that his life would have been happier, and his teaching and gifts more appreciated, had he decided to remain in Bradford. But his ambition to return to Oxford was not to be quelled.

Vernon Bartlet was due to retire at the end of Trinity term 1928. When Cadoux heard this, before the end of 1927, he wrote to Selbie asking that his name might be considered by the College Council, when the question of Bartlet's replacement was discussed. Feeling uneasy and anxious at hearing nothing after Selbie's brief acknowledgement of his request, he wrote again in March 1928 – 'As I think I mentioned in my last letter, I have for some years been nursing the presumptuous ambition that some day I might be called back to Mansfield'. Still he heard nothing, apart from an acknowledgement. It was made all the more tantalising by the fact that the position was not advertised, and therefore he was unable to make a formal application, putting forward his claims to his own satisfaction. Unable to wait without doing something, he approached certain members of the Council, including Leyton Richards, enlisting their interest and if possible support. When he went to the Mansfield Old Men's Meeting in June, presumably feeling a mixture of apprehension and ambition, he tried to arrange an opportunity for conversation with Selbie. On the second day of the meetings, he wrote in his diary, 'Selbie tells me "Nothing doing re me" . . . Bartlet tries to console me'. It was a very great disappointment, made no easier by the fact that Marguerite had just gone into hospital for an operation and was not in a position to offer much sympathy. However, Ida came to stay to look after the family, and he poured out his thoughts and feelings to her.

His diaries do not make it clear whether or not he knew yet what decision the Council had made, but the news of the appointment was published in *The Christian World* a fortnight later (12 July 1928). J. S. Whale, a much younger man than Cadoux, who had gained a First in Modern History at Oxford, followed by training at Mansfield and a pastorate at Bowdon Downs, was appointed Lecturer in Church History, the position of professor being held in abeyance for the time being. There was no personal resentment about this particular appointment on Cadoux's side – it was rather a feeling of deep disappointment that his own college had apparently rejected him, in spite of his obvious academic achievement.

Vernon Bartlet did his best to support and console his old pupil. He explained that Cadoux's lack of pastoral experience had been a handicap, and added:

I am very glad you are not going to let the decision affect your outward conduct and relation to the College; that would, I feel sure, be an error and add to your own sorrow. Go quietly on, with peace in your *inmost* heart, which will in the end extend through all the channels of your being; and one knows not for what you may thereby be preparing.

Arthur too tried to console him:

I hope time will speedily make you feel happier about the disappointment. I do not blame you for feeling it. It is the price you pay for being keen.

It is perhaps significant that the theme of several of his sermons during this summer and autumn was 'Don't worry'.

In this rather depressed mood he returned to Oxford for the second Oxford Congregational conference, this time on the theme of 'Authority', the theme he had suggested. He made contributions to the debate, offering his particular theory of the ultimate authority of the inner light. Soon after the conference was over, he set off for an energetic walking tour with his two sons. Marguerite's illness had precluded any family holiday at the seaside that year; instead she and Ruth stayed in Purley with Maud, while he and the boys set off from there for a fortnight's walking tour through Surrey, Hampshire and Berkshire to Oxford and Benson, then back to Purley by train. Cadoux managed to visit several friends on the way, and called on Bartlet again in Oxford. It was a reviving holiday, and the whole family felt better for it.

Back home in Bradford, he set to work again with renewed energy. He had been asked to make a translation, in colloquial speech, of the book of Deuteronomy for the National Sunday School Union; and he had decided to take up his work on Smyrna again. He had always wanted to visit his birthplace. If his book on the city was to be as thorough and accurate as he wished, it was essential for him to see the site and the ancient remains himself. He therefore asked the College Governors if he might take a month's leave for the purpose; his request was granted at the Governors' meeting in the summer of 1929. Now he could begin making his plans, and an exciting prospect began to open up. But the feelings of disappointment about Mansfield continued, feelings which he confided to numerous friends. None of them could effectively console him.

In that summer of 1929, he attended two conferences in Cambridge, taking place simultaneously. He spoke to the East Anglian Congregational ministers' summer school meeting at Westminster College on 'The challenge of Catholicism' and 'The reply to Rome', and to the third Congregational Conference, this time meeting at

Cheshunt College, on 'the person of Christ as determining our idea of God'. Griffith-Jones attended the latter, and wrote to him from holiday, 'Your own contribution to the Cambridge School was very highly appreciated . . . Theologically it is quite the best thing I have heard from you'.

In August, A. S. Peake, Rylands Professor of Biblical Criticism and Exegesis at Manchester University, died before reaching retirement age. A Methodist and a distinguished Biblical scholar, he was the first Nonconformist to occupy a theological chair in England. Though Manchester did not offer everything which Oxford did, its university had an excellent reputation, and the John Rylands Library was one of the best theological libraries in the country. When it was known that the university was looking for a successor to Peake, Cadoux decided to apply. He wrote to Selbie asking for support in his application, though making it apparent that even if he were appointed, it could only be second-best to Oxford; and that he was still feeling upset at having been 'overlooked' when Bartlet's post was being considered:

I want to thank you for the kindly expressions in the letter you wrote to me some time ago. Of course I accept the assurance that the action taken was taken with a view to the best interests of the College. But I cannot say that I have ceased to feel acutely the sorrow of it. The disappointment of being unable to return to Oxford, as I had all along hoped I might do and still more, the discovery that what I had to offer to Mansfield was, by comparison, so lightly esteemed by those I trusted most, made the blow one that I am afraid I shall feel to the end of my days. So that were I successful in getting appointed to the Rylands Chair, that would not be in any way an equivalent for what I have missed; but it would be a very distinct improvement on my present position, chiefly because it would give me some contact with University life again.

Selbie replied by return that he had recommended Cadoux for the post in Manchester some time previously. It was not until the following May that Cadoux learned that Manchester had appointed another Congregationalist to the professorship – C. H. Dodd. Though causing Cadoux some disappointment, mixed with pleasure on behalf of his old Mansfield colleague, this appointment did involve the creation of a further vacancy at Mansfield;[1] his hopes were raised again.

Concurrently with his teaching and writing, Cadoux was still much involved with the FOR. He was elected chairman in the summer of

[1] Dodd had been Yates Lecturer in New Testament Studies at Mansfield since 1915.

1927 and held that position for the following six years. This meant that he was closely involved in formulating policy and in dealing with certain personal difficulties among the staff, which seemed to take up a disproportionate amount of time.

The Fellowship had not really worked out its role in the post-war world; the differences between those who wanted it to be a campaigning body organised centrally, and those who saw it as a means of strengthening personal fellowship among Christian pacifists at a local level had not been properly resolved nor a compromise agreed. The membership was comparatively small: after a weeding-out of lapsed members in 1928, the roll stood at 3,300 subscribers, a small society from which to support a professional secretariat.

An internal enquiry into the purpose of the Fellowship reported to the general committee on 22 January 1929:

> We have asked ourselves: is it that of a propagandist group, seeking along the ways of manifestoes and resolutions to get its message 'across' to the surrounding community? Or is it rather a kind of Order, a Fellowship of men and women, with a certain unmistakable attitude to life based upon a profound religious conviction? If this latter, then the aim would not be primarily that of securing a number of agreed conclusions on a number of intricate problems – it would be rather that of a living Fellowship, where organisation would count less, but the spirit would count more.[1]

Percy Bartlett, the general secretary, wanted to follow the first policy. He wrote to Cadoux a few days later, suggesting a peace campaign involving Dick Sheppard, Herbert Gray if he could be so persuaded, and others. (The 'Christ and Peace' campaign launched in October 1929 fulfilled this plan, but was not officially sponsored by the FOR.) The idea had not yet been put to the general committee, and Cadoux was cautious about any centrally planned initiative.

In the spring of 1929, the Fellowship held a conference at Caerleon to discuss its own future. Unfortunately Cadoux was unable to leave Bradford at the time, and Henry Hodgkin, one of the original founders of the FOR, who was visiting England temporarily from his work in China, took the chair for him. It was clear from Hodgkin's long, thoughtful letter to Cadoux about the discussions at the conference that the members had thought hard about what they ought to be doing. After listening carefully to the discussion, Hodgkin had appealed to those present to agree to an approach to the churches 'on FOR lines', and had asked Percy Bartlett to see 'how a campaign can be

[1] Quoted in Martin Ceadel *Pacifism in Britain 1914-1945* (1980) p.64.

run on decentralised lines rather than simply by promotion from headquarters'.

The tenth anniversary of the armistice, in November 1928, had provoked a flow of anti-war literature, and the general mood became more favourable to pacifist ideas. A Congregational Pacifist Crusade had already been launched in 1926. The Congregational Union's autumnal assembly at Norwich in October 1929 (which Cadoux attended) was almost entirely devoted to a discussion of issues of war and peace. In the event the FOR was unable to launch any major appeal, but in practice its members supported the many peacemaking initiatives of the time as individuals, rather than through any corporate initiative.

The local FOR group promoted a conference in Ilkley in June (1929). The theme was 'Peace work from day to day'. Cadoux opened the conference with a talk on 'promoting the peace spirit'. Four points he emphasised; the peace spirit would be shown in inner harmony within oneself, in peaceableness of temper, in charitable dealings and example, and in contending for pacifism – 'intelligently and sportingly'. His approach, as shown here and at other times was 'quietist' rather than political; it was by personal appeal to individuals and small groups. He never lost an opportunity to promote a pacifist interpretation of the New Testament in his writing, or to open up a discussion of the subject.

In spite of all his efforts, he was not able to achieve that peace of mind which he preached. Within himself, he was struggling to accept the disappointment about Mansfield. At home, his efforts to promote and maintain peace faltered. But if the strains at home sometimes shook the foundations, they did not crack them. Though Marguerite may have felt exasperated at times, her deep love for her husband did not waver. He was immensely fortunate in his life-partner; while he was a theorist of pacifism, she was a practitioner in peace-making.

X

Smyrna
1930

CADOUX'S VISIT to Smyrna was planned to occupy the whole month of April 1930. His scheme to take Edward Yuill with him fell through because the York cocoa works where Yuill was employed decided, after much hesitation, that it could not spare him for such a long leave. Instead, Cadoux invited Francis (now Sir Francis) Boyd to accompany him. Francis Boyd had been a pupil at Silcoates, the Congregational boarding school near Wakefield at which Cadoux frequently preached, and had also attended the Free Church schoolboys' camps; his father had died young, and Cadoux had taken an interest in his career. He was now almost twenty, a junior reporter on *The Leeds Mercury*. A visit to Smyrna and the country inland could provide an unusual opportunity for foreign journalism. The two got on well together: Cadoux the mentor and scholar, Boyd the willing pupil and fledgling journalist. The visit proved a memorable experience for both of them.

Smyrna had suffered many changes since Cadoux's parents lived there. Nineteenth century Smyrna had a population which was almost half Greek, partly Armenian and partly Turkish. Most of the inhabitants were Orthodox Christian, only a quarter were Muslim. During and after the first world war, Asia Minor and eastern Europe was the battleground for competing claims amid the wreckage of the old Ottoman Empire. The Treaty of Sèvres of 1920, which was accepted by the Sultan though not by the Turkish nationalists, granted the administration of Smyrna and the surrounding area to Greece; this zone was to remain under nominal Turkish sovereignty for five years, after which it might opt to be transferred to Greek sovereignty. Greek troops had in fact been in occupation since 1919; and in view of the attitude of the Turkish nationalists, mounted a campaign against their forces in 1921. This went disastrously and on 9 September 1922 the Turks, led by Mustapha Kemal, retook the city. Five days later, a terrible fire broke out which destroyed about three-fifths of the city, including many of the best streets and buildings; not only this, but the Armenians and Greeks were forced to leave without any hope of being able to return. The old Smyrna (including the house in which the Cadoux family had lived) was virtually destroyed. Finally the Treaty of Lausanne of 1923 recognised Turkey's claim to Smyrna.

In that same year, 1923, Kemal became president of the new Turkish republic. Smyrna, the Greek name of the city, was replaced by the Turkish name Izmir (though for the purposes of this account the Greek name will be used).

The new city revived the prosperity of the old one; it remained the chief trading city of Turkey after Istanbul. New inhabitants moved in so that it still had a population of between two and three hundred thousand. The Turks rebuilt the devastated areas, creating a modern and spacious city.

The English community had not been forced to move out, and there were still people in Smyrna who remembered the Cadoux family. Bernard's wife's family, who were Belgian, lived there. Bernard still visited Smyrna, and gave his brother advice; as a result he was able to book rooms at Miss Grace Williamson's, an English nursing home which also took paying guests. Grace Williamson remembered William Cadoux as a much-loved Sunday School teacher.

Cadoux's regular diary is blank for the period 7–26 April, the period of their actual stay in Smyrna, and the detailed account of this visit he must certainly have written has not been found. It is fortunate that Francis Boyd's own journal, detailed, lively and informative, has survived intact.

The two men left Purley, where they had stayed with Maud, on Sunday 30 March. It took them a week from leaving London to reach Smyrna. First they travelled by train overnight to Venice. At Basel they got into conversation with an English professor, who entertained and instructed them on the pronunciation of English place-names. When they reached the Italian frontier at Chiasso, they observed a large number of Italian soldiers, wearing 'rough grey-green cloak, breeches, puttees and hat like our Robin Hood dressing-up hat' (Francis Boyd). Each one was armed with a rifle with fixed bayonet. According to the professor, Mussolini had stationed soldiers at every railway station, with the result that the trains were much more punctual.

They spent a night in Venice, which gave them the opportunity for some sight-seeing. They visited St Mark's Cathedral, the Doge's palace and the Rialto. Francis Boyd remembers that Cadoux, a devotee of Ruskin, 'would not dally to gaze at the Santa Maria della

Salute across the water from St Mark's, still less to visit the church. The Salute was one of the finest sights I had ever seen'. He remembers that when they stopped for a coffee in St Mark's Square, the Italian waiter corrected Cadoux, who was stirring whipped cream into his coffee – 'You must NOT stir it in Signor. You must let the cream rest on top of the coffee and drink the coffee *through* the cream'. For Boyd, this was 'my first lesson in worldly wisdom', but it is unlikely to have made much impact on Cadoux, who rarely drank coffee in any case.

From Venice they took the boat 'Gastein' down the Adriatic, calling at Brindisi, Santi Quaranta and Corfu before moving towards the Ionian sea and the Greek coastline: an exciting journey for anyone versed in classical literature and history. Cadoux was moved to get up in the night to catch a glimpse of Ithaca, like many generations of travellers before and since. When there was nothing to watch along the coast, they found people to talk to, and predictably the conversation frequently turned to matters of war and peace. 'Get into argument in French w' Turk ab't morals, God, fatalism and pacifism', Cadoux wrote in his diary (3 April). When that discussion finished, another one began, also in French, with two Italian students.

In Athens, they had a whole day ashore for sight-seeing. A Mr Stokes, the resident representative of MacAndrews and Forbes, was supposed to be meeting them to direct their sight-seeing. In fact, he missed them at the disembarkation point and spent the day chasing them round Athens, finally encountering them as they were about to re-embark. Nevertheless they managed to see many of the sights of Athens; the Propylaea, the Parthenon, the Erechtheum, the Areopagus, and the so-called Theseum. It was a hurried but exciting day.

The following day they reached the Gulf of Smyrna, and Cadoux's excitement mounted. Francis Boyd wrote in his diary:

> Impossible to give any impression of CJ's excitement throughout the whole of our trip down the Gulf. At breakfast he was not feeling well, but soon cheered up afterwards. From then on he was always on the look out for ancient sites, and the first glimpse of Smyrna which thrilled him to the core. Such excitement is good to see. We are both determined to make this a first-class holiday.

It was the culmination of years of study and planning. A return to one's birthplace, for the first time and in middle life, is an event out of the ordinary.

They managed to reach Miss Williamson's pension and settle in after a cup of tea. The other residents in the house were English or American, and proved friendly to the newcomers, though Cadoux's already encyclopaedic knowledge of the topography of the city may occasionally have proved disconcerting. As Francis Boyd remembers, 'he was able to correct, accurately, any of Miss Williamson's guests who were rash enough to say "Turn right at the Caravan Bridge for the Baths of Diana", instead of "Turn left"'.

It was a surprise to discover in conversation that Miss Williamson's cousin lived in Ilkley, and that her cousin's daughter was an acquaintance of Francis Boyd. She and other residents talked to the two visitors in the evenings and gave them graphic descriptions of the Turkish occupation and the fire of 1922, which had clearly been a traumatic experience for the English community.

Cadoux and Boyd spent the first ten days of their stay in and around the city of Smyrna. They saw some of the devastation, and the new buildings and wide roads which were gradually replacing the ruined narrow streets. They took their bearings and admired the setting. It was a colourful sight. Smyrna, Francis Boyd wrote, 'is set alongside the deep-blue waters of the gulf, bounded by great green-grey hills, with here and there a fertile strip of land splashed with the purple and crimson of its poppies and the white of its orchards, the whole lit up by brilliant sunshine'.[1] They went to the British consulate, where they met the consul's clerk, Adil Bey, who could speak quite good English, and was prepared to show them some of the archaeological sites of the city.

There was much to see and study. As a classicist, Cadoux was interested in the first Smyrna, founded in the tenth or eleventh century BC on a site three miles to the north-east, a city destroyed early in the sixth century; and in the second city, founded on the present site after the death of Alexander the Great. The new Smyrna was an important Ionian city, and later one of the chief cities in the Roman province of Asia. As a church historian, Cadoux was fascinated to study the remains of this second Smyrna, for it was one of the earliest Christian cities of Asia Minor, the site of one of the seven churches of Asia described in the book of *Revelation,* and the episcopal see of the martyr-bishop Polycarp. Several centuries as part of the Byzantine Empire were followed by further centuries as part of the Ottoman Empire. Smyrna had had a cosmopolitan population and thriving prosperity as a trading city and port.

When Cadoux wrote his history of ancient Smyrna, taking his account up to AD 324 (he always hoped to be able to continue the story in a second volume down to the present day) he wrote that his attempt to write a comprehensive history of the city 'has brought with it

[1] *Manchester Guardian* 2 July 1930.

painful confirmation of the truth of what a former Oxford teacher once told me – that one can never really exhaust a subject'. Nevertheless, he would do his best to master the surviving evidence, and to collate and interpret it.

He already had a permit to visit the interior and to take photographs. That did not necessarily mean they could go everywhere they wanted to, for the Turks still felt insecure in their possession of Smyrna. Francis Boyd wrote in an article for the *Manchester Guardian* (2 July 1930) not long after their return:

> The visitor to Smyrna will be struck with the loss of his freedom perhaps more than anything else. The Turks do not want a recurrence of the Greek occupation of 1919, and to prevent it they have put the hills to the south of the gulf under the control of the army. These military zones, embracing places of interest to the visitor, are only accessible by military permits, which are frequently refused to the applicant. Especially vexatious is the constant refusal of the authorities to allow anyone up Mount Pagus, an old acropolis of Smyrna, from which a magnificent view of the city, the gulf, and the hills beyond can be obtained, and which is full of interest for the archaeologist.

Their first sight-seeing expedition was to the Smyrna museum, housed in a former Greek Orthodox Church. Now that the Greeks had left, there was not a single Orthodox church in use for worship. The museum had preserved many inscriptions and sculptured heads from Smyrna and the surrounding area. They found the museum inspector 'a man of considerable charm', who spoke to them in French and allowed them to take photographs. They left 'on the best of terms'. Other visits followed to the sites known as Diana's Baths (below the local waterworks), Agamemnon's Baths, the Acropolis of old Smyrna, and the Tomb of Tantalus.

The Baths of Agamemnon made a great impression on the young Francis Boyd:

> These 'baths' mentioned by the geographer STRABO in his survey of Asia Minor are hot springs which appear *right at the side of a pleasant mountain stream,* flowing at the foot of The Three Brothers. At some points baths of brick have been erected, but at others the springs have not been touched. They are in fact extremely hot, so much so that it was impossible for us to hold our hands in the water for more than a few seconds. Near the water were many bull-frogs making the dickens of a row. A tortoise also hopped along and was photographed by me – successfully I hope. An extremely interesting visit.

On one of these outings, they visited the International College at Paradise (originally founded in order to Christianise the Turks, but now stripped of its proselytising function and confined to purely educational activities), in order to borrow a copy of Weber's *Sipylus et ses Monuments*, which would help them to identify the earliest remains. Cadoux wheedled the librarian, a Mr Lawrence, 'a very weary man without any fun in living', into allowing him to borrow the book for an extended period.

Family piety was not forgotten. After visiting the International College, Cadoux and his young companion went on another two miles to Buja, where the Cadoux family had lived for a time. Francis Boyd wrote in his diary:

> We saw the site of the house and made for the abode of Mrs Hanson, wife to Hanson of MacAndrew and Forbes, Church-warden of Buja, and she gave us tea and permission to go to the English Church. There we went to see the graves of three of CJ's sisters. The eldest of them died at the age of 12. Found easily and photographed.

There were other old contacts to be renewed. They visited Maurice Eppstein, whose sister Katie had acted as a housekeeper to the family in London after Cadoux's mother's death. A more recent contact was Bernard's wife's family. Cadoux hurt his leg while they were visiting the Tomb of Tantalus, and sent Francis Boyd round that same evening to invite Bernard's sister-in-law, Mademoiselle Lison de Hochepied, to come round to Miss Williamson's. In spite of her own quite severe lameness, she 'proved herself to be one of the jolliest people we have met so far'; she suggested that as they were visiting 'les antiquités de Smyrne' they should call on her.

Their first expedition further afield was to Ephesus, one of the most impressive ruined cities in the whole of Asia Minor. They travelled by train, third class. English residents customarily travelled first or second class, alongside the Turkish officials and clerks, but it was much more interesting to travel with the ordinary Turkish people; in any case Cadoux's 'levelling' instincts would have made him uncomfortable in anything else. They did not realise at first that men and women travelled separately, and had to be turned out of a 'Ladies Only' carriage. The three hour ride provided plenty of opportunity to see more of Turkish life, before leaving the train at Seljuk for the walk to Ephesus. Here they visited the enormous theatre, once capable of holding 24,000 people, the scene of the riot against the apostle Paul; from there they walked along the Marmorean Way to the library of Celsus. As usual, they had their papers with them, printed in the

Roman letters which Kemal had substituted for Arabic ones as part of the policy of westernisation. The local policeman, unused to the new letters, examined their papers, and took them for spies; they repeated one of the few Turkish words they knew, 'konak' (town hall), which convinced the policeman that it might be wiser not to arrest them. They were not able to spend enough time to make a thorough study of the ruins before making for the return train; but such a splendid site is never forgotten.

The following day they were able to join a party of English people, friends of one of Miss Williamson's guests, to make a journey by car to Mahmud Dag, 4500 feet high, which they climbed, and the Karabel pass, driving through beautiful country on the way.

They had now visited the city sites of two of the seven churches which figure in the early part of *The Revelation of John*. Their most adventurous tour was the one which took them to a third – Sardis. They travelled by train to Sardis station where they were met by a Mr Ali, an agent for an employee of MacAndrews and Forbes; also in the party was Mr Nuridin, a clerk for the same agent. The party set off by cart for the foot of the Acropolis, site of the Temple of Artemis, one of the largest Ionic temples in the Greek world. Here they climbed up to the south side and took photographs.

After this they started out for their final destination that day, the village of Ahmetli, where they were to spend the night. This journey, and the hospitality they received at the end of it, was vividly described by Francis Boyd in an article he wrote for the *Yorkshire Post* (21 November 1930) a few months later:

> The sun had already begun to set when the two-wheeled cart started its journey along the rough track that led between fields of crimson, purple and white poppies from the ruins of Old Sardis to the little village of Ahmetli, some six miles to the west. There are five people in the car: the driver; Nuridin, our guide; Ali, our host – all three Turks – and we two, who had escaped from the grime and chill of the West Riding into the burning sunshine and dry air of Asia Minor. Nuridin alone spoke two languages, and his French was as bad as ours. With the others we conversed in signs.
>
> The journey came to an end opposite a small door in a high stone wall, pierced with one lower and two upper windows to the left of the entrance. Ali smilingly bade us enter and beckoned us up a wooden staircase leading from the yard to a wide balcony, in a dark corner of which could be seen a woman bending over a brazier. By her side was a collection of plates and bowls filled

with vegetables of all kinds and meat. She seemed to be preparing the evening meal.

The room we were shown into was small and clean. Along one side of it stretched a divan and wide, flat cushions lined the base of two adjoining walls. A circular table, three chairs, a small dressing table and an oil lamp completed the furniture. The wood work of the door and window surround lacked paint but seemed all the cleaner for that.

Wearied by the events of the day – we had already travelled for five and a half hours in the train up from the coast and had scaled the steep slopes of the Acropolis that watches over Sardis – we were anxious for sleep. Besides, we were to set off next morning at five. But Nuridin, who always made the best of his rare visits up-country, and Ali, jealous of the company of his equally rare guests, had other plans.

To our dismay, preparations were started for a great meal. The round table began to creak under the weight of the heaped-up dishes with which it was being covered. When all was ready, Ali, his tanned face creased up into a most inviting smile, motioned us to the table. My eyes fell on such a collection of food as I had never seen before and hope never again to see. A great oval dish of light-coloured meat – probably goat's flesh – occupied the centre of the table. Near it were well-filled bowls of potatoes, green salad, spiced with very bitter salt, and what appeared to be sliced scarlet runners, though their taste was far different from that of the English variety.

For sweets there were pilafe and yoghurt, a dish made of soured milk. Cheese and coffee followed. The meal had been prepared with characteristic generosity; when my companion, a vegetarian, asked politely for 'des oeufs à la coque', Ali set two in front of him before there was time to say 'Jack Robinson' and produced six more five minutes later.

The end of the meal did not bring with it the hoped-for permission to sleep. Indeed, as we rose from the table, we could hear footsteps coming up the stairs. There entered a well-built, middle-aged man, dressed in blue serge trousers, a cardigan and a smart double-breasted jacket. He had a large fat face, its pallor relieved by a small jet-black moustache. Round his neck he wore a white scarf, and he carried in his hand a 'peaker' [peaked cap]. A sudden lull in the conversation marked his entrance and indicated to us that he was a man of importance – perhaps the Mayor himself? We discovered him to be the 'chef de gare', receiving all the deference that would have been due to the mayor, had such an official existed.

The stationmaster went straight to a chair in the middle of the room, bowed to us, sat down and allowed the company to settle itself before be began to speak. Besides Ali and Nuridin, Ali's father and the driver of the cart were now in the room. All thoughts of sleep had long been banished from our minds.

'Mesdames et Messieurs . . .' He may have begun less formally, but that was the impression one got. Certainly he spoke a vigorous and fluent French, and though Nuridin alone of the Turks understood him, the others gloried in the throaty syllables and cataclysmic sentences that issued from his lips. We were quite overwhelmed by this outpouring, but managed to fix on a sentence or two which seemed to make sense. Turkey, we gathered, did not want war. She wanted peace; was longing for friendship with England; needed England's co-operation and capital in order to develop her resources properly; was rich in minerals but poor in money. Turkey was glad for visitors to come and was especially glad to see us. We bowed. We had perhaps noticed the elaborate arrangements made by the police to know of our movements? We had! Was not that proof of friendship? The police wanted to be able to help us at any minute should an accident occur, and therefore had to know where we were . . . 'Eh bien, mes amis, au revoir!' The stationmaster was so sorry, but he had to go: it was regrettable, but there were trains even in Turkey, and one could not keep them waiting for ever, no?

With him went all the others save Ali, who removed the table and spread on the floor two mattresses. These he covered with two blankets, and with a kindly smile waved us to our beds.

Next day, another cart journey, a long walk to the tumulus of Alyattes, king of Lydia (who had destroyed Smyrna early in the sixth century), and a train journey, brought them back again to Smyrna.

There were three more long excursions. First, a visit to Magnesia ad Sipylum (Manisa), considered one of the most up-to-date towns in Turkey, and the carving of the Hittite mother goddess (sometimes referred to as a representation of Niobe), dating it was thought from 1400 BC; on the way home they just missed an earthquake. Then a shorter excursion, a drive to Bunarbashi, Bel-Kavé, and Burnabat, where Cadoux was excited to discover a Greek inscription he was looking for on a pillar in the mosque. And finally an expedition by fast Renault 80 miles north to the site of another of the seven churches, Pergamum, in the company of Mrs Guiffray and a friend, to whom

Maurice Eppstein had introduced them. Here they visited both the earlier city on the hill, and its later extension on the plain below. The views from the hill were magnificent.

Cadoux's leg was troubling him and he was persuaded to consult a doctor; it made him depressed at times, but did little to impede the remaining sight-seeing. On 26 April, he and Francis Boyd left Smyrna on the ship 'Egitto', and spent the next five days at sea. It was fine weather, and it was an opportunity to relax; 'absolutely slacking, in order to rest brain and heal leg', wrote Cadoux in his diary.

They disembarked at Trieste and took the train to Paris, and on to London, where they were met by Bernard. It had been an exciting, hectic, rewarding trip. Cadoux had checked on much of his accumulated information, acquired more, and experienced the atmosphere of a place which had long captured his imagination. It gave further dimension to his knowledge of his birthplace and its history.

For Francis Boyd it was a journey to remember for a lifetime. He told Cadoux in a letter soon after their return that the trip had been 'in every way delightful', and that it had been fascinating 'to watch your tremendous enthusiasm and excitement' and to pick up 'a few of learning's crumbs'.

The crowning sequel to the visit for Cadoux was, of course, the publication of the book for the sake of which it had been undertaken, and on which he had worked intermittently ever since 1909, when he had chosen the history of his birthplace as the subject of his London MA thesis. It was not, however, until 1928 that he was able to begin seriously to cast his material into a form suitable for publication, and after the visit of 1930 it took him a further six years to complete it. His return to Oxford in 1933 afforded him much easier access to the relevant material. The book was finally completed in the autumn of 1936; after the initial disappointment of having it turned down by the Oxford University Press, Blackwell's agreed to publish it. It was entitled *Ancient Smyrna: a History of the City from the Earliest Times to AD 324* and appeared in May 1938.

It was a monument of careful scholarship, and earned praise from reviewers. Nathaniel Micklem wrote of it in *The British Weekly* that it was 'the most massive, impressive, dignified tribute ever, as I suppose, offered by a scholar to the town where first he saw the light'. Of one review, by his friend Marcus Tod of Oriel College, he must have been particularly proud. Tod wrote in *The Oxford Magazine* (20 October 1938):

> One reader at least has closed the book with a sense of profound admiration for the author's achievement and of pride that Oxford

should have given to the learned world so valuable and scholarly a work.

It was of particular service to the team of British and Turkish archaeologists who excavated the site of Old Smyrna in the years 1948–51,[1] thereby making available much additional evidence for the early history of the city, though unhappily too late to be of help to Cadoux.

It was a book in which Cadoux took a particular pride; a year after its publication, he noted in his diary, 'Anniv^y of public^n of *Ancient Smyrna.*' As a work of filial piety, it was dedicated to the memory of his parents, and to his brothers and sisters. As a work of scholarship it was to contribute to his being awarded the Oxford degree of D.Litt.

---

[1] This work is described by J. M. Cook and others in *Annals of the British School at Athens* LIII/LIV (1958/9) 1-181.

XI

Last years in Bradford
1930–1933

NOT MANY DAYS after Cadoux returned from Smyrna, he received the letter telling him about Dodd's appointment as professor in Manchester. Any thought of going to Manchester himself had now to be dismissed; but what about the New Testament post at Mansfield that Dodd was to vacate?

Mansfield was going through a period of change and re-organisation. The triumvirate of Selbie, Gray and Bartlet, which had given the college stability and distinction for so long, was broken when Gray died suddenly in 1922. Bartlet had retired in 1928, and Selbie was now soon to retire. Selbie's term as Principal had been extended beyond his 65th birthday, but by 1930 the Council was seriously searching for a successor. His health was poor and his grip was not as firm as it had been. The Council itself reflected a variety of different interests and theological positions, and the problem of finding a new principal who would have and retain the confidence of all members of the Council was going to prove formidable.

Unknown to Cadoux, a small subcommittee was appointed to search for a successor to Dodd as New Testament Professor with the Principalship also in mind. Within a month, they produced their nomination to the Council and Board of Education; their proposal was that Nathaniel Micklem, Professor of New Testament Studies at Queen's Theological College, Kingston, Ontario, be appointed to the Yates Chair of New Testament Exegesis. This proposal was confirmed at a further special meeting in September 1930. In addition, Micklem was appointed Vice-Principal. And further, in November, the Council

> while feeling unable definitely to pledge their successors, wish to assure the Rev. N. Micklem in inviting him to the Yates Chair that it is their hope and expectation that he will succeed to the Principalship.

Cadoux's hopes were still firmly pinned on Oxford. In June 1930 he

131

visited Taunton School and consulted the headmaster about Theo's entering the school 'on suppos^n of my coming to Oxford'. He knew only that there was to be a special Mansfield Council meeting on 27 September to review the staffing position. Still he heard nothing. On 19 October he phoned Leyton Richards, a member of the Council. 'Quite indeterminate reply from him. Decide to worry abt Oxford no more', he wrote in his diary. But the anxiety was not so easily suppressed.

It was not until December that he learned, from *The Christian World,* about Micklem's appointment to Mansfield. He felt he had been rejected yet again, and shared his disappointment with a number of people. At the Yorkshire College, early in the new year, he talked it over with a member of the Education Committee: 'Chat w' Donald-son – he tells me he has heard that it was my views re sinlessness of Jesus that cost me the chair at Mansfield' (diary, 6 January 1931). Whether or not that was the case, a controversy with A. D. Martin in *The Congregational Quarterly* on the subject early in 1930 cannot have helped his case.

A. D. Martin, a Congregational minister, had discovered a critical reference to an article of his in *Catholicism and Christianity.* This led him to examine carefully what Cadoux had to say about the teaching and person of Christ in both *Catholicism and Christianity* and *The Guidance of Jesus for Today*; he concluded that Cadoux did not believe in the sinlessness of Jesus, nor in his intellectual infallibility. Martin published an article in *The Congregational Quarterly* (January 1930) under the heading 'The doctrine of the fallibility of Jesus'; while appreciating Cadoux's immense industry and scholarship, he did cast doubt on Cadoux's Christology, and further asked whether scholars like Cadoux realised the effect of their ideas on the churches. This prompted a correspondence in *The Christian World* in which Cadoux and Martin both took part, and in which Griffith-Jones was moved to write defending both Martin's Christology and Cadoux's intellectual integrity.

The offending passage which Martin had quoted was from *The Guidance of Jesus for Today* (pp. 47–48):

> Apologists for the creeds confidently assert that Jesus was sinless in the most absolute sense, despite the fact that we know too little of his life or of the psychology of sin to be able to insist dogmatic-ally on sweeping conclusions in regard to such a point, and to build doctrines upon them: nor do they adequately explain why Jesus submitted to a baptism of repentance, or why he objected to being addressed as 'Good Master', on the ground that '(there

is) none good save one, (namely) God', or why the author of Hebrews described him as 'learning obedience by the things that he suffered'.

Cadoux published a reply to Martin in the following issue of *The Congregational Quarterly* (April 1930) in a discussion article headed, 'The human nature of Jesus'. He defended his search for truth, regardless of the consequences; for how else was it to be discovered? There was no proof that modernist theology was responsible for emptying pews – 'that emptiness may be due just as much to attempts on the part of the pulpit to maintain a historically untenable view of Him'. The article included the sentence:

Let is be clearly understood that to challenge the dogmatic assertion of Jesus' sinlessness as a supposedly historical datum on which a theory of His Person can at once be built is not to call in question for a moment the moral purity, nobility, and serenity of His character, the creative power and unique holiness of His Person, and the saving efficacy of His work.

The controversy seems to have hinged partly on the meaning of the words 'sin' and 'sinless'. Cadoux referred to

the baffling connexion (in human experience) between avoidable and blameworthy wrongdoing on the one hand and, on the other, the more or less venial yet often serious imperfection (in its myriad forms) which is incidental to all natural human growth.

Cadoux's orthodoxy was still left in question for some people, especially those who were not able to give the matter time and close attention, and who relied on second-hand reports.

Maud tried to console her brother:

I am so sorry about Oxford, but don't worry my dear Jack, perhaps it is for the best. I often think in life the things we long for do not always bring the happiness etc we think – but I hate you to be disappointed, only don't let it affect your health.

And so did Arthur:

. . . you must not let a disappointment of this sort destroy the joy of present values, disappointment may sometimes save us from what is worse, disillusionment.

I remember your telling me years ago that when you were working for the BA you thought that, that achieved, the world and life would take on new colours for you, and were surprised, when the results were published, to find how little difference it made. I think you may be pretty sure that had you gone to Oxford, you would now have had much the same experience.

Theo went to Taunton School as a boarder in January 1931. Until

March Ruth was the only child at home. But on 26 March, another daughter, Joan Mary, was born. The happiness of this event was almost immediately overshadowed by another crisis, for Ruth was taken ill with a high temperature and had to be taken to join her mother in the same nursing home. Jack wired to Ida, who was unable to come, then to Connie, who did come to look after the household for the next few weeks. Ruth recovered, and she, Marguerite and the new baby came home amid general rejoicing. Nevertheless, it was a most exhausting Easter holiday – 'worn to a shadow w' strain of the children', Cadoux put in his diary.

These family affairs had no noticeable effect on his intellectual work. He could write articles and chapters according to schedule whatever might be happening in other areas of his life. In the middle of the Easter holiday, and in a single day, he wrote his contribution to a collection of *Essays Congregational and Catholic* (edited by Albert Peel 1931), in commemoration of the centenary of the Congregational Union of England and Wales. There was a distinguished group of contributors, including Dodd, Micklem, Selbie and R. S. Franks. Cadoux's contribution was entitled, 'Congregationalism the true Catholicism'. As with his previous work, he sent the essay to Bartlet, and then revised it in the light of Bartlet's suggestions. His theme was one already expounded in *Catholicism and Christianity*. Congregationalism was 'an attempt to assert the great truth that all Christian men are brethren'; 'the true Church exists wherever and whenever two or three gather together, in the name of Christ and having faith in Him, for worship and work as His disciples'. The key to reunion was

> primarily, not agreement regarding ministerial orders or essential doctrines, but the mutual recognition of Christians by Christians as being really fellow-members of that One Church to which they severally belong.

In retrospect, we can see that this has in fact proved a means of creative reconciliation between churches of different traditions.

While revising this essay, he was also checking the galley proofs of his colloquial translation of Deuteronomy, which was also published in 1931. Though it was a serious and thoughtful attempt to make a document far removed from western culture intelligible, interesting and valuable for 'the general reader', it proved too colloquial for most tastes.

That summer the family were unable to take a holiday all together, particularly as there was a new baby to look after. In June Cadoux paid his regular visit to Oxford for the Mansfield Old Men's meetings; a few days later Griffith-Jones drove him and Arthur to Cambridge for the Congregational conference, where Arthur read a paper on 'The ethical teaching of Jesus'. On returning home, Cadoux prepared to take his sons on a walking tour of Hampshire and the Isle of Wight. It was a nostalgic visit. First they visited his uncle Henry, who had married a younger sister of his father in Portsmouth. They visited the 'Victory' and the dockyard, and then drove out to Hayling Island to see the grave of Effie, his sister who died there as a child. The following day Cadoux visited Royal Clarence Yard, where he had once worked, and met two of his former Admiralty colleagues. Then they crossed over to the Isle of Wight. By great good fortune his old Boys' Brigade colleague Peacock was in camp at Bembridge; they visited the camp and there was a happy reunion with several other old friends. 'A great day!' he wrote in his diary. Then there was a visit to the house in Ventnor where his father had died, before returning to the mainland and paying a brief visit to the New Forest. It was a refreshing holiday, and there was another 'joyful reunion' when they reached home.

That autumn he became involved in an unfortunate and unpleasant controversy with *The Tablet*. It began with Selbie's writing a few columns in *The Christian World*, in answer to a reader's question about worship of the Virgin Mary. As a description of the 'general Roman Catholic belief' about the Virgin Mary, Selbie quoted from Cadoux's 'great book', *Catholicism and Christianity*. This attracted the notice of *The Tablet*, which strongly criticised Selbie's article. Cadoux came to his rescue with a letter, which was printed with editorial comment. A ding-dong controversy followed, with *The Tablet* referring to Mansfield as 'the most pretentious Free Church seminary in all England' and to 'the touchy Dr Cadoux', in a tone hardly conceivable in such a context fifty years later. No constructive purpose was served by the correspondence, and it upset Cadoux considerably.

Throughout that year, 1931, and into early 1932, Cadoux took pastoral oversight of Greenfield Congregational Church in Bradford. Whatever extreme liberal views he might be expressing in his articles found no place in his conduct of worship. Harry Escott, one of his students in Bradford, attended Greenfield sometimes that year. He remembers that

> his conduct of the communion service and his prayers which were always spoken extempore were both marked by sincerity and evangelical tone and grace, I thought, and belied his theological liberalism which at the time bordered on what we thought was Unitarianism.[1]

Another former student, L.J.Malkinson, wrote to him while he

[1] Letter to the author 28 February 1982.

was still acting minister at Greenfield, to thank him for his conduct of the communion service at the meeting of the Bradford Congregational Association, of which he had just been elected President:

> Personally I very much appreciated all that you said, and have never listened to a communion address with so much enjoyment, a pleasure which, I think, was shared by all who were present. The real value of the symbolism does need to be emphasised in non-catholic groups and I feel you will be doing a real service whenever you speak along lines such as those you followed last night.

Many remembered his preaching years later with gratitude. His conduct of worship as a whole, his general bearing and sense of reverence, and his skill as a teacher, formed a lasting impression on the members of his congregation at Greenfield.

He was now also the President of the Bradford Free Church Council. On 11 March Griffith-Jones wrote him a note complimenting him on his chairmanship of this Council:

> Everybody seems very pleased with you as President; certainly you seemed to the manner born yesterday. You'll make a popular leader of affairs after all!

A few hours after reading this appreciative note from his Principal, he opened another letter containing good news. It was a letter from Edinburgh University offering him the honorary degree of DD. This was a welcome recognition of his scholarship and teaching ability by the university for whose degrees he prepared students.

Griffith-Jones had already signified his intention of retiring in the summer of 1932. He had celebrated his seventieth birthday two years earlier and found the day-to-day responsibility of his position was becoming too much for him. It did not take the Governors very long to decide to offer the Principalship to Ernest Price. Though Cadoux might have considered himself a candidate for the position, his sights were set on Mansfield, and it is doubtful whether he would have been prepared to commit himself at that stage to a prolonged stay in Bradford.

Only a matter of days before Griffith-Jones had handed in his resignation in Bradford, Selbie had handed in his in Oxford. He felt he should retire at the end of Hilary Term 1932. Micklem was immediately appointed Principal designate, to succeed as Principal after Easter. A small subcommittee was appointed 'to consider all questions relating to the staff and curriculum' and to report back to the Council.

As Micklem describes in his volume of reminiscences, *The Box and the Puppets* (1957), he and the College Council did not see eye to eye about the teaching arrangements in the college, and the Council over-ruled his own suggestions. He was already teaching New Testament Studies in succession to Dodd; H. Wheeler Robinson was teaching the Old Testament, and J. S. Whale Church History. Although the subcommittee recommended that Micklem should continue to teach New Testament, the Council would not accept this suggestion and asked him to assume responsibility for Systematic Theology, which he later claimed was the only part of the theological discipline in which he was not really interested. However he took up the challenge, though his method of approaching the subject proved not to be at all what the Council had in mind.

The Council's next meeting coincided with the Old Men's Meetings at Mansfield in June. Cadoux as usual travelled south for the commemoration, and learned in conversation first that the Council was about to appoint a New Testament professor (the position he held in Bradford) and secondly that the Council was not going to appoint a Congregationalist at all, but the Presbyterian T. W. Manson, a young but already distinguished New Testament scholar for whom Cadoux had a high regard. But why had it been necessary to look outside the Congregational denomination? Why had he been overlooked yet again?

He believed, probably rightly, that this disappointment was responsible for a rise in his blood pressure, which in turn was the cause of a blurred patch in his right eye. He consulted Dr Eurich, who recommended at least a month's 'slacking'. It worried him a good deal, especially as it prevented him from writing without the help of an amanuensis. In August he was worrying even more and wrote to Dr Eurich to ask about his condition and the prospects for recovery.

> It was at Oxford about June 17 that I experienced a keen and unexpected disappointment; and from my general state of health before and since that date I am inclined to believe that the blood pressure trouble dates from that time.
>
> . . .
>
> I am doing what I can to keep my mind in a cheerful and healthy state but am not very successful in this.

Dr Eurich replied that overwork and anxiety were the most likely causes of his illness, and that he must expect improvement to be slow, and 'no treatment can be effective unless the patient consents to cut down his work'. 'Perseverance and patience' would be called for.

While he was recuperating in August, he received a letter inviting him to go out to Australia as Principal of Camden College, a

Congregational theological college in Sydney. It was not a very tempting offer, for the salary was poor and it was an awkward time to disrupt his children's education. He consulted Griffith-Jones, who advised him against going – 'You are far too modernist in your critical and theological views to suit the Antipodeans'. It did not take him many days to decide to reject the offer.

When he went to stay with Arthur for a few days' rest the following week, he discovered that the New Testament chair in Glasgow University was being advertised, and wrote to tell Marguerite that he was thinking of applying for it. She replied that she was willing to go anywhere with him, but wondered whether 'they could swallow your teaching'. Though he was warned that it was almost certain that a Presbyterian would be appointed, he discovered that legally the post was open to non-Presbyterians, and put in an application. Within a month, the appointment of the Presbyterian G. H. C. Macgregor (another influential pacifist) was announced. He should not have been surprised, but this further setback did nothing to improve his health.

Before Christmas a glimmer of hope appeared. At the beginning of December *The Christian World* published news of the appointment of J. S. Whale as President of Cheshunt College, Cambridge. His post at Mansfield would soon be vacant. Within two days came a letter from Leyton Richards saying he wanted to nominate Cadoux for the vacant chair of Church History. Did Cadoux feel he could work happily under Micklem's principalship? Cadoux hastened to reply in the affirmative, notwithstanding their growing theological differences. Apparently he also believed himself fitted to teach Church History, though his work in that field was limited to the early period. Letters between Oxford and Bradford travelled frequently over the next ten weeks, and Cadoux's hopes were slowly but steadily raised.

The Mansfield Council met in London on 10 February 1933. Certain members of the Council were by this time determined to push Cadoux's nomination strongly, and after a good deal of discussion, the proposal that he be appointed was carried unanimously. When Cadoux arrived home for supper that evening he found a telegram from Albert Peel – 'Good news on the way'. His diary recounts – 'Later wire fr Richards saying Mansfield had appointed me Mackennal Professor. Delirious!' The next day he received a letter from Dr Sidney M. Berry, chairman of the Council, passing on the unanimous invitation of the Council to accept the Mackennal Chair of Church History, as from the beginning of the new academic year in October, at a salary of £600 per annum. Needless to say, he lost little time in writing a letter of acceptance.

Griffith-Jones wrote from his retirement home in Wales, summing up the place of the Bradford experience in Cadoux's career, as he saw it, and offering a hope for the future:

'All things come to them who wait', and at last your life's desire to get on the permanent staff of your Alma Mater is a *fait accompli.*

. . . It was easy to see, in spite of the happy relations that have always characterized your work at United, that the Yorkshire environment has not been altogether congenial to a man of your scholarly mind and temperament, and that there are many sides of your personality that have been more or less starved there . . . Not that your sojourn at United has been without its profound influence and value to you, even as scholar and thinker. I have seen the gradual and in many ways beneficent effect on your mental and spiritual sense of values, to be thus plunged for so many years into the rough but potent practicality of the York-shire world-view after the thin academic air of Oxford ecclesi-asticism. This rough bath has corrected your natural tendency to a vague idealism, and – pardon the suggestion – to the tyranny of abstract principles aloof from the practical issues and problems of actual experiences. I sincerely hope that you will take back with you the full values of this fruitful episode in your life into Oxford, and that you will never allow yourself to degenerate into a 'donnish' type of creature in your old age.

Many letters of congratulation arrived, from Arthur ('quite the best thing I have heard for a long time'), Connie ('so you have got your heart's desire at last'), from members of the Council and the Senior Common Room at Mansfield, and from numerous ministerial friends, even from the Bishop of Bradford (A. W. F. Blunt), a fellow-member of the Bradford Theological Circle.

In March, he went to Oxford to look at possible houses, and took Marguerite a few weeks later to make a final choice. They decided on 179 Woodstock Road, about a mile from the centre of the city. During the same visit, Cadoux read his first paper at the Oxford Society for Historical Theology (or rather T. W. Manson read it for him, as he had lost his voice) on 'Some problems of the early history of the Church at Smyrna'. That same day Micklem had written him a letter to say he was appointed Vice-Principal. There were 'no official duties except to take my place when I am absent. Its real significance is that it gives you seniority in the Common Room'.

He returned to Bradford to celebrate his fiftieth birthday, and to wind up his affairs at the college. There were farewell meetings to attend, and the removal to prepare for. Two days before leaving

Bradford on 24 July, Cadoux consulted Dr Eurich again. His heart was 'practically right' and the prognosis 'reassuring'. It was with higher spirits than for a long time that Cadoux returned to live and work in Oxford.

XII

Return to Oxford
1933–1934

THOUGH CADOUX'S HEALTH after he left Bradford was never really good, he thoroughly enjoyed the theological life of Oxford. It had so much to offer to the theological scholar; one of the best libraries in the world, several societies dedicated to the discussion of theological subjects, and other stimulating minds. On the other hand, he found less satisfaction in his life in college, and began to find himself out of sympathy with many of his colleagues, in a way he had not experienced in Bradford.

The family home was a substantial red-brick semi-detached late Victorian house. It was in that part of north Oxford which had been developed in the late nineteenth and early twentieth centuries, after university dons were allowed to marry; they were family houses sufficient for several children and at least one maid. The Cadouxs' house, in common with many others in the area, had been built by St John's College. It was on three floors, and had a small garden in front and a good-sized one at the rear. The ground-floor rooms included a dining room and a bedsitting room at the front, and a drawing room opening onto the back garden. On the first floor, Cadoux had a large study at the front. There were sufficient bedrooms for all the family, the maid and a guest, in addition to the room downstairs, which was usually occupied during term by one or two Mansfield students; there were often eight people sitting down to meals together.

The boys were still away at school during term-time. Ruth, who was eight when she moved to Oxford, went to the Oxford High School for Girls, where she remained for the rest of her school career; Joan was only two, but eventually followed her sister to the High School when she was old enough.

The distance from the house to Mansfield was just over a mile. Cadoux frequently walked or cycled, otherwise took a bus. (The family never owned a car). When travelling by bus, he would wait until the very last moment, often posting one of his children at the gate to watch for its approach, even occasionally instructing them, to their embarrassment, to ask the bus to wait for him.

Not far to the west of the house lay Port Meadow, one of the largest expanses of common land in England. On either side of the meadow was a waterway: to the west the river Thames (known as the Isis within the boundaries of Oxford) and to the east the canal, with the railway running between the two. From the meadow one looked across to Wytham Woods and Cumnor Hill. It was an unspoilt oasis of peace which Cadoux enjoyed to the full, walking on or near it almost every afternoon. Sometimes he would go farther afield. He would take a student or one of his children with him whenever possible. He was not a great respecter of boundaries, and had no compunction in walking across private land; if challenged he claimed to be doing no harm, and usually proceeded without interruption. His younger daughter had many anxious moments when accompanying her father across land labelled with the words 'Trespassers will be prosecuted'; she thought 'prosecuted' meant 'executed'.

Except when interrupted by illness, Cadoux's daily schedule was adhered to strictly. The general framework of his day was as follows: at 6.30 he made a pot of tea, then retired to his study for prayer. He had a schedule of hymns and would often sing the appropriate one for the day while dressing. Breakfast was always served at 7.45, after which he would return to his study for work. At 10.15 he would come downstairs to listen to the BBC daily service, and drink more tea. He would work again, either in his study or in college, until lunch was served at 1 pm; after lunch he enjoyed 30 minutes sleep before going out for a walk, preferably with a companion, and returning for afternoon tea. After tea he returned to his study until supper time. And unless he had an evening meeting, he did more work in his study after supper.

There was never a feeling of rush or panic about any of his activities; he was always able to meet the deadline for articles or books, and never had to stay up working late into the night. His students at Mansfield believed that for his history of ancient Smyrna, he had calculated the length of time necessary to finish his research, the length of the projected book, and the amount of time needed to type it; and then worked out how many words he needed to write each day in order to keep to his schedule. No doubt this is mythical, but it indicates appropriately the method and discipline of his work.

Though writing and research were always an integral part of his life, the meeting of teacher and pupil were important too. His own teachers had been, and continued to be, very significant for him; he wanted to offer the same help to new generations. He had always enjoyed getting to know young people, especially his students. Now he not only took the opportunity of talking to Mansfield students, but also to undergraduates reading subjects other than theology, with whom he or his family had some contact. There were young men newly arrived from St Dunstan's, Catford, and from Bradford Grammar School; there were his sons' friends, and his friends' sons. During term, he and his wife would arrange tea parties twice a week for these young people; there was plenty of good food, and a relaxed, friendly atmosphere. Cadoux and his wife 'seemed genuinely glad to be visited. And if he seemed glad, then he was, because you always knew where you were with C. J. Cadoux'.[1]

Cadoux's life in Oxford, outside the family, was centred on Mansfield, and on the wider theological circles within the university and associated theological colleges. His poor health prevented him from travelling about as much as he had done in previous years, or from taking much part in wider church life. Only six weeks after the move, his eyes began to give cause for anxiety; the oculist found a slight leakage (retinal haemorrhage), this time in his left eye, and he was ordered to limit his reading to only two hours a day – disastrous for a scholar. This led to a very frustrating first term; he could do little research, he gave no lectures, and felt listless. Arthur sent him wise counsel:

> Part of the art of getting the best out of oneself is to have the right amount of lying fallow. I think this is especially the case with anyone who has worked hard over a long period. If we keep the most conscious part of us too occupied, it does not give the subconscious a chance of digesting and working up what we shove into it.

He never fully recovered his health, though he did his utmost to live a healthy life. It was unfortunate that he felt unable to accept an invitation offered in May 1934 to become the secretary of the theological committee of the World Conference on Faith and Order, in preparation for the conference in Lausanne in 1937.

He took fewer preaching engagements than in earlier years. For one thing, members of staff were expected to attend Mansfield College Chapel on most Sundays in term time; for another Cadoux's larger salary (£600, raised to £650 in 1936 and £700 in 1937) meant that preaching engagements were no longer a financial necessity. Though Harold complained that the family finances were always (quoting his father) 'in an awkward transitional stage' whenever he had reason to ask for money, the financial pressures seem to have been eased.

[1] Letter from Dafydd Ap-Thomas 14 February 1983 to the author.

At Mansfield Cadoux was required to lecture twice weekly on Church History, to give tutorials, taking students singly or in pairs to discuss a weekly essay and guide their reading, to attend meetings of the Senior Common Room, and to share in and occasionally lead worship in the college chapel. It was not until the beginning of 1934 that he was well enough to assume these responsibilities fully. The college was not residential, but there were meals in Hall for both staff and students and their guests, and Cadoux would sometimes dine there, and share in entertaining college visitors.

When Cadoux had left Mansfield in 1919, Selbie was fully established as Principal with several more years to look forward to. In 1933 Selbie was still living in Oxford, but in retirement. Cadoux still regarded him as his mentor and consulted him frequently. The Selbies lived in Banbury Road, half way between the Cadoux home and Summertown Congregational Church, of which they were all members, though the Cadoux family attended Mansfield Chapel during term. When Selbie had become too old to attend church regularly, Cadoux often called at the Selbies on his way home from church to chat and talk over his worries over college affairs. The advice he received was not always theological; on 11 December 1933 he wrote in his diary – 'Sleep well to my gt surprise – thanks to read'g Wodehouse on Selbie's advice'.

Nathaniel Micklem, the new Principal, had been Cadoux's exact contemporary at Mansfield when they were both theological students, though Cadoux was five years older. The two had been on friendly terms since they first met; for some unknown reason Micklem always called Cadoux 'Charlie', a name no one else seems to have used. But they had never been close friends. Their backgrounds, minds and temperaments were very different; and theologically they were moving far apart. Cadoux remained a theological liberal to the end of his life; Micklem's response to the 'Blackheath' controversy[1] showed that he was already committed to the recovery of theological orthodoxy. His book *What is the Faith?* (1936) was to reveal how far he had moved away from the liberalism of his earlier years. Cadoux was a meticulous historical scholar, with a strong belief in the virtue of logical argument; Micklem had a more speculative, imaginative, subtle mind, which found a deep expression in poetry. Cadoux was a man of simple pleasures and disciplined lifestyle whose circle of friends was largely drawn from the world of Free Churchmen and Oxford theologians; Micklem's more sophisticated background and education (at Rugby and New College, Oxford) had opened to him a

[1] See below p.146.

richer cultural life and a wider circle of friends, political and literary as well as theological.

Two further factors made their relationship difficult. One was that the College council had appointed Cadoux to be Vice-Principal without specifically defining his responsibilities. This led to friction when he felt that he was not being sufficiently informed about college affairs, and discovered that other members of the college had been told things before he was. It was not until he had been Vice-Principal for nine years that he finally asked the Council to define his duties and responsibilities. Perhaps he took small problems too much to heart; perhaps he wanted matters to be more cut-and-dried than others did; perhaps he was too much conerned with his own status. But a title without a task can be frustrating to any conscientious person.

The other factor was more complicated. The members of the Mansfield College Council, elected by different 'interests' (subscribers, the Congregational Union, etc.), inevitably represented different theological points of view. In the later years of Selbie's principalship, these differences were contained within a reasonably stable, some thought too stable, framework. With a new Principal, eager to educate future ministers to meet new challenges, things changed. Some members of the Council could not keep up with the quick, questing mind of the new Principal. Nor could they comprehend his decision to base part of his teaching in theology on Aquinas. What was the Principal of a Congregational college doing choosing to lecture from a mediaeval Roman Catholic text? Nor did some of his liturgical innovations meet with favour, and his alterations to the college chapel, particularly the refurbishing of the antechapel for daily use, were regarded with suspicion by some.

In this situation, some of the Council regarded with relief the appointment of someone who was known to be a theological liberal, to be a stout defender of Congregational principles, and to have the intellect to be able to expound and defend his views against critics – in fact the sharper the criticism, the more effective Cadoux's weapons of defence became. Cadoux was a man of consistency. While the Principal could survey the truth from many different vantage points, the Vice-Principal kept faithfully to his own path, never progressing without testing the ground carefully, slowly but surely clearing the way forward. It was believed by some that Cadoux had been appointed to act as a restraining influence on some of Micklem's more adventurous ideas – not an altogether congenial atmosphere in which to co-operate. Undoubtedly their uneasy partnership was a cause of unhappiness and friction for both of them.[1]

The day before Cadoux had been appointed to the Mansfield chair, a group of Congregational ministers had published a letter in *The Christian World* (the main Congregational newspaper) publicising a re-statement of faith, drawn up during several discussions over the previous month. The document's provenance, Blackheath Congregational Church, whose minister, T. Wigley, was the chief spokesman of the group, caused the signatories to be dubbed 'the Blackheathens'. The Blackheathens were all known to be modernists, and their statement proved unacceptably modernist to many; it was reminiscent of the New Theology of the first decade of the century. The first to reply to the letter in the following issue of *The Christian World* (16 February 1933) was Nathaniel Micklem, who wrote that 'Their rather jejune *credo* represents, I take it, a modern Christian philosophy or the conclusion of rational discussion unassisted by revelation'.

Cadoux was never a member of the Blackheath group and took no direct part in that controversy. In the heated argument that followed, however, the theological ideas which Micklem expressed in response to the Blackheath statement were not at all to his liking, and it was in this situation that he was regarded by some members of the denomination as a counterweight to the Principal.

As far as the rest of the staff were concerned, none had been there when Cadoux had left in 1919. T. W. Manson was New Testament Professor; Old Testament studies were in the hands of H. Wheeler Robinson, a distinguished Baptist scholar who had been a student at Mansfield under Fairbairn. He was Principal of Regent's Park College, a Baptist theological college which had recently moved from London to Oxford, though without a proper home until 1939. For the time being Wheeler Robinson was a member of the Mansfield Senior Common Room, and his students were members of the Junior Common Room. He was much respected in the university, and was the first Free Churchman to be elected chairman of the Board of the Faculty of Theology (in 1937). Of all the members of the Mansfield Senior Common Room, he was the one whose mind and temperament were most congenial to Cadoux. The Principal's brother, Romilly Micklem, was chaplain, and lecturer in Psychology and the Philosophy of Religion; and W. H. Cadman, officially a research fellow, also took a share in teaching New Testament.

[1] Micklem wrote briefly about this in his autobiography, *The Box and the Puppets* (1957) pp. 81-3. The book was written soon after he retired from Mansfield, when the experiences of his early years there were still vivid. In his later reflective years, he may have been able to think of Cadoux with more sympathetic understanding.

Though officially Mansfield was still not a part of the university, something of the quality of its reputation in this decade can be sensed from the college jubilee production – a series of studies in Christian worship, edited by the Principal.[1] The section dealing with the biblical background had contributions from Wheeler Robinson, T. W. Manson, W. H. Cadman, and C. H. Dodd; the historical background was covered by J. V. Bartlet, R. S. Franks, James Moffatt, Cadoux, J. S. Whale, and A. G. Matthews; in addition, there were studies by Romilly Micklem, Edward Shillito, Kenneth Parry and the editor. All were past or present students and/or members of the college staff.

Cadoux's own contribution was an essay on Zwingli. Many have remarked that in some ways Cadoux resembled Zwingli, that the qualities which Cadoux praised in Zwingli – 'his broad healthy simplicity', 'the reasonableness of his mind' and 'the personal reality of his religious faith and devotion' could equally have been applied to himself. It was the Zwinglian strand of the Reformation, rather than the Calvinist or Lutheran, which most appealed to Cadoux, and it was Zwingli's emphasis on the commemorative aspect of the Eucharist which he found to be the most helpful and authentic. In this he differed from most of his Mansfield colleagues.

In 1933, when Cadoux returned to Mansfield, there were 23 students preparing for the ministry, and four others taking special courses. The Council's concern that these numbers were not being maintained led to the college having its own 'Franks report'[2] in 1937, with a thorough examination of the intellectual rigour demanded of the candidates, of the place of the chapel in university and college life, of the scholarships available, and of the publicity issued about the college. Mansfield was more expensive than other Congregational colleges; but as the Principal explained in one of his annual reports (1937–38), Mansfield was the only such college offering teaching to research graduates, and at that time probably the only one offering a chaplaincy to Free Church undergraduates reading subjects other than theology.

Cadoux's brief was to lecture on the history of the Church from its beginnings until the twentieth century. He took his subject chronologically, giving special emphasis to the Reformation, and the development of the Puritan tradition since that time. His lectures were

---

[1] *Christian Worship: Studies in its History and Meaning* (1936), ed. N. Micklem.

[2] The chairman was Oliver (now Lord) Franks, son of R. S. Franks, and then a Fellow (in Philosophy) at the Queen's College.

thorough, scholarly and fair rather than exciting; every statement was justified by carefully collected and examined evidence. In retrospect, one feels that it was unfortunate that when Cadoux was finally offered a teaching post at Mansfield, it was in Church History. He had taught New Testament Studies in Bradford, and this was always his first love. He had a thorough knowledge of pre-Constantinian church history, but the Reformation period did not excite him as it did some other theological scholars; neither had he an extensive knowledge of the source material for that period. Had he been able to continue lecturing in the New Testament field, he would have enjoyed his later years at Mansfield more.

In the wider circle of theological discussion in Oxford, Cadoux became a familiar figure. He had immediately re-joined the Oxford Society of Historical Theology, of which his old tutor, Bartlet, and B. H. Streeter were now co-secretaries. Here scholars of all denominations met together and enjoyed the papers and discussions. In 1936, when R. H. Lightfoot was elected secretary in succession to Bartlet and Streeter, Cadoux was elected treasurer. This society was confined to senior members of the university. The Origen Society, to which Cadoux also belonged, was a meeting place for undergraduates, postgraduates and senior members for joint discussion of theological problems. Cadoux was also a member of the Nicene Society and the Reunion Society. All these societies met regularly during the university term; members read papers, followed by discussion. Cadoux himself was a regular contributor. He thoroughly enjoyed the stimulus of discussion with other first-rate minds; he could test out his own theories and findings, and keep in touch with developments in theological scholarship, and his encyclopaedic knowledge earned him considerable respect.

During his earlier years as a tutor at Mansfield, he had attended William Sanday's New Testament seminar at Christ Church. Now, on his return, he was able to attend another equally important seminar held at the Queen's College. The Provost, B. H. Streeter, himself a former member of Sanday's seminar, was a brilliant New Testament scholar who had done pioneering work in synoptic criticism. His book, *The Four Gospels: a Study in Origins* (1924), set forth the results of his research. His weekly seminar was a valuable forum for discussing and appraising new developments in New Testament criticism, and it helped Cadoux to keep up his New Testament study, and to prepare the ground for his major work in this field, *The Historic Mission of Jesus* (1941).

Apart from lectures and seminars, there was the Bodleian Library.

Return to Oxford

There can be few places more congenial to the historical scholar than Duke Humphrey's library in the Old Bodleian, a long late fifteenth century gallery with its panelled painted ceiling and its quiet secluded desks divided by stall shelving; here the reader can absorb the atmosphere of many generations of scholars before him. Cadoux loved to spend hours working here, especially on his book on Smyrna. Here he was away from controversy, argument or pressure, able to devote himself to the research he loved.

The company of his friends was always welcome. His old tutor, Vernon Bartlet, lived on the route to Mansfield, and the two frequently discussed problems and ideas over a cup of tea. 'To Bartlet's – a long healing talk w' him' (21 September 1933) was a typical entry in his diary. It was to Bartlet that he turned before sending anything controversial to print knowing that his tutor's eirenic temperament would restrain any unwise aggressive argumentativeness on his own part.

Another stimulating companion was W. G. Moore, a younger scholar whose father was headmaster of Silcoates School, the Congregational boys' boarding school near Wakefield at which Cadoux had frequently preached. Will Moore was a distinguished modern linguist who had gained his doctorate for a thesis on the influence of Luther in France; a Fellow of St John's College, he was also a leading Congregational layman and member of the Mansfield College Council; he often attended the Congregational Theological Conferences and enjoyed discussing theology, politics and other affairs with Cadoux. The two families lived near each other and became very friendly. Cadoux often called on his friend for 'a refreshing chat'.

If drinking tea can be considered a vice, then that was Cadoux's vice. He enjoyed nothing better than conversation over several cups of tea. When he was seriously ill at the beginning of 1939, Francis Boyd wrote him a letter of commiseration and sympathy and described the pleasure he gave his friends at these tea-drinking sessions:

> I am losing the art of tea drinking and need a few sessions with you to get back the charm and delicacy of that process. Not that I don't drink tea – quantities of it – but I don't suck in the fragrant liquid with anything like the same swoosh which is a feature of drinking tea with you. For not only does one drink tea in your company, one swallows it down with the sanction of virtuousness to gloss over what would otherwise be a normal human vice. Moreover, one drinks in knowledge at the same time. The tertiary Franciscans, Barthianism, prestidigitation and other matters of useful information have all become part of my being through drinking tea in your company.

Cadoux's other recreations were drawing (especially portraits of his family, in which he was most accomplished), collecting and pressing wild flowers, and walking. Not only was there his daily walk, but where possible, a walking holiday during the Christmas and Easter vacations. He would take as his companion either one of his children, a younger friend such as Francis Boyd or Will Moore, or his old friend from Catford days, Charlton Short. The walks were centred on Inkpen, in the Berkshire countryside which he had come to love so much during his earlier career in Oxford. Inkpen lies north of a cluster of hills where Berkshire, Wiltshire and Hampshire meet. Inkpen Beacon was a focal point from which one could enjoy a commanding view. To the west lay Shalbourne, where Cadoux also stayed sometimes, especially in later years. The peace of this unspoilt area revived his spirits and brought him relief from intellectual activity. Family holidays were usually spent on the Isle of Wight, the scene of those happy Boys' Brigade camps in years past.

It was a disciplined, purposeful life, with much to do and much to enjoy, so long as his health did not grow worse.

XIII

In defence of liberal theology
1934–1939

JUST BEFORE CHRISTMAS 1938 the Mansfield Junior Common Room put on a pantomime for the amusement of themselves and of their tutors. Adapted from Cinderella, this story had three sisters – Liberella, Quiney and Barthy. Cadoux had just published *The Case for Evangelical Modernism*, and the pantomime made ample use of it. The 'three blind alleys' of the second chapter of the book provided perfect material for a skit; 'the anthropocentric man', 'Barty the Revelation fan' and 'Quiney whose home is the Vatican'

all come under the Liberal ban
as blind alleys three.

The programme note explained, for the benefit of non-theological members of the audience, that the three sisters represented 'the three most powerful theological tendencies in the College today' (liberal modernism, Barthianism and the philosophy of St Aquinas). Cadoux and the other tutors took it all in good part. Underlying it, however, was a serious debate.

For a new theological voice was now being heard, that of Karl Barth. Barth had rejected liberalism; he emphasised above all the transcendence of God, the centrality and objectivity of God's revelation of Himself in the Word, and denied that man could rise to the knowledge of God through the use of his own unaided mind. Natural theology played no part in his scheme. This struck at the very roots of Liberal Protestantism.

Barth's work had been well-known in the German-speaking Protestant world since the end of the first world war. It first became widely known in the English-speaking world in 1933 when Sir Edwyn Hoskyns' translation of Barth's *Commentary on the Epistle to the Romans* was published. In fact, the *Oxford Magazine* of 19 October 1933, within days of Cadoux's taking up his new appointment, carried a prominent advertisement of this as one of the most important new books published by the University Press since the previous term.

First published in 1919, the work had been written in Switzerland during the first world war, by which it was deeply influenced, and represented a revolt against the liberalism in which Barth had been educated. Barth had later moved to teach in Germany, where he stayed until his stand against Nazism led to his expulsion and return to Switzerland. His succeeding books, such as *Credo* (1935, English translation 1936) and *The Knowledge of God and the Service of God* (the Gifford Lectures, published 1938) gained a wide circulation.

Not only Barth, but his compatriot Emil Brunner too had challenged the Liberal immanentist theology. Brunner supported Barth in emphasising the transcendence of God; but whereas Barth rejected natural theology, Brunner maintained that fallen man could attain to some knowledge of God. His work too was becoming known in Britain, and at least four of his books had been translated into English by 1937, the best known being *The Mediator* (1927, English translation 1934).

The theology of both Barth and Brunner found many supporters in the Congregational and Presbyterian denominations. In the later 1930s, admirers and followers of Barth were to be found in both the Junior and Senior Common Rooms of Mansfield; it was an important day for the college when Barth himself visited Mansfield in March 1938 while he was in Oxford to receive the honorary degree of DD.

Cadoux could never accept the absolute distinction which Barth made between theology acquired through human reason and experience, and revelation received in faith. The whole argument which Cadoux had built up in *Catholicism and Christianity*, with its discussion of the nature of authority in religion, was inimical to such an approach. Neither could he accept Barth's extreme emphasis on the sinfulness of man as an absolute barrier between man and God, to be broken only by the 'leap into the void'. And so it was that Cadoux now found himself more and more occupying a defensive position, against Catholicism and neo-orthodoxy as well.

As Professor of Church History at Mansfield, Cadoux was concerned not only with history, but with the doctrine of the Church, and so with the nature of doctrine itself. These were questions he dealt with in his inaugural lecture at Mansfield, and in two articles he wrote for *The Christian World* in October 1934. His vigorous defence of the liberal interpretation of Christianity was expressed in no uncertain terms.

The inaugural lecture[1] was delivered on 16 January 1934, having been postponed from the previous term because of ill-health. The

[1] Published in *The Congregational Quarterly* July 1934 pp. 284-297.

theme was 'The doctrine of the Church in the light of human history'. 'No intelligent Christian', he declared, 'least of all perhaps a Mackennal Professor, can afford to be without a well-considered doctrine of the Church Catholic'.

In the lecture he returned to themes he had developed a decade earlier. Before one can answer questions about the nature of the Church, one must ask about its composition:

> Who are in it? Who are not in it? The fundamental question is not, What is the correct view regarding episcopacy, credal confessions, the Lord's Supper, Baptism and so forth? important as such matters are. It is this, What are the grounds which justify one Christian body either speaking or tacitly acting as if the members of another body did not belong to the Church of Christ?

He then went on to trace in the history of the church, two strands of belief, one exclusive, one inclusive.

> We can . . . see two mutually inconsistent doctrines of the Church contending for mastery in the Christian mind down the ages – one (the exclusive) which says 'The Church consists only of those professed Christians who agree with me on certain matters which on various grounds I regard as essential', and the other (the inclusive) which says 'The Church consists of all professed Christians, whether they agree with me or not'. Which of the two views is the true one? It is manifestly impossible to answer this question by means of a majority-vote; for majorities are often wrong, and the imposing advantage which mere weight of numbers gives to certain types of exclusiveness is casual, meretricious and indecisive. Moreover . . . not one of the great exclusive bodies abides *consistently* by its exclusiveness. All make to Christians without their doors concessions radically inconsistent with the closing of those doors. *Cadit quaestio.* A view which it is admitted cannot be consistently maintained must in all honesty be abandoned. The only doctrine of the composition of the church Catholic, which Christian love and Church History jointly do not make untenable, is that which concedes the name of Christian to every person who professes to have faith in Jesus Christ, and which identifies the Church with the sum-total of all Christians who, on the strength of such faith, claim to belong to it. [1]

All this had implications for re-union. In Cadoux's view, the re-union of the church would not be found by agreements between two

[1] *Ibid.* pp.292-3.

or more denominations to form a single organisation on the basis of agreed creeds or church structures (though that might be desirable), for such agreements 'never allow properly for the Churchmanship of dissenting individuals'. The Church's faith was safeguarded by 'the Spirit of Truth'. Re-union would be achieved by

> a frank and explicit acknowledgement of the churchmanship of all our fellow-Christians. Such an acknowledgement will not indeed involve the abandonment of our sectional beliefs and usages; but it *will* involve our willingness to associate with Christians of every colour, not only in practical Christian service, but also in the offices of prayer and preaching and in the fellowship of the Lord's Table. [1]

This lecture was inevitably something of an ordeal; to Theo (still at boarding school in Taunton) Cadoux wrote on 27 January:

> My inaugural lecture came off last evening. The big lecture-room at Mansfield was almost full, and I had a kind hearing and generous applause. Selbie and Bartlet and all my colleagues were there, but only one Anglican professor, so far as I could learn. It went off all right; and I am glad to have it behind me.

The next ordeal was to take a service in the college chapel. To Theo he wrote again a fortnight later (11 February):

> It is with great joy that I sit down to write to you this week . . . because I took the service for the first time in Mansfield chapel this morning and got thro' without disaster.

In October 1934 Cadoux published two articles in *The Christian World* with the heading 'Dogma and Truth: the doctrinal task of the Church'.[2] Though no other theologian was named in the articles – apart from two references to 'Barthian quarters' – they were at least in part criticisms of a paper which Micklem had read at the Congregational Theological Conference in the previous summer. Cadoux wrote about 'the unreal antithesis between objective truth as revealed by God and objective truth as discovered by man' – a reference to Barth's claim that 'the Gospel is not a truth among truths. Rather, it sets a question-mark against all truths'.[3] Whatever objective truth was enshrined in the traditional doctrines of the Church would

> commend itself evermore to the truthloving minds and hearts of Christians, and does not need to be defended against occasional and partial disbelief by being hedged around with a barbed-wire entanglement of dogmatic or traditional authority.

[1] *Ibid.* p.297.   [2] 18 and 25 October 1934.
[3] K. Barth, *Commentary on the Epistle to the Romans*, trans. Hoskyns (1933), p.35.

Above all, he claimed, it was dangerous to interfere with 'the freedom of Christian speculation'. This was not to deny 'the objective realities on which Christianity rests', but it was to assert that 'only what is true is an essential part of Christian Faith'.

Cadoux believed it was right that he should defend this freedom of Christian speculation against any threat to it. Micklem, however, felt that the articles were disloyal. It is not clear whether Cadoux showed them to his principal before sending them off, though he did discuss them with Selbie; the Principal did know, however, that they were being prepared for publication. On 10 October, Cadoux wrote in his diary: 'Long talk w' Nat in his upper room in the Tower, ab't our corresp^{ce}, my CW arts, & wh'r I hold the substance of the Xn faith etc'. He found himself in a similar situation to that of his early years in Bradford, of being under suspicion for holding unorthodox opinions. It had been easier to handle then, when his principal had been almost old enough to be his father, but now he was working for a principal who was a somewhat younger contemporary. He knew that Micklem doubted his orthodoxy.

There is a valuable insight into Cadoux's attitude towards traditional Christian doctrine in a letter he wrote to Theo on 13 May 1934. For some reason not explained Theo had asked his father about the doctrine of the Trinity. His father replied:

In regard to your question about the Trinity – it is important to realize that this doctrine is not *explicitly* taught in the NT (tho' there are passages like I Cor xii 4–6, II Cor xiii 13, Rev i 4–5, which do mention Father, Son and Holy Spirit together); but it is contended that the place given to Jesus Christ and to the Spirit in the NT is such as to necessitate the ascription of full divinity to them; and when one raises the question, How then are these two related to the Divine Father? it is difficult to see how you can answer it without either affirming the Trinity in Unity, or affirming the existence of three Gods, which last is absolutely impossible. I do not know what you want the information for; but I want to point out that, while the doctrine of the Trinity has great difficulties of its own, such as (for me) make it hard to affirm it emphatically as a great clarification of the issue, yet

1) when correctly understood, it is not so impossible for thought as it appears to the uninitiated at first blush

2) it deals with matters really beyond the reach of man's intellect, and therefore *necessarily* wears a paradoxical look

3) any criticism of it which does not rest upon a sympathetic

and understanding knowledge of how it came into existence, is unwarranted.

See me about it later.

Cadoux was engaged in controversy again in 1935, in writing a short, more popular work on Roman Catholicism, entitled *Roman Catholicism and Freedom*, which was published early in 1936. This sold more copies than any of his other books except *The Life of Jesus* and ran to four editions.

He had never ceased to collect and classify examples of Roman Catholic restriction or denial of freedom; and to record the attitude of contemporary Roman Catholics towards persecution in the past. A number of these examples were quoted in the book. Since the book was a comparatively short one, he confined himself to 'the Roman record during the nineteenth century', and to quoting twentieth century apologists for persecution. Much of this material had already appeared in *Catholicism and Christianity*. He recognised that many Roman Catholics had followed in the tradition of Erasmus and More, Newman and Acton in rejecting the cruelties of past persecutions; and he recognized that Protestants as well as Roman Catholics had been persecutors. But whereas he believed that 'there is absolutely nothing in Protestantism – as all the world knows – to make a revival of Protestant persecution in the least degree likely', there were

the strongest possible grounds for believing that the theory behind the Catholic persecutions of the past is still fully approved in the Roman Church, and both is and will be acted upon wherever and whenever political circumstances permit.[1]

Protestantism stands by toleration; 'the use of coercion and punishment for the purpose of silencing error is futile, and because futile, morally wrong'. Protestants trust 'the convincing and unifying power of the Truth itself'.

If Catholics have in their dogmas the faith they profess, they ought to be willing to trust to the power of their truth to convince men, without needing the extraneous aids of coercion and punishment to protect them from criticism and denial. God Himself has the human race in hand: the only Truth there is His Truth. If we stray from it, He will teach us through experience that we are straying, and will lead us back. 'But the straying is harmful', you will say. Doubtless it is; but the prevention of it by coercive means is, as we have shown, still more harmful. Far better is it to defend the Truth by loving, exploring, proving, declaring, and obeying it, than by rousing against it, through the

[1] C. J. Cadoux *Roman Catholicism and Freedom* (1936) p.49.

imposition of constraint, the enmity of the rebel and the still more subtle enmity of the coward and the hypocrite. [1]

The last section of the book dealt in some detail with Roman Catholic propaganda and influence on the press, and the campaign to persuade the state to pay for the building of new Catholic schools. This last was something he felt very strongly about; in Bradford he had taken part in a counter-campaign to resist such pressure.

Cadoux believed that his case against Roman Catholic influence on the press was proved by the fact that 'the Press as a whole has practically boycotted the book'. [2] Apart from Protestant denominational papers, there were very few reviews. Three months after the book was published, he learned from one bookseller in Oxford that it had not been judged expedient to display the book in the window, as might otherwise have been done, for fear of offending the shop's Catholic customers.

Reading the book today, one realises what great steps have been made since 1936 in mutual understanding between Catholics and Protestants. Cadoux's warnings of the dangers of Catholic intolerance at the time were recognised as important by his fellow Protestants, and it was agreed that he had shown courage in being prepared to expose real weaknesses and abuses in Catholic practice at the time, whatever the consequences. At the same time, the necessarily polemical tone of the work makes it one of his less enduring works.

Cadoux's tour de force in defending liberal theology was *The Case for Evangelical Modernism*, published in November 1938. It was the revised text of four lectures delivered at the University College of North Wales in December 1937, under the title, 'Christian faith in its relation to history and to truth'. He thought carefully about the title of the book, and his final choice was intended 'to make the designation somewhat more specific'. In the book itself he more frequently used the term 'Liberal Modernism' for that which he was defending.

The tone of the book was controversial, even aggressive; *The Times* reviewer (3 December 1938) praised the author for displaying 'both pugnacity and persuasiveness, an excellent combination of qualities'. Cadoux had always enjoyed controversy and did so here: 'In all Christian charity . . . I mean to put up as good a case as I can for the opinions I wish to express'.

The first task was to define that which he wished to defend:

By Liberal Modernism . . . I mean that attitude to Christian

[1] *Ibid.* p.123.
[2] *Ibid.*, foreword to the second impression (August 1936).

doctrine which, taking due account of the occasional conflict between truth and tradition, rejects the customary identification of tradition and orthodoxy, and sees the real test of orthodoxy (i.e. right belief) in truth.[1]

Therefore

> ... whatever validity the traditional Christian doctrines possess they owe ultimately, not to their antiquity, nor to their ubiquity, nor even to their Scripturality, but to their capacity to vindicate themselves to Christian hearts and minds as true. The essence of the Gospel consists, not necessarily in what our Christian predecessors proclaimed, but in what the Spirit of the living God reveals to us as true, rejoicing the heart and enlightening the eyes.[2]

How then was truth to be discovered? Cadoux believed that the theologian could learn from the scientist, for

> the customary distinction drawn between religious knowledge as based on revelation and scientific knowledge as based on reason proves on examination to be illusory, so far as concerns, not the nature of the things known, but the epistemology involved. Revelation and faith are present in science as well as in theology; reason is present in theology, as well as in science.[3]

The scientist is free to pursue his own enquiries, while respecting the conclusions of those who have explored the field before him; the final authority which he recognizes is that of the objective facts which scientific theories attempt to explain. Likewise the theologian can enjoy the freedom to question traditional beliefs, but *'only in the sense in which that liberty is already taken for granted in science'*. The final authority lay not in any established body of doctrine, but in 'our records and experiences of God's dealings with us' (pp.32–33).

This was the point which critics of Liberal Protestantism challenged. T. W. Manson, for example, wrote a few years later that this was its wrong theological turning: 'the mischief was begun when the working hypotheses of natural science were allowed to become the dogmas of theology'.[4] The relation between God's revelation of Himself and man's reflection upon His nature was at the heart of the difference between the liberals and the neo-orthodox.

Cadoux however stoutly defended Liberal Modernism against its

[1] C. J. Cadoux *The Case for Evangelical Modernism* (1938) p.10.
[2] *Ibid.* p.17.
[3] *Ibid.* p.21.
[4] T. W. Manson 'The failure of Liberalism to interpret the Bible as the Word of God' in *The Interpretation of the Bible* (1944) ed. C. W. Dugmore.

foremost critics. These he put into three categories; to the left, the non-Christocentric humanists, to the right the Barthians and the neo-orthodox, whom he preferred to call the traditionalists (under which heading he also dealt with fundamentalists). He gave little space to the non-Christocentric humanists, for they did not constitute a real Christian alternative to Liberal Modernism. The serious challengers were the traditionalists and the Barthians.

By traditionalism he meant

the view that, over and above personal self-commitment to God through Christ, essential Christianity requires the acceptance of a certain *definable minimum* of doctrines, failure to accept any one of which calls for the surrender of the claim to be a Christian.[1]

Here he was on familiar ground, and his response to this view was to assert, as he had asserted before, that *the only true safeguards* against our possible loss of any Christian essentials were 'trust in the guidance of the Spirit and in the "anima naturaliter Christiana"'.

The other great challenge to Liberal Modernism came from 'the Barthians'. Cadoux treated the views of Barth and Brunner and their supporters as a unity. He had read, and quoted from, one book of Barth's – *Credo* (1935, English translation 1936) – and two of Brunner's – *The Word and the World* (1924, English translation 1931) and *Philosophy of Religion from the Standpoint of Protestant Theology* (1926, English translation 1937). He had also listened to lectures by one of Barth's disciples, Professor Günther Dehn,[2] who lectured at Mansfield in 1935 on the theme 'The Gospel of the Reformers and the Modern Man'. But he was out of sympathy with their approach, and failed to derive any real inspiration or enlightenment from it.

I regard Barthian theology, despite the truth of many of its positive affirmations and despite even the need for new stresses on them, as on the whole unacceptable. It is not only paradoxical, but self-contradictory; it is needlessly dualistic, bristles with false antitheses; it displays strong tendencies to obscurantism.[3]

He did not accept the Barthian distinction between religion, 'what man thinks about God' and revelation, 'what God says to man'; 'No part of Barth's system is more strongly emphasized than the total dissimilarity between Natural Theology acquired through reason and experience on the one hand, and revelation received in faith on the other'.[4] Cadoux went to the other extreme, believing that religious

---

[1] *The Case for Evangelical Modernism* p.54.
[2] Professor at Halle until ejected by the Nazis.
[3] *Ibid.* p.54.
[4] *Ibid.* p.49.

truth was attained by the same principles and methods as in other fields of enquiry (though he accepted that in religion the data include what God has revealed to man through the life and teaching of Jesus). It seemed to him that

> As once in Calvinism, so now in Barthianism, God's majesty is exalted at the cost of His love, and appeal is made not to man's gratitude to God so much as to his fear of him.[1]

What of the doctrine of the inner light, the inner witness of the Holy Spirit, to which Cadoux attached so much importance?

> The admission that the Word of God is *not co-extensive* with Scripture, and the frank acceptance of Biblical Higher Criticism, are consistent with the doctrine of the Inner Witness of the Spirit, but are not consistent with the repeated Barthian declaration that the Scriptures are the supreme authority for Christian belief.[2]

There was recognition for many of the positive affirmations of 'Barthianism', together with gratitude 'for recalling me to phases of the truth which I had perhaps been prone to neglect'; and above all admiration for Barth's courage in standing firm against the Nazification of the church in Germany; 'the name of Karl Barth will go down to history as that of a noble servant of God'. But as one who continued to be influenced by Harnack, Cadoux remained out of sympathy with one who showed as little interest as apparently did Barth in 'the historical Jesus'.

The third section of the book was an appraisal of the traditional Chalcedonian doctrine of the Person of Christ, the doctrine (formulated AD 451) which spoke of Christ as 'truly God and truly man', 'co-essential with the Father as regards his Deity, and the same co-essential with us as regards his humanity', acknowledged to exist 'in two Natures unconfusedly, unchangeably, indivisibly, inseparably'. Many Protestant theological scholars of the early twentieth century found the traditional doctrine unsatisfactory. Cadoux's dissatisfaction with it was chiefly on the ground that 'instead of synthetizing the historical data, it defies them, and in doing so rules itself out as inadmissible';[3] there was 'an increasing tendency to locate the Divinity of Jesus in the metaphysical composition of his person rather than in the spiritual and moral quality of his character'.[4] So 'the quest for the historical Jesus' should be a part of the quest for understanding the nature of Christ – Cadoux's familiar theme that history and theology could not be separated.

---

[1] *Ibid.* p.49.   [2] *Ibid.* p.52.
[3] *Ibid.* p.91.   [4] *Ibid.* p.112.

The last chapter was entitled, therefore, 'The way to the real Jesus'; this Cadoux paraphrased as a study of 'the factual roots from which the traditional Christology sprang'. It was important to study the historical Jesus and

> to accept the critically sifted history of Jesus (despite its minor elements of uncertainty) as a datum no less real and usable than all the other objective data of our experience . . .[1]

Many elements in the Gospels would have to be rejected as unhistorical – for example the Virgin Birth and the nature-miracles.[2] On the other hand, there is much of which we can be historically sure. Jesus' ministry

> was shaped primarily with an eye to the moral and spiritual needs of Israel and the world at that particular juncture in human history; but in being so perfectly adapted to them, it displayed then, and for all time will display, the universal sweep of God's love and the eternal meaning of His will.[3]
>
> . . . In his death at the hands of sinners, men have read the cost of human sin to God, have heard God's loving rebuke, and been moved by it to respond in penitence, and so have been led to receive His forgiveness and be reconciled with Him through His grace.[4]

What theory of the Person of Christ could be constructed on these data? Cadoux found Paul's description of Jesus as 'the firstborn among many brothers' (*Romans* 8.29) a pointer:

> Why, therefore, should we not, tentatively at least, affirm that 'God's Presence and His very Self' – the Presence and Self manifested with unique clarity and fullness in the overwhelming goodness of Jesus – is after the same fashion though with less clarity and fullness manifested in those in whom Jesus himself has called forth a longing to follow him?[5]

This formula was less precise than the traditional one, and left many questions unanswered. But to Cadoux it satisfied his criterion of truth; and in his experience, 'the Gospel of the redeeming grace of God in Christ can be as efficiently conveyed to men in Evangelical Modernist, as in traditional terms'.

The book was a very clear, vigorous, critical defence of Liberal Modernism. The general impression left by reading it is that most of the writer's energy is given to refuting other people's theories. Cadoux does not deny value to the views of his 'opponents', but one cannot help feeling that the 'joy of battle' and 'the friendly clash of conflicting

---

[1] *Ibid.* p.125.   [2] See *ibid.* pp.128-134.
[3] *Ibid.* p.148.   [4] *Ibid.* p.149.   [5] *Ibid.* pp.156-157.

views' to which he referred in the opening pages of the book had led him to give too little attention to his positive affirmations. This is not to deny that he had deeply felt affirmations to make; but in controversy they were often overlaid by negative assertions.

It was generally agreed by reviewers that the author had stated his case clearly and well, and that the book showed that theological libreralism was still a force to be reckoned with. The Principal of Pusey House, F. L. Cross, writing in the *Oxford Magazine* (May 1939), found himself in sympathy with Cadoux's emphasis on 'the inherent rationality of the Christian faith' but was more critical of 'his tendency to find the exclusive norm of truth in history'. E. J. Price, writing in *The Congregational Quarterly* (January 1939) wished that Cadoux 'had more fully developed his positive affirmations in the closing part of his book'; but concluded that there could be no doubt about the author's 'firm belief in the saving activity of God as manifested uniquely in Christ'. On the other hand, H. Cunliffe-Jones, a former Mansfield student now teaching at the Yorkshire College, representative of a different theological standpoint, wrote in the *Mansfield Magazine* (December 1938) that

> theologically speaking this is not a good book because it rests upon assumptions the ground for which are never stated and defended, yet on the question whether you will agree or disagree with the book as a whole absolutely depends.

Albert Peel, editor of *The Congregational Quarterly*, and a student of Elizabethan Puritanism, used his review of the book in *The Christian World* (17 November 1938) as an opportunity for comparing the variety of teaching offered to Mansfield students by the Principal and Vice-Principal with that offered to the congregations of the Temple in the reign of Elizabeth I by Richard Hooker and Walter Travers:

> In the Temple there was Canterbury in the morning and Geneva in the afternoon, so that, in old Fuller's words
>> What Mr Hooker delivered in the forenoon, Mr Travers confuted in the afternoon . . . the nails and pins which one master builder drave in were driven out by the other.
>
> The brains of Mansfield students must be sharpened as they ponder the writings of their learned members.

Such a treatment was hardly tactful, and called forth in the following week's edition not only a carefully considered, typically pacificatory letter from Vernon Bartlet, but also a sharp denial by representatives of the Mansfield Junior Common Room.

It was in the aftermath of this unfortunate publicity that the Common Room must have prepared their pantomime 'Liberella' for the end of that Michaelmas Term 1938. No wonder that the president of the J. C. R. could write in the *Mansfield Magazine*, in reference to this pantomime, that 'Providence has been very good to us this term in supplying us with sources and materials'.

Cadoux's ideas found a more positive expression in a lecture which he delivered to the Assembly of the Congregational Union meeting in Bradford in October 1938, just before *The Case for Evangelical Modernism* was published. The theme was 'The Reformation'; the two chosen speakers were Cadoux, and the Cambridge historian, Bernard L. Manning. Cadoux was always sure of a warm welcome in Bradford, and he enjoyed seeing old friends, both at the Yorkshire College and at Greenfield Church.

The subject of his speech was 'The spiritual principles of the Reformation'.[1] The Reformation, he said, was characterised by two great principles, the doctrine of justification by faith, and a new stress on the sovereignty of the Scriptures. To assert and insist that God's personal and gracious love was offered to each individual, effective forgiveness and evoking man's moral obedience 'was the great and capital service which the Reformers rendered to the Christian Church'. But the doctrine of predestination, associated with it by the Reformers, was not a gift to be so treasured:

I shall never forget the painful shock I experienced when my eyes were first opened to the facts by a perusal of the Catholic Adam Möhler's *Symbolik*, where the deterministic teachings of the three great leaders of Continental Protestantism are set forth in their awful reality, with ample and unescapable quotations from their own writings.[2]

The 'new and direct dependence on Scripture' was central to the Reformation, and following from it, the right of the individual to interpret Scripture without the control of any external authority. The Reformers themselves did not interpret Scripture 'in the way in which we have since learnt to be historically the true way', though Calvin 'broached a theory about "the internal witness of the Holy Spirit" as the basis of our ability to learn from Scripture – a theory which might have carried him a long way, had he followed it up'. This new insight did open the way for the critical study of the Bible in a later age.

In essence the fundamental principle of the Reformation was the principle of 'immediate spiritual contact between man and God as the ultimate religious reality'; faithfulness to the Reformation insights must lead to

[1] Published as *The Reformation: Addresses by C. J. Cadoux and B. L. Manning* (1938).   [2] *Ibid.* p.10.

a heartier allegiance to the New Testament standards of religion and life, a bolder quest for truth irrespective of tradition and custom, and a deeper and more constant trust in the God and Father of our Lord Jesus Christ.[1]

In the summer of 1939 Cadoux enjoyed one of the proudest days of his life. He and both his sons received degrees at the same ceremony in the Sheldonian Theatre in Oxford on 29 July 1939.

Cadoux had two doctorates already, his London DD and the honorary DD from Edinburgh, but neither was recognized by Oxford. His previous application for permission to supplicate for the degree of DLitt at Oxford had been refused. Now in the spring of 1939 he tried again. He submitted *The Early Church and the World*, *Catholicism and Christianity* (with special reference to the section on authority), *Ancient Smyrna*, and several articles. When he was given leave to supplicate, he found that the Board of Theology had accepted all his submitted work except *Catholicism and Christianity* (arousing in Cadoux a certain justifiable disquiet; was the Board alarmed at the possibility of Catholic disapproval, and was this not a further example of the influence he criticised in *Roman Catholicism and Freedom*?). But at last he would now be 'Dr Cadoux' in Oxford as well as elsewhere.

Both boys had left their respective boarding schools in 1935. Theo had won an exhibition to Queen's to read 'Greats' (the classical languages and literature, history and philosophy), much to his father's delight. After the rigorous four year course, Theo had been placed in the first class of the honours list. It seemed that he was all set to follow his father as a scholar. Harold was not an academic in the same way, and had already decided on a career in engineering. However, he yielded to his father's desire for him to take a degree, and after a year as an apprentice with the firm of British Thomson Houston, electrical engineers, of Rugby, he came up to Oxford as a member of St Catherine's Society and read engineering science. His course was a three year one, so he took his final examinations in the same term as did Theo. Father and sons thus received their degrees on the same day. There was a family celebration at home after the ceremony, and a report of the family's achievement appeared in *The Manchester Guardian* on 1 August (by courtesy of Francis Boyd, then on the staff of that newspaper).

Theo went straight off to France to stay with friends. He had, naturally, begun to lose interest in family holidays, and after a token

[1] *Ibid.* p.20.

appearance in the Isle of Wight, had gone to Paris in each of the two preceding summers. His father was, equally naturally, worried about his conduct there and on this occasion there was additional anxiety because of the uncertain international situation. Cadoux himself drew up a new schedule as 'a free man', as he put it in his diary. In fact he had already finished a draft of another book, this time in New Testament studies – *The Historic Mission of Jesus*; and two days after the degree ceremony he resumed work on the second volume of his history of Smyrna, a work he was unfortunately never able to complete.

The war-clouds over Europe caused him deep distress. To this subject the next chapter will be devoted. There were also some clouds over his personal and professional life. He was still worried when there were disagreements at home, taking them very much to heart; but they did not disturb him to the extent that they had done ten years earlier. There is no doubt that his daughters brought a new and gentler influence into his family life.

He had had a serious attack of bronchitis early in 1939. His life was in danger for some time, and letters and telegrams poured into the house. He spent more than two weeks in the Acland Nursing Home and for a further six weeks he was confined to his bedroom. This meant that within the space of six years, he had spent two complete terms away from his work at Mansfield. This illness particularly sapped his strength, but did nothing to diminish his intellectual activity, to which he returned in his convalescence.

As he recovered from his illness, he was greatly distressed about the prospect of war. His first outing was to go with the rest of the family to tea with their next-door neighbours, a German Jewish family, refugees from Berlin. He wrote in his diary (3 April 1939): 'Mrs Munz tells me terrible a/cs of German concentration camps'. How could he now defend Christian pacifism?

XIV

Christian pacifism re-examined
1939–1940

'THE CHRISTIAN ETHIC is essentially one which has to deal with the rampant evil of the world', wrote Cadoux in the early months of the second world war.[1] For him, pacifism was an essential part of that ethic; it was a commitment of faith, not a practical policy for the prevention of war. Nevertheless, the acts of aggression by Mussolini and Hitler, and the horrors of Nazi persecution, had challenged his conscience at a deep level. Was the defence of his pacifist convictions offered in 1914 still adequate, or appropriate to the situation? Was the apparent deadlock between the Christians who were reluctantly prepared to go to war when faced with evil of this magnitude, and those who could never countenance war in any circumstances, to continue unresolved, or could some way be found of reaching reconciliation?

During the first world war, it had been possible to make the claim that those who refused to participate in war were showing the greater loyalty to Christ's teaching, teaching which had an even higher claim than the claims of patriotism. But by the late 1930s, there were strong theological voices claiming that pacifist Christians were 'soft utopians', lacking a sufficiently deep understanding of Christianity. Karl Barth, dismissed from his university post in Nazi Germany in 1935, believed that pacifists were failing to recognize the reality and strength of the evil confronting them. The American Reinhold Niebuhr, once a member of the FOR in the United States, and now much influenced by Barth, believed that Christians had to risk involvement in the power struggles of the age, even by taking part in war if that be necessary as a last resort. Both these theologians abhorred war as an instrument of international policy, but were not prepared to renounce it as a final strategy for combating evil.

Cadoux's pacifism and his theology were closely connected. He believed that Jesus had left a body of teaching which constituted 'a Law or revealed Will of God', and that this teaching included the

[1] C. J. Cadoux, *Christian Pacifism Re-examined* (1940) p.x.

requirement of non-resistance to evil; further, he believed that Jesus' whole mission was a living interpretation of this teaching.[1] 'Non-resistance and the Cross are two inseparables'; 'love involving non-resistance (the moral ground of the Cross in history) must be the essence and centre of the Christian ethic', he had written in *The Message about the Cross* (pp. 82 and 83).

He had in the past been accused of adopting an aggressive style in his defence of pacifism. In 1938, a Bradford correspondent reminded him that in the local branch of the FOR in the 1920s he had been known as 'our pugilistic pacifist! You did enjoy a fight and I hope that you still do'. By the late 1930s there was a greater willingness to recognize the complexity of the issue. His old Principal at Bradford, Griffith-Jones, corresponded with him about the issue in 1935, and in the course of a long letter (12 March) remarked, 'You have made great progress in my judgment in the way you put the case for Pacifism since I have known you'.

It is possible to discern this more moderate approach in a letter to Theo in January 1934. Theo had written from Taunton to tell his father about a speech he had made in the school debating society, favouring the abolition of the Officers' Training Corps. Cadoux replied:

> I was much interested in your speech about the OTCs. As you know, I share your view that they ought to be abolished. But I feel a little sympathy with those who hesitate because they cannot regard the whole question as a simple and obvious one. The issue is simple if one artificially isolates certain horrible accompaniments of war: but such isolation of a part of the problem is never quite satisfactory; and one hardly wonders that it does not always prove convincing. I have spent years going into the ramifications of the problem, and have come out a convinced pacifist; but I think it is only fair to recognize that (1) the ethical question is complicated and therefore not easy, and (2) that the pacifist solution, if it is to be carried thro' convincingly, must be the outcome of a very clear and resolute and convinced vision of certain religious realities and values, which will take us all our time to live up to. It means, e.g. one must, if needful, face martyrdom.

Here the real nature of the pacifist's commitment was recognized.

Cadoux seems to have played no part in the Peace Pledge Union, which was officially launched under Dick Sheppard's leadership on 22 May 1936, nor in any of the peace fellowships which were growing in

[1] See the discussion of *The Historic Mission of Jesus* (1941) below, pp. 194-198.

numbers. His pacifist links remained with the FOR, which was about to experience something of a revival (the membership rose from 3,300 in 1934 to 10,000 in 1939). In March 1936, he attended a meeting in the Old Library of the Church of St Mary-the-Virgin to discuss the formation of an Oxford branch of the FOR, though this seems not to have come into being officially until October 1938. In April 1936 he addressed an FOR Youth Conference in Oxford on the theme 'Is pacifism obsolete?'. A few months later he was consulted about the formation of an Oxford University Pacifist Association (OUPA). This association seems to have been officially launched at the beginning of 1937, and Cadoux was among the first speakers, on 'The pacifist ethic'. From that time onwards, he attended regularly, sometimes entertaining the speakers to dinner at Mansfield beforehand. A year later he was a member of a study circle which met to discuss G.H.C. Macgregor's *The New Testament Basis of Pacifism* (1936).

By 1938, contingency plans were being made throughout the country to meet the possibility of war. Cadoux, in response to an appeal from the Vice-Chancellor, issued at the end of July, had agreed to undertake clerical work in the medical services. He had never taken an 'absolutist' standpoint, and was prepared to take a share in coping with the consequences of war.

He was concerned about his sons. It would have shaken him badly if his sons had accepted combatant service. Both in fact registered as conscientious objectors, were allowed non-combatant service under civilian control, and joined the Friends' Ambulance Unit. Harold was in the age group which was called up first and was summoned to attend a tribunal a month before war was actually declared.

There was the underlying worry about what was actually going on in Germany and elsewhere. The news filtering out of Germany about concentration camps was sickening; the news about refugees was little better. Three weeks before war was declared Cadoux wrote in his diary, 'Very sad at terrible news of Jewish refugees off Smyrna'.

When war was actually declared on 3 September, Cadoux's immediate response was twofold. Within hours he was round at the nearest air-raid station volunteering for service as an air-raid warden; he served in this capacity throughout the war. And within three days he was planning a book on Christian pacifism. He felt he must justify, to himself and to others, his continuing pacifist convictions. He worked at the book throughout the autumn and finished it early in the new year. It was actually printed and 'passed' by the Government's Press and Censorship Bureau early in June as the Dunkirk evacuation was taking place, but the publisher (Blackwell) deemed it advisable to hold it back until the military and political situation was more stable. Though not published until September 1940, when it appeared as *Christian Pacifism Re-examined*, it represents his mind in the first months of the war.

In the introduction, Cadoux explained how he had been led to re-examine his pacifist convictions. First there was the obvious fact that the revulsion against war in the 1920s and early 1930s, and the growth of movements such as the Peace Pledge Union, had failed to prevent war; they had failed because war seemed to be the only weapon that could be used to combat the evils of the totalitarian régimes of Italy and Germany. Cadoux did not attempt to whitewash Hitler or to minimise the brutality of the Nazis. He was quite sure that 'it will be much worse for the world if Hitler wins the war than if the Allies win it'. But he felt 'profoundly distrustful of the possibility of getting any lasting peace on the basis of a military victory' (p.210).

It was widely recognized that war and Christianity were fundamentally incompatible. The COPEC conference of 1924 and the Lambeth Conference of 1930 had issued declarations to that effect. But for many Christians, that did not mean that there were not some circumstances in which to fight must be regarded as the lesser of two evils. Nazi brutality and aggression in Europe seemed to most people to be one of those circumstances.

Cadoux therefore set himself to defend his beliefs in the light of changed circumstances. He had to face the question 'whether, if this re-examination were to show me that I had been mistaken, I should have the courage to abandon a position which I have for so many years strenuously defended'. Equally, was it possible 'that advancing years and somewhat impaired physical health and vigour may be casting a cloud of conservatism over the idealistic vision of my earlier years?' (p.9).

After an introductory chapter, he began the discussion with two chapters on 'The nature of the problem'. The Christian, he contended, was rightly concerned with his fellow-men. His efforts at reformation will begin with himself; but they will then turn outwards to the world about him, expressing 'a loving concern for our fellows'. The important question is to consider

> what form or forms of pressure it is ethically legitimate for a Christian man to use, in his individual and also in his corporate capacity, as a means of causing others to act in ways which he deems essential to their own and to the general welfare.[1]

War was one of the possible options in deciding how to exert

[1] C. J. Cadoux *Christian Pacifism Re-examined* (1940) p.15.

pressure for change. Other options, in Cadoux's analysis, were personal appeal (as through lectures, pamphlets or petitions, for example), rewards and punishments, and non-co-operation. We may distinguish between 'influence', which is not necessarily resented by those whom one attempts to influence, and coercion, which is usually resented and which rarely changes anyone's attitude for the better. It was with coercive pressure, the most extreme form of which is war, that the book concerned itself.

Cadoux then asked how we can discern God's guidance on this problem, and suggested five 'tests': the general sense of the Christian community, the promptings of 'the Christian heart', the character and teaching of Jesus, the Christian doctrine of the character of God, and the test of expediency.

The heart of the book was in the fourth chapter, 'The primâ-facie case for pacifism', where four of these five tests were applied to the problem of war. The reader was not to expect 'an unambiguous conclusion', but was justified in hoping that 'some sort of unity by way of a solution' would emerge.

The first test – the general sense of the Christian community – revealed no clear-cut answer. The vast majority of Christians throughout history had accepted the validity of war as an instrument of policy, within certain limits and in certain circumstances; the concept of 'the just war' was a part of Catholic teaching. But there were other voices, notably from the pre-Constantinian Church, whose attitude Cadoux had studied so carefully and exhaustively during the first world war; Origen's defence of pacifism (in *Against Celsus* Book VIII ch. 68–76) was published as an appendix to Cadoux's book. Since the Reformation there had been small but persistent minorities who refused to participate in war; in 1940 they were 'a minute minority':

> ... but they are drawn from all sections of the Christian Church, and they command the puzzled respect of vast numbers of Christian people who cannot agree with them and yet cannot with full completeness and confidence condemn them.

> ... notwithstanding its acceptance of the present struggle, the conscience of Christendom has been more profoundly stirred regarding the legitimacy of war in our day than at any previous period in its history since Constantine.[1]

For Cadoux, this implied that 'the broad feeling of the Christian community' needed correction on the subject. The reader's conscience was stirred, but he was left free to draw his own conclusions.

The 'utterance of the Christian heart', the instinct of compassion

[1] *Ibid.* pp.68-69.

and reverence for life, would be to recoil from the idea of causing suffering. Cadoux reminded his readers that war involves inflicting as well as experiencing suffering. However, the argument from compassion could be used against pacifism as well as for it; compassion for the defenceless may lead us to use coercion in their defence. Cadoux recognized the force of this appeal; 'the strength of the emotions connected with the question . . . are such as to render it perhaps the most perplexing item in the whole enquiry'.[1] It is indeed one of the most frequently used arguments against pacifism.

To this Cadoux replied, first, that it was not in question that the weak should be defended, but the matter at issue was 'By what means ought we to defend them?'

> . . . speaking generally, and taking a long view, we may claim that the method of gentleness, as an expression of active good-will, is at least as effective for defence as is violence . . . And it is to be observed that such a method of protection often depends for its success on not being used alongside of the weapons of violence, but adopted as the sole and exclusive policy.[2]

Secondly, the defence of the weak was rarely the main issue at stake in war. Thirdly, it is a good controversial weapon in the non-pacifist argument but as a principle it is not applied consistently. Fourthly, it is arguable whether 'right conduct regarding others can be allowed to involve a radically different ethical standard from that required for right conduct regarding ourselves'.[3] Cadoux recognized that this was an exceedingly difficult problem, but one which had to be thought through without being dominated by a sometimes superficial sentiment.

In discussing the third test – the character and teaching of Jesus – Cadoux was returning to themes he had discussed in previous books. He had argued at considerable length in *The Early Christian Attitude to War* that Jesus rejected war. Jesus taught and practised the way of non-violence, and intended that his followers should do the same; 'the appeal to the test of conformity with the teaching and example of Jesus results in a very strong vindication of the rightness of our provisional pacifist theory'.[4]

The fourth test was the Christian doctrine of the character of God. In a necessarily very brief treatment, Cadoux posed the problem of bringing to a synthesis the revelation in Scripture of God as 'the awful

[1] *Ibid.* pp.122-123.
[2] *Ibid.* p.118.
[3] See pp.117-123 for these arguments.
[4] *Ibid.* pp.86-87.

Judge Whose punishments strike terror in the guilty heart' and 'the self-sacrificing and forgiving Father' as revealed in the teaching of Jesus. If one regards the Divine severity as operating through the laws of nature, and the Divine forgiveness through God's personal relation to us, and is then reminded that Jesus taught his followers to reflect God's forgiving love, rather than His judgment, to others, it is then possible to reconcile pacifism with our understanding of the nature of God.

> If therefore, as pacifists, we claim to conform to one phase of the Divine character rather than the other, the choice is not an arbitrary one, but has the sanction . . . of Jesus himself.[1]

The final test, to which Cadoux devoted a separate chapter, was the test of expediency. Though the main force of Cadoux's argument was theoretical rather than practical, ethical rather than political, he believed that 'the probable or certain results of any course of practical conduct *are* relevant material for a true judgment as to its ethical value', for concern about results is itself a moral concern.

History provides many examples of progress being achieved by the use of force and fewer examples of the practical success of pacifism. But may the cause of this not be simply 'the fewness of pacifists rather than the ineffectiveness of pacifism'? The final appeal must be to the Cross and the Atonement, for 'the paradoxical principle of love's success through failure' is one of the crucial characteristics of Christianity. As he had argued in an earlier book, 'the Cross and non-resistance stand or fall together'.[2]

These arguments convinced Cadoux that it was right to maintain his belief in pacifism. But they had manifestly not persuaded others; this might be explained partly by the fact that the arguments were comparatively new to most people. The notion of war as an instrument of policy, even of religious policy, was too deeply embodied in conscious and unconscious attitudes for it to be easily abandoned. Nevertheless, much common ground could be shared by pacifist and non-pacifist; the chief area of disagreement was 'the test of expediency', whether or not war could be regarded as the only conceivable way of overcoming certain recognised evils.

Here Cadoux returned to the 'theory of ethical relativity' which had brought him criticism in 1917. It was this theory, he felt, which might best enable non-pacifist and pacifist to respect each other's opinions and work together for the common good. In Cadoux's own words:

[1] *Ibid.* p.90.
[2] *The Message about the Cross* (1924) p.90.

It cannot be denied that, in deciding for himself what he ought to do, a man cannot do better than decide sincerely to act according to his lights, and that, in so far as anticipation of results enters into his method of decision, he ought to take that course which he sincerely believes will on the whole lead to the best consequences. That being accepted, I want to invite the reader to agree to this further affirmation – that a man so acting is not only subjectively justified, as doing what is, for him, with such light as he has, right and good, but is also instrumental – by virtue of his sincerity (coupled, of course, with an average measure of intelligence) – in producing some objectively useful result, even if he is mistaken in his calculations, and even if much evil which he did not anticipate or rightly assess follows therefore as a consequence of his action. [1]

. . .

Just as only the Christian can do the fully Christian thing, so only the convincedly-pacifist Christian can practise Christian pacifism. This means that the majority are at least *relatively* right in employing on occasions the method of war. [2]

What should the pacifist then do, finding himself the citizen of a country fighting a war against a government which he recognizes as evil? The pacifist should be prepared to co-operate with others 'so long as the co-operation is concerned with good objects which he values in common with them'. He would tend wounded soldiers, or victims of air-raids, and must be prepared to put himself in danger; but he would not take part in any action which involved killing or wounding the enemy.

Above all, the pacifist has a moral obligation to help all those who work for peace; this may well mean involvement in political activity. It could involve campaigning, when the time came, for a 'healing peace', a different kind of treaty from that at the end of the first world war, which had been a factor contributing to the second world war; it could involve campaigning for a better international scheme for preserving peace in the future. It might involve pressing for a humane conduct of war (for example, opposing air attacks on civilians) and the better treatment of refugees.

When the book was finally ready for publication, a year after it was begun, and six months after it was finished, Cadoux wrote in the preface that 'riper reflection' had convinced him that there were three crucial points in the argument: 1) that the conduct of war could not

[1] *Christian Pacifism Re-examined* pp.128-129.
[2] *Ibid.* p.131.

be harmonized with any Christian standard, 2) that war provokes further war, and 3) that the Christian ethic involved the overcoming of evil *with good*.

The book was unusual, from Cadoux's pen, in having no footnotes (except in the appendix). But the argument was highly concentrated, and the reader could find it difficult to keep track of all the threads being woven into the fabric at any one time. This was partly a consequence of the complexity of the problem. It may be that the author recognized that in the last resort, the case could not be proved; it was possible to set forth the rational arguments for the pacifist ethic, but ultimately its acceptance had to be an act of faith. At the end of the book he wrote:

> It has been good to travel all round our problem, and make use of all the help intellect could offer. But that very trust in the intellect rests after all on an act of faith; and it is at bottom the same faith which bids us do the best we know, and leave the issue thereof in God's hands.[1]

Griffith-Jones, who was not a pacifist, thought it was Cadoux's best book – 'far the greatest you have so far written, tho' there may be – I hope so – still greater to emanate from your fruitful mind and dexterous pen'. Part of the 'greatness', Griffith-Jones wrote, was the spirit in which the book was written – 'tolerant yet convinced', 'courteous yet positive', 'thorough yet modest'. This opinion was echoed by reviewers. The book was commended for its fairness, its courage, its sincerity, its comprehensiveness.

Shortly after publication, it stood side by side with Leonard Woolf's *The War for Peace* in Blackwell's bookshop window. Almost simultaneously another book on the same subject appeared, but written from a different standpoint. John Lewis, author of *The Case against Pacifism*, was a former member of the FOR who was now persuaded that pacifist principles could no longer be sustained. Cadoux's work and the book by Lewis were frequently reviewed together; on the whole, whatever the attitude of the reviewer, Cadoux's book was judged to be the more effective and convincing.

In *Christian Pacifism Re-examined* we encounter a mellower Cadoux. There is still the same deep commitment to non-violence, the same exhaustive argument; but also a more sympathetic understanding of other points of view, and a greater humility.

It is unlikely that anyone was 'converted' to pacifism by reading the book. It did, however, help many young people, faced with conscription and feeling that they could not conscientiously take part in

[1] *Ibid.* p.229.

acts of war, to sort out their ideas, and perhaps to give a clearer justification for their beliefs than they might otherwise have done. Cadoux was always ready to help anyone preparing to face a tribunal. But he did not try to put any pressure on any of his young friends who felt that their conscience prompted them to support the war effort.

The life of faith is a life of taking risks. The Christian does not work from clear-cut instructions about how life should be lived; he has to work out a Christian response to each new situation. Cadoux had wrestled again with the burning question of war, and had made his decision. He now faced the unknown future firm in his own commitment, but able to respect and co-operate with those who differed from him.

XV

War years
1940–1945

THE WAR DID NOT greatly affect Cadoux's professional life. He continued to teach and write as before and the interruptions were caused more by his illnesses than by any exterior circumstance.

There was more of an effect on family life. 179 Woodstock Road was a large house with several bedrooms. Oxford was not thought to be a likely target for air raids (it was not in fact ever bombed). In a 'safe' area, all empty bedrooms were compulsorily filled. Marguerite Cadoux found and selected her own lodgers wherever possible. Throughout the war the house was full; many of the lodgers were civil servants working in requisitioned colleges. For a time Maud and Annabel, and Ida, stayed with them, to escape the bombing in Tonbridge and Edgware. This meant an extra burden for Marguerite, who had to undertake the further catering involved in addition to the regular entertaining, especially as there was no longer a living-in maid.

In spite of the extra work, it was usually a happy household (except when marred by Cadoux's illness). Marguerite wrote to Theo (2 October 1940) that 'we are all very happy and they help so much that it is not too bad'. A few days later, Cadoux wrote to Theo that 'the family party is very happy – with much laughing and a certain am't of leg-pulling'. Cadoux himself often enjoyed discussions and arguments with some of the lodgers during and after meal times.

The boys were both in the Friends' Ambulance Unit, but undergoing very different experiences. Theo, being two years older, was not called up till January 1940. After initial training in Birmingham, he spent the greater part of the next four years in London, working in 'rest centres' for the bombed out and in the FAU headquarters. Though it was a busy life, he found time to continue with his research and to correspond at length with his father, who more and more was enjoying his intellectual companionship and stimulus. He was able to come home at regular intervals. After further training in the latter half of 1943 he was sent abroad in January 1944 and served in Egypt, Palestine and Greece until his return home in December 1945. He was mainly engaged in relief work. Contact was maintained by the exchange of air-letters and 'airgraphs' (reduced photocopies of written sheets).

Harold went to the training centre in Birmingham (September 1939), then to London, and in February 1940 was sent to Finland, which Russia had invaded. When the war there ended, the German invasion of Norway and Denmark in April prevented half of this group from returning home, and after some months in Sweden they had an adventurous and fascinating journey through Russia and Turkey to Egypt. After a winter in Alexandria acting as the transport section of a military hospital, they moved in the spring of 1941 to Greece, where there was fighting with the Italians. Once again their situation was transformed by an invading German army. For several weeks there was no news of the fate of their group, and it was an anxious time for the family at home. Finally, on 20 June, a telegram arrived. Cadoux wrote to Theo two days later:

> I cannot tell you how intensely relieved we were to hear by wire fr Brandon Cadbury on Fri ev'g that our dear old Harold with his 15 friends were safe and well at Corinth . . . I found the joyfulness of the news quite overwhelming at first.

Though safe and well, Harold was now a prisoner-of-war, and was soon moved to Germany. It was to be another four years before he returned home, and communication during those years was slight and irregular. This was a constant underlying anxiety for the family.

The girls stayed at home throughout the war. For one brief period, after the retreat from Dunkirk and threat of invasion in 1940, the idea of sending them to North America was seriously considered. In June, offers came from universities in both Canada and the United States to take children of university dons immediately for the duration of the war. Cadoux had gone off to Inkpen at the end of Trinity term for a short walking holiday; almost immediately meetings were hastily convened to discuss the arrangements for sending children overseas. Marguerite attended at least two and wrote to her husband explaining what was involved. Some of their friends and colleagues had already decided to send their children. What could or should they do? Ruth was fifteen and soon to take School Certificate, an awkward time to move to a completely different educational system; Joan, on the other hand, was only nine and would be able to adapt more easily. Perhaps they should send Joan alone? It was an agonising decision to have to make. When Cadoux returned from Inkpen the threat of possible invasion any day hung over them. After much discussion and heart-searching, they decided to keep the girls at home. A few days later, they received a generous offer from friends in New Jersey to take the girls immediately. Grateful as they were, they did not change their minds. As things turned out, it was a decision they did not regret. Ruth did well at Oxford High School and in 1943 delighted her father by being accepted by St Anne's Society (as it then was) to read Zoology. Joan continued at the High School till the end of the war, after which she was sent to boarding school.

Cadoux had hoped to arrange a family gathering in July 1940 to celebrate the hundredth anniversary of his father's birth. The difficult war conditions made this impossible, much to his disappointment, but he used the opportunity to correspond with his brothers and sisters about it. Similarly, his and Marguerite's silver wedding six months later, on 23 December, had to be celebrated quietly.

Life at Mansfield was disrupted, but not essentially restricted, by the war. Even before war was actually declared, the government had taken over all the college buildings except the chapel, library and Principal's lodgings. Later, the library was taken over too. Fortunately, Regent's Park College now had a reasonably spacious and central new building in Pusey Street, just off St Giles, and in view of the long co-operation of the two colleges, Mansfield's teaching and lecturing was immediately transferred there. When the library was eventually taken over, a home for the books was found in New College Old Library. All this involved a certain amount of extra walking round Oxford, but the basic work and life of the college continued unimpeded, and there was always a number of students in residence. The Junior Common Room moved into the basement of the Principal's lodgings, enjoying what one member called 'an eschatological existence in the catacombs'.

In place of T. W. Manson, who left Mansfield in order to replace Dodd as Rylands Professor in Manchester in 1936, and Romilly Micklem, who returned to the pastoral ministry in 1938, A. M. Hunter came from Scotland, and John Marsh, whom Cadoux had met earlier, from Yorkshire. When Hunter returned to Scotland in 1943, there was some re-arrangement of the teaching, and Alec Whitehouse, a former Mansfield student, returned to the college as chaplain.

Though Wheeler Robinson retired from the principalship of Regent's Park College in 1942, he remained in Oxford, and Cadoux used to visit him regularly. He was a friend and frank critic, and once told Cadoux that 'I am no philosopher, and put myself out of court for theolog'l issues (diary 29 December 1943).

More and more, Cadoux felt himself the guardian of the tradition he had inherited from men like Selbie and Bartlet, of the Congregationalism and liberal theology which he had absorbed in his student days. He had spent most of a lifetime expounding and defending that theological position. Now he found that many of those around him at Mansfield, whether students or members of staff, were adopting a different standpoint, which seemed to him to be reactionary, obscurantist and backward-looking, the very bondage from which he had struggled so hard to be free.

This trend was epitomised for Cadoux by *The Presbyter*, a journal started in 1942 for the discussion of Reformed theology and churchmanship. Many of its contributors were connected with Mansfield. Cadoux made no secret of his view that *The Presbyter* was identifying itself with 'a trend in modern religious thought which, in common with most Mansfield men and most Congregatl ministers I know, I regard as definitely reactionary and erroneous.'[1] That trend involved a belief in Scripture as 'God's objective will and self-revelation' which as formulated by the contributors to *The Presbyter* Cadoux could neither accept nor fully understand.

It was not that he wanted his pupils and colleagues to think as he did in every respect; if they did there would be no controversy and therefore no stimulus and excitement in intellectual debate. He wrote to Theo once (12 March 1944) – 'I am in rather a whirl of controversial articles and lrs to press ("spice of life" – what ho!)' indicating how much he thrived on the cut-and-thrust of intellectual debate.

But he was now beginning to feel more isolated within the college. The feeling was deepened by the deaths of both Bartlet and Selbie. Bartlet died in August 1940; he had been 'father in God' to Cadoux as to others, and was much missed. No longer could Cadoux call round to the house in Museum Road for advice (which was often, though not always, followed) on his latest article or book. He was however able to honour his former teacher by editing for publication Bartlet's lectures on *Church Life and Church Order during the First Four Centuries* (published 1943), originally delivered as the Birkbeck Lectures in Cambridge in 1924. The lectures exemplified the 'historic method' which Cadoux had learned from Bartlet. As an introduction to the published work, Cadoux contributed a 45 page biographical memoir, not altogether accepting Arthur's advice that 'to be in style with the subject, you will need to make it least half parenthesis'.

Four years later Selbie died, in April 1944. Cadoux gave the address at the funeral, paying tribute to his former Principal as one who

[1] Letter from Cadoux to Alec Whitehouse 2 February 1944.

'worthily cherished and garnered the harvest' planted by his predecessor Fairbairn, and referring to his own and a younger generation 'into whose imperfect hands the maintenance of this great heritage has been entrusted'. To Cadoux's mind, that heritage seemed under threat.

His difficulties with the Principal were no nearer resolution. Against the advice of his friends, he made a formal complaint to the College Council on two occasions. The first involved a request that the Council should define the responsibilities of the Vice-Principal (reflecting Cadoux's disappointment at being so rarely invited to occupy the college chapel pulpit, and being excluded from actual decision-making); Cadoux did make a point of telling Micklem exactly what he was doing, and to Theo he wrote (24 May 1942) – 'I had a v. friendly talk w' NM after dinner last Fri so he knows what is coming'. The Council referred the matter back to the Senior Common Room, who passed a non-committal resolution that the Vice-Principalship should carry with it 'the right and the duty of acting for the Principal whenever he is prevented from fulfilling any engagement or performing any duty as Principal of the College' (21 November 1942). Cadoux was present at the meetings at which this was discussed and wrote to Theo that they were 'very amicable in tone'. All this did something to clear the air, but Cadoux was not much happier about his status in college.

The cause of his second formal complaint, which led to no further action, was that two of the Mansfield students had been sent to lectures given by a Roman Catholic priest, Father Gervase Mathew, a distinguished Byzantinist at Blackfriars, the Dominican house in Oxford. Cadoux found sympathy, but not support, for his feelings of dismay about this.

This unhappiness and sense of grievance were exacerbated by his increasingly poor health; and the anxieties were also, at least in part, the cause of the ill-health. His wife pleaded with him in a letter (2 August 1943) – '. . . if you could only go quietly and not worry so much over other people it would be better'. And his old friend Wheeler Robinson wisely urged him (9 February 1944) – '. . . don't worry too much over other people's misdeeds, for which we shall not be held answerable'.

Twice he had long serious illnesses. The day after his silver wedding in December 1940 he had to stay in bed with an ulcer on his leg, which proved very stubborn, so that it was four months before it began to heal and he could get dressed again and resume normal life. He had a spell in the Acland Nursing Home for ultra-violet ray treatment, but improvement was slow. He suffered intense pain and at times acute depression. He managed to study intermittently and friends visited him regularly. But it was a great drain on his temper, sense of proportion and spiritual resources, and added to the strain under which his wife was now living.

Two years later he had an even worse illness, when his life was seriously in danger. Late in November 1942 the doctor was summoned and told Cadoux that he was suffering from cardiac degeneration and arterio-sclerosis and would need to take great care. Ten days later Marguerite wrote to Theo that his father was very ill and might not recover. Cadoux himself wrote to Theo – 'I am inwardly upheld and kept peaceful'. Theo wrote a letter full of concern and affection to his father, which prompted Cadoux to write in his diary: 'Get a wonderful lr fr Theo, express'g affection and gratitude: better disposed to Xty: has been and will be praying for me. How long have I waited for this!' The essential unity of this family was a great support and strength to him, particularly in these last years.

Cadoux himself was moved to write to Maud and Connie (he had recently been going through some of his early papers) to ask their forgiveness for his attitude at home forty years earlier. Both replied with kind, appreciative letters. Connie reminded him that 'there is *no-one* who does not regret doing or not doing something in their lives . . . at least no-one with a conscience which we Cadouxs seem to possess in the superlative degree(!) and suffer accordingly'.

The crisis eventually passed, and he recovered his health sufficiently well to be able to give his lectures in Hilary Term. Despite indifferent health henceforward, there was still much to enjoy in life. Lecturing and teaching still brought him great satisfaction. His Reformation lectures were now listed in the University Gazette under History as well as Theology, and he was always pleased when any undergraduates studying history came.

As a teacher he conveyed his own love of truth and Christian values. In a letter written to thank the Cadouxs for a wedding present, one of his students (W. T. Pennar Davies) wrote (12 July 1943):

> Nothing greater can be said of a theological teacher than that he communicates to his pupils a passion for the service of the kingdom of Christ – and that can certainly be said of Dr Cadoux. I shall always honour him as a great lover of truth and goodness.

It was on his walking holidays in the Inkpen district that he offered those students whom he invited to accompany him the opportunity to discuss and hear him discourse at greater length on all his favourite subjects – ethics, theology, literature, philosophy.

Marguerite did not now enjoy walking and never accompanied him on his walking tours, but took her holiday at a different time, visiting friends or a relation. Family holidays belonged to the past. It was a deprivation to their marriage, and to Marguerite in particular, that the two of them were not able to enjoy a relaxing holiday together now. But she was glad that her husband could unwind at the end of each term in those peaceful surroundings.

A particular friend was the rector of Inkpen, Francis Driscoll. Driscoll was unusual in having been a chef at Claridge's for some years before entering the priesthood at the age of about forty. He enjoyed theological discussion with Cadoux, and welcomed Cadoux to his pulpit. Cadoux wrote to Theo from Inkpen Rectory, where he had been invited to stay, on 24 August 1943 – 'I have had some very interesting talks w' the Rector, and we are on an excellent footing. I go gently as a controversialist – but have given him one or two home truths about Romanism, of which he didn't seem to be aware'.

In August 1943, shortly after that visit to Inkpen, Cadoux went with Ruth and Joan to spend a few days with his old friend Charlton Short at Short's caravan near Dorking. It proved a disastrous few days. One evening, Short reprimanded Ruth for not helping sufficiently with the chores, reducing her temporarily to tears. Cadoux felt that it was a very unfair criticism, and tried to persuade his friend to apologise; Short refused, saying that his criticism was perfectly justified. That episode rankled in Cadoux's mind more and more, out of all proportion to its importance. The breach was never healed. He talked it over with innumerable friends, expended an inordinate amount of energy in writing letters to Short, and in worrying about it. His friends' appeals to him to 'bury the hatchet' fell on deaf ears.

Marguerite told Theo that she thought her husband had idolised Short far too much. It was true that he felt a close sentimental attachment to him as a fellow worker in boys' classes and boys' camps in the old days before the first world war. This made the breach all the more painful and his desire to heal it all the stronger. But his natural indignation on Ruth's behalf and his insistence on an admission from Short that he had been at fault, combined with Short's equal obstinacy, brought the relationship to an impasse. It was a cloud over those last years.

His intellectual work was following the same themes as before, all planned according to detailed schedules. Amidst all the ill-health and anxiety those schedules provided an anchorage for his daily life. More important, his scholarship was recognized as a valuable contribution to 'the theological enterprise'. Even those who disagreed with his conclusions accepted this; T. W. Manson, for example, in his review of *The Historic Mission of Jesus* (*Mansfield College Magazine* July 1942) remarked that even those like himself who regarded the work as 'the last kick of expiring Liberalism, will have to allow that for a last kick it has uncommon force and shrewdness' and that

> . . . there are some who will not abate a jot of their admiration for its author and his devotion, though they fill his margins with marks of interrogation, exclamation, and all the apparatus of contradiction. For apart from the matters of theological dispute, there is a great deal of solid and valuable instruction concerning matters of fact, a great deal of acute and judicial discussion of critical points, and a great deal of earnest, sincere and sensitive treatment of moral and religious issues. It is a liberal education in theological liberalism to read it.

Quite apart from its external value, Cadoux's work, like that of every writer, fulfilled an inner need. Having found in early life a way of reconciling his Christian faith with his intellectual quest for truth, of remaining loyal to the faith of his father (for whom he retained a deep respect, almost reverence, to the end of his life), and yet of enjoying a freedom to use his intellectual powers to question traditional forms of Christian doctrine, he could not let that go – he must defend it with all his considerable intellectual powers. He made several references to the way in which 'Christian liberalism' had saved him from revolt against 'the old evangelicalism' in a series of articles in *The Christian World* from 1944 onwards.

He had found his own solution by making a distinction in theological thought between

> the foundation realities on the one hand, and the resultant doctrines involved in and implied by them on the other. The difference between these two lies in the fact that the former are directly rooted in man's religious consciousness and experience, whereas the latter are the fruit of his subsequent reflection on this consciousness and experience . . . We contrast religion with theology: we speak of kernel and husk, of substance and form, of things essential and things optional.[1]

He was drawing on a distinction which his teacher, Bartlet, had made between 'idea', the religious reality experienced by all Christians, and 'conception', the means by which human beings attempted to expound the meaning and significance of 'idea'. The new orthodoxy, on

[1] 'The present cleavage in Congregationalism' in *The Congregational Quarterly* July 1942 p.231.

the other hand, was based on different presuppositions; 'it starts not with experience but with the witness of the Church to Christ'.[1]

This new orthodoxy represented a dangerous threat and challenge to Cadoux's scheme; all his intellectual powers must be summoned to show that the liberal position was the right and safest way forward, for

the safest path of theological progress is a bold and trustful use of reason and intelligence, combined with reverence for the great central sanctities, human and Divine.[2]

Liberal Protestantism asserted the freedom to

sift, abandon, and reformulate the traditional Christian doctrines, according as its knowledge of the relevant facts and its grasp of truth expand, and to do so unhindered by the antiquity of the doctrines or concepts in question, and undeterred even by the fears of those who are unwilling to abandon or alter them in any respect.[3]

Whatever else he was working on during these years, he always had some book or article on hand which expressly supported this viewpoint. In the years 1941–43 he was at work on three books; to Theo he wrote on 11 September 1942 – 'I keep all my 3 bks going in due proportion, under a specially devised schedule'. The three were his second volume of the history of Smyrna (which he never completed), a work on Philip II of Spain, and a book of dialogues on Christian teaching, eventually published as *A Pilgrim's Further Progress*.

A Pilgrim's Further Progress came out at the end of 1943. Some thought its title unfortunate, even presumptuous, though in the introduction Cadoux disclaimed any desire to 'challenge comparison with the immortal Bunyan'. He dedicated the work to his children; it was cast in the form of dialogues between an enquirer named 'Pilgrim' and a teacher (i.e. himself) whom he called 'Interpreter'.

The pilgrimage was primarily an intellectual one, covering theological and ethical issues. Having made his familiar distinction between the absolute 'foundation-realities' and the relative 'doctrine', Cadoux devoted the first half of the book to doctrine. Though cast in a new form, the ground covered was familiar; the search for the historical facts about Jesus, the need for a new Christology and doctrine of the Atonement, and the relative value of the doctrine of the Trinity. It brought together ideas which had already appeared in his previous books and articles.

---

[1] Review of *A Pilgrim's Further Progress* in *The Presbyter* July 1944 by Alexander Miller.
[2] *A Pilgrim's Further Progress* (1943) p.vii.
[3] *The Congregational Quarterly* July 1942 pp.232-233.

The second half of the work dealt with ethics and the Christian life, prayer, church reunion, and 'our world and the future'. Much of this material too had appeared in earlier books and articles, though the chapter on prayer treated that subject at greater length than is found anywhere else in Cadoux's writings.

The chapter on sex was largely an attack on 'the new morality', especially as expressed by Kenneth Ingram in *Sex Morality Tomorrow* (1940). Here Cadoux parted company with some of his modernist friends, and argued vehemently for the traditional Christian ethic of chastity before marriage and faithfulness within it. He founded his argument on his interpretation of the teaching of the Bible. The Christian ethic itself was based not on a rejection of 'life in the flesh' but on 'the healthy Hebraic conception of the goodness of creation and the sacredness of personality'. The Gospel record of Jesus' teaching about sex he took to be 'historically true' and entitled to the Christian's obedience. 'The Christian ideal is constructive enough: the only thing that is wrong with it is that so many persons won't pursue it. But that is *their* fault, not Christianity's . . .'.

The reader who worked through to the end of the book would have covered a wide sweep of Christian doctrine and ethics, presented from a Liberal Protestant point of view. The references to newer 'neo-orthodox' points of view were of course unsympathetic.

By casting the book in the form of a dialogue, Cadoux aimed at enlivening what would otherwise have been a continuous exposition of his own views. He did not attempt to present contrary arguments with force and conviction, so as to produce the appearance of a spirited encounter of minds, and perhaps could not have succeeded in doing this if he had tried. As it is, 'Pilgrim' is throughout brief, tentative and deferential, like the interlocutors of Socrates in Plato's dialogues.

The book sold reasonably well, and a second edition came out two years later in a religious book club version.

The book on *Philip II of Spain and the Netherlands* was an unusual work and one extremely difficult to evaluate. Its real theme was the way in which Roman Catholicism had been and was still being used to defend the repression of freedom. One of the book's reviewers, G. F. Nuttall, writing in *The Congregational Quarterly* in January 1948, suggested that it might best be considered as 'an extended footnote to the chapters on persecution in *Catholicism and Christianity*'.

Theo had suggested that his father might approach Roman Catholicism through the writings of more recent exponents. He wrote on 30 October 1942 – 'Is it possible that there is a forward movement in

Catholicism working towards a new philosophy of the relationship between the authority of the Church and the individual?' He suggested that his father might read something by Maritain, for example. Cadoux replied (1 November) – 'I think you are prob. right that there is an intelligent wing in Cath^m. But the adherence to the false system on the part of the intelligent is itself a lack of straightforwardness'. He was not to be deflected from his mission.

He was intensely sensitive about cruelty, and felt very strongly that the facts about Spanish persecution were being obscured by a modern 'whitewashing' of Philip II. He had first conceived the idea of writing a book on this subject before the war and by 1940 was working on it steadily. It was finished by the middle of 1944 and accepted for publication by Lutterworth in 1945, but was not finally published (partly owing to shortage of paper) until a few months after Cadoux died in 1947.

The work was sub-titled 'An essay on moral judgments in history'. It was avowedly controversial, an attack on moral relativism. In reply to the publisher's suggestion that some of the pointed phrases and forcible expressions might be toned down, Cadoux replied (31 August 1945):

... as the book is a fighting book, these features are quite in place ...

Whatever a book on this subject says, it is bound to draw fire: and therefore it seems to me it is best to make the attack as pointed and telling as possible, provided the decencies of debate are observed.

In order to write the book, Cadoux had researched very carefully into the secondary sources, in English, on the subject of his book. He freely admitted that he had not examined the primary sources, but claimed that this made no difference to the value of his argument, which rested on generally acknowledged facts. An Oxford historian who specialised in sixteenth and seventeenth century history, whom Cadoux consulted, believed that the historical background was accurate. Certainly the detailed chronological table at the end of the book revealed an extensive knowledge of the field and helped the reader to follow the argument.

The first chapter of the book dealt with the problem of moral judgments in history. How far was the historian entitled to pronounce human beings or their actions morally good or bad? Cadoux recognized that the historian must normally forbear to pass judgment on a person, but believed that he did have the right to censure actions; for we cannot rightly draw a sharp distinction here between the historian as judge and the ordinary man as judge, and say that, while the ordinary man is welcome to think and say what he likes about any historical character, yet *in his capacity as an historian* he must keep his mouth shut in regard to all value-judgments.

. . . I cannot see why the historian should be called upon to leave unused his ethical judgment any more than any other power he possesses for discerning the truth.[1]

In making this claim, he was challenging the view being expressed by other contemporary historians – notably Herbert Butterfield in *The Whig Interpretation of History* (1931), a book which Cadoux discussed in this first chapter.

He went on to demonstrate what he believed was pro-Catholic bias in two recent works on Philip II. The first was *The Golden Century of Spain* (1937) by R. Trevor Davies, an Oxford history don who taught at St Catherine's Society (which meant that he taught some Mansfield ordinands who read history). Cadoux had told Trevor Davies what he intended to say, and actually had 'a friendly discussion' with him about it. The other work was *Philip II* (1938) by an American professor of English, W. T. Walsh. Trevor Davies was an Anglican priest, W. T. Walsh a Roman Catholic layman. Cadoux contended that

both are animated by a great admiration of Philip, an approval of the Spanish Inquisition, and a dislike of sixteenth century Protestantism in general, and of the Protestants of the Netherlands and their great leader, William of Orange, in particular.[2]

In addition, *The Times Literary Supplement* had given 'unstinted and even extravagant praise' to the first, and 'an almost unqualified eulogy' to the second.

Cadoux then examined several aspects of the relationship between Spain and the Netherlands in the later sixteenth century: the character of the Inquisition, Spanish administration of the Netherlands – especially under the duke of Alva, the personal characters of Philip II and William of Orange, and the nature of the Netherlands resistance to Philip. His objective was

to arrive at some just and tenable judgment regarding the ethical issues involved in the struggle itself and the ethical quality of the conduct of the main protagonists on either side.[3]

He felt that both Trevor Davies and W. T. Walsh, in common with

[1] C. J. Cadoux *Philip II of Spain and the Netherlands* (1947) p.11.
[2] *Ibid.* p.32.
[3] *Ibid.* p.40.

some other Catholic apologists, had gone much too far in attempting to vindicate the Spanish side against the charges levelled against them by earlier historians such as Lecky and Motley. They had tried to show that the horrors of the Inquisition had been exaggerated, that its courts were more humane than the secular courts of the time, that some Elizabethan tortures may have been worse than the Spanish, that Philip's motives in persecution were political rather than religious; none of this, to Cadoux, could alter in any degree the judgment that the Spanish Inquisition under Philip was a heartlessly cruel institution. He asked the reader

> ... to say candidly whether or not it was for the good of mankind and for the advancement of the religion of Jesus Christ that such an institution should be resisted and ultimately abolished. Let him bear in mind by all means that virtually the whole of Europe took for granted the legitimacy of torture as a part of judicial procedure, that rules had been laid down against excessive severity in the use of it and in penalization generally, that Protestant writers have exaggerated the severities of the Spanish Inquisition and the numbers of its victims, that it was not as cruel as the Roman Inquisition, that the Inquisitors were actuated by the noblest motives and were personally virtuous in many ways, and so on. Yet the question remains: what is to be our resultant judgement on the ethical character of the Inquisitional practice in Spain and the Netherlands? Is a national uprising which aimed at bringing it in the latter country to as speedy an end as possible deserving of our censure, or of our warm admiration and gratitude?[1]

Cadoux believed that the deeds of both Philip II and the Duke of Alva were deserving of the strongest moral condemnation. Philip II 'felt conscientiously certain that God had charged him with a sacred mission – to glorify the House of Hapsburg and to destroy Protestantism':

> With such ideals fixed in his mind, he drew the conclusion that no considerations of mercy (which, had nothing else been at stake, would doubtless have weighed with him) could be allowed to stand in the way of the zealous fulfilment of his divinely-given mission. Nay, nothing less than the full range of the coercive power of despotic rule was to be employed in its service. It is this thoroughgoing policy which makes the story of his reign such terrible reading; and all the efforts of his apologists to emphasize his more amiable qualities, and to depreciate the character of his

[1] *Ibid.* pp.62-63.

enemies, do not avail to render his severities other than most repulsive.[1]

His rule over the Netherlands was not only 'tyrannical and bloody'; it was also 'perfidious'.

The worst condemnation was reserved for the Duke of Alva, Philip's representative in the Netherlands from 1567 to 1573:

> ... if Alva was not cruel and bloody, then I know of no cruel and bloody man who has ever existed on this earth from the beginning of history until now.[2]

More than half his chapter on the Duke was devoted to a discussion of the way in which 'this monstrous purveyor of homicide' was treated by W. T. Walsh and Trevor Davies, and their attempt to justify many of his repressive measures. None of their arguments convinced Cadoux that Alva was other than a cruel tyrant, deserving of the strongest condemnation.

William of Orange, on the other hand, had been unjustly treated by these same historians. He was not, according to Cadoux, 'the coarse and brutal materialist' of Trevor Davies, but a man whose true place

> is among the heroes, who, notwithstanding certain undeniable defects of character, enthrone themselves in the heart of humanity, by dint of the far-seeing, long-sustained, and self-denying service which they render to their afflicted fellow-men.[3]

These judgments were based on a particular understanding of the nature of the conflict in the Netherlands. Cadoux saw this in the traditional terms of a conflict between potential democracy and monarchical despotism, between religious freedom and intolerance, and between humaneness and savage cruelty. The 'obsession of the modern mind with economic problems' could bring grave distortions of judgment to bear on an age in which religious ideas played a dominant role. While recognizing (in theory at least) the value of appreciating an economic factor in the conflict, and while conceding that the contrast between the protagonists was less a matter of 'black and white' than had sometimes been suggested, Cadoux believed that the issue of religious and political freedom was the crucial one. This had contemporary relevance:

> Now that the true character of Nazi despotism in all its naked and hideous brutality has been unmistakably seen, we shall probably be a little more willing than we were in the pre-war years to appreciate the blessings of religious and political freedom, the abolition of torture and other forms of wanton cruelty, and the

[1] *Ibid.* p.119.   [2] *Ibid.* p.110.   [3] *Ibid.* p.213.

enthronement of a standard of humaneness and of respect for personal life.[1]

It was true that Protestants as well as Catholics had used persecution. But only within Protestantism, argued Cadoux, was toleration *inherent,* even if not at first recognized.

Since the purpose of the book was to consider moral judgments, Cadoux invited the reader on the last page to deliver his own: 'which side was it, in the great struggle we have been studying, in whose behaviour there can be seen some promise of better and humaner things?'

Cadoux would not have agreed with the judgment of Salvador de Madariaga in the latter's review of the book in *History* (October 1948) that he 'did not possess the chief qualification for such an essay [in moral judgments] – detachment', for he wrote it in the conviction that detachment must mean lack of ethical concern. It has to be said however that by 1947 most historians were concerned with many wider aspects of Netherlands history and not just religious factors; valuable as was Cadoux's work in exposing some recent unfair historical judgments, his concentration on those alone made it a book which was neither purely history nor purely ethics.

Professor Norman Sykes, reviewing the book after Cadoux's death in *The Journal of Theological Studies* (July–October 1948) thought it could be an interesting exercise

to construct a series of imaginary conversations between Dr Cadoux and the historical figures described in these pages, as they hold high argument in the Elysian fields; and to conjecture whether the author has been driven to modify some of his assertions in the light of that fuller knowledge which such encounter might convey.

He added

It is certain that this posthumous work recalls to mind the most engaging and endearing of the writer's qualities, as well as some of his most cherished dogmatism . . .

Whatever else the book had, it had Cadoux's touch.

Alongside all these enterprises, Cadoux continued with his New Testament studies. *The Historic Mission of Jesus,* one of his major works, appeared in 1941. His last work of all, *The Life of Jesus,* presented to the general reader the fruits of that lifelong study. To these works the next chapter will be devoted.

[1] *Ibid.* p.219.

XVI

New Testament scholar

'COUNCILS, WE ADMIT, and Creeds, cannot go behind, but must wholly rest upon the history of our Lord Jesus Christ'. These words, written by Canon R. C. Moberly in *Lux Mundi* (1889) were quoted by Cadoux more often than any other sentence, in both books and articles. They epitomised the justification for the quest for the historical Jesus.

Cadoux had made a life-long study of the Bible, and of the Gospels in particular, and had taken part in a long series of Oxford seminars on Gospel criticism which made an important contribution to New Testament studies in this country. His pacifist convictions were, as we have seen, integrally connected with his interpretation of the Gospels.

He had begun his academic career as a tutor in Old Testament studies, while at the same time writing his thesis for the London DD on the attitude of the early Church to pagan society. His very first published scholarly article, in *The Interpreter* (January 1916), 'The Ethics of a Hebrew Lawyer', took an Old Testament subject; it was an interesting discussion of the *development* of religious ideas revealed in the Book of the Covenant (*Exodus* 20.22–23.19). This was his only excursus into Old Testament studies if one excepts his colloquial translation of Deuteronomy, his exposition of the Suffering Servant passages of Isaiah in *The Guidance of Jesus for Today,* and a short article on Saul and Samuel in *The Hibbert Journal* (January 1939). He did not neglect Hebrew, however, for he read a short passage from the Old Testament in Hebrew each day.

His teaching in Bradford was in New Testament studies. As we have seen, he published *The Guidance of Jesus for Today* early in his career there. This laid the foundation of all his subsequent work on the Gospels. There followed a number of articles on New Testament subjects. He read and kept files on all the important books and articles in this field of study.

It was an abiding interest which he shared with Arthur. Most of

Arthur's books were on New Testament subjects.[1] Though Arthur did not accept his brother's pacifist interpretation of Jesus' teaching, their expositions of the mission of Jesus nevertheless bore many striking similarities. Arthur's book on *The Gospel that Jesus Preached* (1925) and his contribution to *The Lord of Life* (1929), for example, foreshadowed in many respects the argument in his brother's *The Historic Mission of Jesus* (1941). It is difficult to say how much Jack Cadoux was influenced by Arthur's writing. It seems that it was through mutual encouragement and appreciation, and through sharing broadly similar liberal views, that they helped each other.

When he returned to Oxford, Jack Cadoux began to collate all his New Testament material, and to plan a substantial work on the Gospels. Though he was teaching Church History at Mansfield, his private study of the New Testament continued unabated, and he was now able to attend New Testament seminars again. Alongside his writing on Liberal Protestantism, Smyrna and Philip II, Gospel studies always found a place. His daily reading from Greek (as well as Hebrew) provided a regular, fertile background to his study.

When A. M. Hunter resigned from the Yates Chair of New Testament studies at Mansfield in 1942, Cadoux seriously thought of applying for the position. He wrote to Theo (18 October 1942) – 'I felt at first disposed to press to be given his chair, for wh as you know I have long longed'. But he realised that it would mean a great deal of extra work and strain at a time when his health was poor; Theo advised against any move on his part. He decided to make no formal request, and no approach was made to him.

The Historic Mission of Jesus was written between 1937 and 1940 and published at the end of 1941. It was a long book (376 pages), though only half the length of *Catholicism and Christianity*; the argument was densely packed and carefully documented. Each chapter began with a brief résumé of the ground covered, so that the reader could work systematically through the steps of the argument. It was a book for the scholar, student or theologically informed layman who was prepared to give it close attention. The whole edition of 1500 copies was sold over the next six years.

The Life of Jesus was for the general reader. It owed its existence to James Wickett (the 'JJW' of the dedication), a lodger in the Cadoux household during the war who later married Ruth. He had a great admiration for Cadoux, and suggested that Cadoux should share his insights and ideas with a much wider audience by writing a more popular book. His own experience of marketing a different kind of

[1] A list of A. T. Cadoux's published works appears in Appendix D.

product (engineering components) prompted him to suggest that Cadoux should write for a market, not of one or two thousand, but of tens of thousands.

A few months after the end of the war, Cadoux wrote to Penguin Books to ask whether they would have any interest in a 'life of Jesus'; their reply was favourable. With some speed and a good deal of enthusiasm Cadoux set to work on the task, and within six months had despatched his manuscript to the publishers. That was in May 1946. Penguin confirmed that they would publish the book; though both their readers dissented from many of the views expressed in the book, both recommended it for publication. With shortage of paper and other problems it was nearly two years before the work was finally published, in 1948. It was sad that Cadoux did not survive to see his only best-seller in print; it sold almost 100,000 copies. On the other hand, he had told Theo (25 November 1945) that he shrank from 'making money out of Jesus, lest I become what the Didache calls a Χριστέμπορος'.

Although different in length and form (*The Life of Jesus* had no footnotes and few references), these two books covered much the same ground, and revealed the same presuppositions. It is appropriate, therefore, to consider them together.

Cadoux had a firm conviction that the Jesus of history could be distinguished from the Christ of faith. 'The quest of the historical Jesus' was, he argued, a valid part of the search for the truth about God; he was confident that the Gospels contained 'a good deal of historical truth' and that it was possible 'to disentangle it by the use of the ordinary standards of sanctified common sense from the less-historical matter by which it is accompanied'. He wrote of examining the life and teaching of Jesus through 'the lens of history'.[1]

Some years earlier he had written:

> Notwithstanding the tendency of some moderns to belittle the religious value of what they call 'knowing Christ after the flesh', and the tendency of other moderns to declare that it is impossible to know for certain more than a very little about Him, a sound instinct still continues to rivet Christian attention to the story of Jesus and to keep alive an untiring quest for the truth concerning Him.[2]

He recognised that Schweitzer's work had destroyed the old 'liberal' picture of Jesus. No subsequent account of Jesus' teaching could

[1] *The Life of Jesus* (1948) p. 19.
[2] *The Expository Times* (1 June 1935) 'The Historical Jesus: a study of Schweitzer and after'.

ignore the powerful eschatological elements in the Gospels.

But it is a mistake to suppose that the overthrow of the 'liberal' picture of Jesus makes it easier than before to synthetize His earthly history with the precise traditional doctrine of His Person. One outstanding result of the abandonment of the 'liberal' view is to prove that Jesus' intellect was more conditioned by the ideas of His time than it was formerly thought to have been: and this makes it harder, not easier, to synthetize His history and the traditional dogma so long (of course) as men do not help themselves out by ignoring Moberly's great canon: 'Councils . . . and Creeds cannot go behind, but must wholly rest upon the history of our Lord Jesus Christ'.[1]

The problems of history in the Gospels, not least the understanding of the apocalyptic elements, had to be honestly faced.

The Historic Mission of Jesus was subtitled, 'A constructive reexamination of the eschatological teaching in the Synoptic Gospels'. It began:

Notwithstanding the vast amount of useful work – linguistic, documentary, historical, and expository – which has been done during the last 50 or 60 years on the contents of the New Testament and of the Synoptic Gospels in particular, we are still without any comprehensive and generally-satisfactory account of the real purpose of Jesus in his public Ministry and the real content of his teaching. . . . the endeavour to obtain a complete and systematic view of the real content of Jesus' own teaching – in distinction (so far as possible) from the interpretation put upon it by his first followers – remain a vital pre-requisite for the true understanding of the whole Christian movement.[2]

As we have already seen, Cadoux believed that Barth's and Brunner's apparent lack of interest in the historical evidence for the life and teaching was 'erroneous and regrettable'. He was likewise unable to welcome the work of Bultmann and the Form Critics, who attempted to trace the history of biblical material before it was written down:

When one asks how exactly the new study has helped us to distinguish better between factual record and legendary accretion, the answer is meagre and disappointing.[3]

Neither was he prepared to accept the view of Sir Edwyn Hoskyns, expressed in *The Riddle of the New Testament* (1931), that Mark's

[1] *Ibid.*
[2] *The Historic Mission of Jesus* (1941) p.1.
[3] *Ibid.* p.7.

Gospel as much as John's was primarily a work of theological interpretation. What he did accept were 'the ripest findings of Drs Streeter, Vincent Taylor and T. W. Manson', whose theories he regarded as 'certainly the best yet reached by critical research'.

It was Cadoux's suspicion of the apparently 'anti-historical' theological ideas emanating from Germany, and therefore his rejection of the most original ideas in Protestant theological scholarship in the 1930s, which led the Dean of Christ Church, John Lowe, reviewing Cadoux's book in the *Journal of Theological Studies* (January–April 1943), to say that though few people could have read recent New Testament studies of the previous twenty years more carefully than Cadoux, yet his book 'smacks of the 1920s rather than of the present day'.

The Historic Mission of Jesus had four sections: 'the bringer of the Kingdom', 'The nature and presence of the Kingdom of God', 'The future of the Kingdom as first envisaged' and 'The future of the Kingdom as last envisaged'. The material on which it was based came largely, though not entirely, from the Synoptic Gospels. In an early article,[1] Cadoux had argued that there was a certain amount of reliable chronology in John's Gospel, especially the framework of Jewish festivals within which the discourses and miracles of Jesus are structured. Some evidence was used therefore from the Fourth Gospel in support of the main argument.

The Kingdom of God was the central theme of Jesus' teaching. Cadoux felt that it was right to devote the first part of the work to an examination of Jesus' teaching about himself; Jesus knew himself to be in 'the closest filial intimacy with God as his Father'; it led him to stress for himself and others the Fatherhood of God, charging that relationship 'with a fulness and depth of meaning for which his hearers had no precedent'. As the Fatherhood of God was the supreme reality, Jesus lived in unqualified obedience to his Father.

This sense of being engaged entirely in God's service led him to apply to himself, and enable him to derive support and guidance from, the Deutero-Isaianic passages portraying the Servant of the Lord and describing his experience.[2]

Out of this understanding flowed Jesus' compassion for individual men and women and his longing for their salvation – that is 'the fulfilment by man of God's purpose for him, i.e. man's filial, loving, obedient, and intimate relationship with God'.

[1] *Journal of Theological Studies* (July 1919), 'The Johannine account of the early ministry of Jesus'.
[2] *The Historic Mission of Jesus* p.37.

Though Jesus knew himself to be the Messiah, 'we ought to think of his Messianic consciousness as secondary and subordinate to his filial consciousness . . .'. He also claimed that ambiguous title, 'the Son of Man', for himself. Altogether

> he assumed an authority over men superior to that of any other authority they knew; yet this authority was not in the last analysis arbitrary and despotic, since he referred men to their own powers of insight for the verification of his pronouncements.[1]

The Aramaic and Greek words translated into English as 'kingdom' were understood better, Cadoux claimed, as 'sovereignty' rather than 'domain'. The Kingdom, for Jesus, was 'a society of human beings, and a growing society at that'. It was a present fact, but also a future realisation; Jesus looked forward to a future climax, when the Kingdom would 'come with power'. Thus Cadoux did not altogether accept the theory of his former colleague, C. H. Dodd, of 'realised eschatology' – that the life, teaching, death and resurrection of Jesus themselves constituted the coming of the Kingdom, and that Jesus' mission was to proclaim this fact; that God had intervened in history to inaugurate His Kingdom.

Cadoux laid much more stress on Jesus' proclamation of the way of life required in the Kingdom. The ethic taught by Jesus was not 'an interim ethic', to be followed in the short time before the expected apocalyptic climax of history; it was the 'ethical imperative' of the Kingdom.

This 'ethical imperative' was not a series of laws in the old sense, but yet, Cadoux claimed, there was a sense in which Jesus could be considered a legislator:

> . . . knowing as he did that the purified heart is dependent on a wisely-guided judgment if it is to eventuate in a righteous life, he devoted a fair proportion of his time as a teacher to specifying the kind of conduct which the children of God ought to exhibit. We may, if we will, call these detailed injunctions of his simply illustrations of the all-important inward spirit; but that is not to deny that they are at the same time definite laws, not indeed imposed in any arbitrary or external way, nor capable of being coercively enforced, but worded – like the laws of the Old Testament – as definite imperatives, addressed to the free and responsible wills of men, and seriously intended by Jesus, not simply as suggestions, still less as impossible demands beyond the power of men to obey, but as requirements which they can and ought to fulfill.[2]

[1] *Ibid.* p.103.   [2] *Ibid.* p.119.

These requirements had both an individual and a corporate application. The Kingdom exists wherever and whenever men are obedient to that ethic. Jesus began his ministry expecting that Israel would 'receive, honour and follow him'. The Kingdom would come by God's power and in God's own time, yet 'not so as to dispense with the need of man's strenuous efforts and prayers'.

In an interesting, even provocative, chapter on 'The political significance of the Kingdom', Cadoux argued that Jesus was involved in the political aspirations of the people of Palestine; as Messiah, Jesus was assuming a role with strong nationalist implications. At the same time, he taught love for one's enemies, rejected the temptation to snatch at world dominion, and enjoined the payment of tribute to Caesar. Was it not reasonable to conclude that he wished Israel to give up her desire for vengeance on Rome, to accept injustice without retaliation, and to reveal the loving nature of God through humility, forbearance and love?

> The coming of God's kingdom on earth involved such healing ministry as this on Israel's part – a zealous, united and triumphant execution of that mission to heathendom which had been so sporadically and half-heartedly attempted in the course of the few preceding centuries. [1]

This was not to be. Jesus and his message were rejected.

The Kingdom 'as last envisaged' was therefore to be inaugurated not through success but through suffering and death. Obedience to God's will led Jesus to the Cross; he believed that by accepting it, he would be the means of bringing men to repentance, and so of heralding the final coming of the Kingdom, when he would return to earth in glory. Careful meditation on *Isaiah* 53 illuminated this idea further. The writer of *Isaiah* and his contemporaries had come to the understanding that the sufferings of the servant were not for his own sin, but for theirs; 'his death was a sacrifice to bring forgiveness (*Isaiah* 53.10)'. This was not a purely subjective theory of the Atonement; the 'willingness of God to meet out of His own resources the cost of the damage wrought by human sin' was an objective basis of redemption.

Cadoux wrote this book as war threatened in Europe.

> The heart turns sick when we are reminded of the concentration camps of Central Europe and the firing squads of Spain. Is there not some vital connexion between the revolting character of these horrors and their total and flagrant incongruity with the values for the sake of which Jesus undertook his great enterprise? [2]

[1] *Ibid.* p.173.   [2] *Ibid.* p.350.

> The Kingdom of God is still at hand . . . The prospect of the Coming Kingdom still remains the lode-star of all healthy human effort.[1]

What began as an academic treatise finished as a passionate plea for the search for righteousness and peace.

T. W. Manson wrote in the *Mansfield College Magazine* (July 1942):

> I am very glad that the book has been published; and I venture to commend it specially to those who, not having been brought up in the Liberal tradition, and having heard that Harnack is dead, are inclined to the view that he and the other Liberals died theologically bankrupt and intestate. There is a lot to be learned from this book, and not least by those who will disagree before they open it, and still disagree when they have finished it.

Some thought it was Cadoux's best book. Though written from a standpoint which few would share today, there is much in the detailed discussion which still repays study.

A very full and detailed criticism of *The Historic Mission of Jesus* appeared in the *Church Quarterly Review*, in a review article by A. C. Headlam (January 1943). In a sense it was a tribute to the book that a prominent Anglican scholar should have been allowed thirty pages in which to discuss it. Headlam himself was a New Testament scholar whose widely-read *Life and Teaching of Jesus Christ* was first published in 1923.

Headlam recognized Cadoux's work as 'an English contribution to the "Quest of the Historical Jesus"', and 'a work of learning and of painstaking investigation' from which much might be learned, 'partly from what we may agree with, partly from what we may disagree with'. He examined very carefully some of Cadoux's specific claims about Jesus' ministry – that Jesus first expected the Jewish nation to accept him, that he did not foretell his rising from the dead, for example – in order to examine Cadoux's methods of historical criticism; he came to the conclusion that Cadoux was too ready to propose that passages in the Gospels which were inconsistent with his theses were therefore not genuine, to eliminate from the record anything which might conflict with his conclusion.

> Dr Cadoux is very critical of the Fundamentalists and Roman Catholics because they arrive at their conclusions on dogmatic grounds. He fails to see that his conclusions are equally arrived at on dogmatic grounds, although his dogmas are different from those of Roman Catholics and Fundamentalists.[2]

[1] *Ibid*. p.353.
[2] *Church Quarterly Review* (January 1943), p.202.

Cadoux was much upset by this review, but at least he was allowed the right of reply; the *Church Quarterly Review* published his rejoinder, eighteen pages long, in the July issue.

He answered Headlam's detailed criticisms of his use of the Gospel texts, and rejected the charge that he and other modernist scholars approached these texts with their minds made up:

> The historian's task is to reconstruct the past. For this purpose he must not only consider the relative dates and comparative value of his sources; he must put the story together out of the statements they contain. In doing this, he cannot simply make a mosaic of these statements, and present that as his picture. He has to allow for some pieces of his material being less reliable than others, and for some of them possibly being wholly unreliable.[1]

Cadoux believed that the New Testament could yield strictly historical truth; his critics believed that history and theology were inseparable in the New Testament.

The Life of Jesus was designed for the general reader, but in essence covered most of the same ground as the *Historic Mission of Jesus*. It was an attempt to write an account of the historical facts of Jesus' life based on a critical study of the Gospels.

> I am convinced that a simple application of the normal standards of judgment with which historical and scientific study has made us familiar will enable us to arrive at a fair amount of accurate narrative.[2]

The pattern of *The Historic Mission of Jesus* was adopted in a less technical account. The book began with a preliminary chapter on sources, and then continued with a chapter on 'Birth and home life' which may have startled the general reader with its opening statement that Jesus was probably born in Nazareth, the first child of Mary and her husband Joseph. Cadoux was not prepared to treat the tradition of the Virgin Birth as a mystery which cannot be explained.

> If a miracle is asserted to have occurred, and cogent evidence for its occurrence cannot be adduced, and belief in it can be readily accounted for along other lines, the duty of scholars is not to leave the reality of it an open question, but to reject it, not as inconceivable, but as in all probability not true.[3]

After chapters on Jesus' early years and his association with John the Baptist, there was a section headed 'The outlook and purpose of Jesus', which distilled the essence of the first section of *The Historic*

---

[1] *Church Quarterly Review* (July 1943) p.188.
[2] *The Life of Jesus* (1948) p.10.
[3] *Ibid.* p.30.

Mission of Jesus. There followed an account of Jesus' miracles and teaching before the entry into Jerusalem: 'The brighter months of the ministry' – the Kingdom as first envisaged, and 'Growing shadows' – the Kingdom as last envisaged.

The miracles present a peculiar problem to the historian; he will ask and try to answer the question, did these special events recorded in the Gospels actually occur? Cadoux laid it down as an axiom that 'the more unlikely an incident, the stronger will be the evidence we shall require as a condition of believing it to have occurred'. Working from that axiom, from the known laws of nature and from examining the evidence carefully, Cadoux came to the conclusion that while the healing miracles could reasonably be accepted, the evidence for the nature miracles was not strong enough to justify belief.

In constructing the second half of the book, Cadoux found himself (like the Gospel writers) bound to include some kind of interpretation as well as narrative. Between the chapter on 'The growing shadows' and that on 'The last days' came a discussion of 'The altered forecast'. Jesus' initial hopes of acceptance by the Jewish people were dashed and he faced mounting opposition. Yet he deliberately set out for Jerusalem.

> His reason for doing so was simply unflinching adherence to the path of duty. His love for men ruled out the idea of armed revolt; the mission to his countrymen with which he was charged ruled out silence and departure. The fatal consequence of the only remaining alternative he found foreshadowed in the fifty-third chapter of 'Isaiah' as the lot of God's special Servant and as the destined prelude to that Servant's final victory.[1]

What then did Jesus look forward to? Three times he predicted that he would be put to death, but would rise again three days later (or on the third day). Several times he alluded to the return of the Son of Man in glory within the lifetime of his listeners. How are these predictions to be interpreted, in the light of subsequent events? Cadoux's hypothesis, now repeated, had first been put forward in his pamphlet on *The Resurrection and Second Advent of Jesus* (1927);[2] that the phrase 'three days later' or 'on the third day' need not be understood literally, but could mean 'after a short indefinable interval'. Thus Jesus' prediction of rising again could be understood as synonymous with his forecast of returning in glory. The empty tomb and the appearances to the disciples, reported in each of the gospels, were not, according to Cadoux, the fulfilment of Jesus's prophecies of

[1] *Ibid.* p.154.
[2] See above, pp.102-103.

rising again, nor evidence of any physical resurrection. He found the evidence for the empty tomb 'weaker than that for the appearances, and not strong enough . . . to command belief'.[1] The resurrection appearances he explained as 'objective visions' – objective in the sense that the disciples did really and collectively have these experiences, that they regarded them as proof of Jesus' continued existence and conquest of death, and that they were henceforth inspired to preach the Gospel to the world. Cadoux held that this interpretation was compatible with his and others' faith that Jesus had 'overcome the sharpness of death'.

He recognized that the more one pondered on this mystery, 'the more are we made aware of an atmosphere of vagueness or mistiness pervading the whole subject'. His solution would not have satisfied all his readers. While he felt that he had managed 'to push the resources of critical scholarship to their very utmost limits', some may have felt that he had pushed them even further. We may have to add that the question, 'what happened when Jesus died?' cannot be answered by the ordinary canons of historical research.

It is not easy to decide at what point a life of Jesus should end, for this is where the attempt to distinguish between history and theology, between the temporal and the eternal, the human and the divine, comes to an impasse. The resurrection brings us to the encounter between two realms which defies any ordinary category of thought. Cadoux accepted that it was impossible to try to construct a narrative of the appearances of the Risen Christ, for these events had passed beyond the realm of history as humanly understood.

After an epilogue which discussed some of the problems inherent in the task he had set himself, Cadoux finished the book with these words:

> . . . whatever be the mysteries and the difficulties, the disagreements and the controversies, the problems and the perplexities, involved in the quest for the historical Jesus, that quest, honestly and lovingly pursued, is one fraught with abundant blessing for us – one which cannot be dropped or by-passed without our forfeiting in large measure those glorious gifts of life, light and peace, which God Himself imparts to us in and through him who, in great loving kindness and amid sharp self-sacrifice, claimed to be – and is known to have been and still to be – the rightful Lord of men.[2]

It was not a work of imaginative or poetic insight, such as his former

[1] See *The Life of Jesus* (1948) pp.164-167, 207.
[2] *Ibid.* p.224.

critic, A. D. Martin, wrote in *A Plain Man's Life of Christ* (1941); but it was a thought-provoking, honest attempt to grapple with the intellectual problems presented to any serious enquirer by the basic texts of the Christian faith. While it appeared radical to many, and others felt that he had underestimated the difficulty of being objective, all recognized his honesty, sincerity and erudition. Above all, the subject of this book inspired and sustained Cadoux's own life to the end.

XVII

Last years
1945-1947

CADOUX WAS DUE to retire from Mansfield in 1948, when he would reach the age of 65. He would receive a modest pension, but there were still Joan's school fees to be paid. How would he manage? At one time he even wondered about making a living as a portrait artist.

He realised that his strength was waning. A note of despair sometimes appeared in his diaries. 'Dreadful sense of frustration; and fear that my strength won't last out to complete my "Mediaeval and Modern Smyrna". Yet wife, Ruth and Joan all very kind to me'.

His family life now meant more and more to him. Three weeks after writing that entry in his diary came the news that Harold had been released. On 27 April 1945 Cadoux was at Oxford station with Ruth to meet him; it was five years and four months since they had last met. There was 'great rejoicing' at the reunion. Further rejoicing came a fortnight later when the war in Europe came to an end. 'It is all very moving. We cannot take it in', Cadoux wrote (9 May) to Theo.

After the first excitement of Harold's return home there were inevitably some difficulties of readjustment, for they had all changed in a period of five years, during which communication had been almost non-existent. It was most difficult of all for Harold, who had lived such a restricted life for the previous four years. He was moody sometimes and difficult to understand. But as the atmosphere became more relaxed, and communication became easier, Cadoux found a new happiness in his relationship with Harold.

Harold remained in the Friends' Ambulance Unit for a while. After a long rest at home he returned to the Unit headquarters in London, and then volunteered for service in reconstruction work in Germany. His intention in the long term was always to return to engineering work at British Thomson Houston in Rugby.

In the FAU he met and became friendly with Lilian Humble; he took her to Oxford to meet his parents; and soon afterwards they became engaged. On 13 January 1946 Harold wrote to his father – 'I have just written to Lilian to ask her to put a notice of our engagement in the Unit Chronicle. You can tell your friends and relations proudly that your younger son is engaged – and I know you are proud'. Cadoux had welcomed Lilian into the family as an 'honoured guest' (as she herself later described it) but was alarmed at the thought of their getting married before Harold had a settled job and a regular income; he did his best to persuade them to wait, as he himself had done. Harold courteously but firmly told his father that he and Lilian had considered all the arguments to the contrary, but were quite sure about their decision to marry that spring; they asked for, and received, Cadoux's blessing.

They went through a civil ceremony in Germany in March, and planned a religious ceremony later at home. When they eventually reached Oxford in June, Cadoux was confined to the house again with heart trouble. His entry for 18 June reads: '6.15 Moxley[1] calls and marries Harold and Lilian in presence of family in my study'.

Theo was still in Greece at the end of the war, and had to wait until December 1945 before being allowed home. He resumed his research work with the support of Queen's, and lived at home for the whole of 1946. In the course of this year he applied for a number of academic positions in Oxford and elsewhere. Cadoux was very thrilled when Theo was eventually offered, and accepted, an assistant lectureship in Greek in the University College of South Wales at Cardiff. He began work there in January 1947.

Ruth had delighted her father by her success in the examinations at the end of her second year at St Anne's. He wrote to Theo on 9 July 1945 – 'The great news is that our darling Ruthie has pulled off a *first* in her Science Honour Mods. We are all very glad and congratulations have been pouring in'.

Joan embarked on a new phase of her school career by going off to boarding school in September 1945. Milton Mount College had been founded in order to educate the daughters of Congregational ministers, and such girls were given substantial bursaries. So it was within the family means to send Joan. The school, which had been evacuated to Lynton, in north Devon, early in the war, did not return to its old home at Worth Park, Sussex, until the summer of 1946. It was therefore to Lynton that Joan travelled on 18 September 1945.

It was not possible for Cadoux to avoid controversy for long. He was now involved in the discussions about possible reunion between Congregationalists and Presbyterians. Formal discussions on this

[1] H. R. Moxley, minister of Summertown Congregational Church.

theme had taken place before the war, without achieving agreement; they were now revived at the suggestion of the Presbyterians. At the May meetings of the Congregational Union in 1945, Cadoux had spoken in the Assembly against reunion with the Presbyterians. Now he was being regarded as one of the chief spokesmen of the 'anti-union' party.

During the next six weeks he wrote a 10,000 word pamphlet entitled *The Congregational Way*, eventually published by Blackwells in January 1946. It was a contribution to the debate on the proposed union.

Cadoux's oft-repeated views on church reunion formed the opening of the pamphlet. Inter-communion and interchange of pulpits, implying mutual recognition of ministries, would be the corollary to recognizing the true nature of the Christian Church as 'the whole company of professed disciples of Christ'; thus mutual co-operation between Congregationalist and Presbyterians was much to be desired. Organic unity, on the other hand, might well involve the sacrifice of much of the rich variety of Christian thought and practice. He then addressed himself to two questions. Would the proposed union, as distinct from the existing co-operation between the two denominations, promote real unity and more efficient Christian work; and further, would it involve the sacrifice of essential Congregational (or Presbyterian) principles?

The most valuable aspect of Congregationalism, he claimed, was its 'catholicity'; it was 'the Universal Church in miniature'. It was 'not a sect or connexion at all, but a body truly catholic in character':

> Not only does it claim that in each of its local congregations, as in each local church of Apostolic times, the Church Universal is operating, but that in its *extensive* aspect the inclusiveness of its basis renders it a truer representative of the Catholicity of the One Church than any other denomination can possibly be.[1]

The word 'church', according to this understanding of Congregational principles, was to be used *either* of the local church, *or* of the Church Universal, never of the denomination.[2]

The refusal to impose credal tests, or to insist on baptism or attendance at the Lord's Supper, were characteristics of the Congregational ideal of 'an inclusive method of organisation'.

> . . . to impose on any man who professed faith in Christ, or faith in God through Christ, any humanly-constructed group of

---

[1] *The Congregational Way* (1946) pp.20-21.
[2] In practice, this changed in 1966 when the Congregational Union became the Congregational Church of England and Wales.

doctrines, however venerable, as an indispensable condition of admitting him to the Church, would be to violate the sacred bond between the believer and his Lord.[1]

This was not to devalue belief or doctrine; it was to affirm the direct link between God and the Christian believer, the 'priesthood of all believers'.

The sovereign independence of each local church was another aspect of this same principle:

> ... its freedom, that is, not from the duty of co-operating with its sister-churches and of listening to their advice, but from the *legal control* of any other body or person whatsoever, whether ecclesiastical or civil.[2]

The Presbyterian Church of England, on the other hand, was 'clearly organised as a sect or connexion'. Cadoux explained that he used the word 'sect' to describe 'a Christian denomination which is admittedly not planned on at least potentially catholic and inclusive lines'. Though no specific doctrinal statement was required of candidates for Presbyterian church membership, baptism was an absolute requirement. The synodical government of Presbyterianism did not commend itself to Cadoux, though he allowed that the authority of the Presbyterian General Assembly was a representative authority, and that it was normally exercised with the free consent of the whole membership.

While both Congregationalists and Presbyterians affirmed the priesthood of all believers, the Presbyterians drew a much clearer distinction between ministers and laymen. For the Presbyterian, the ministry was confined to men who had received formal ordination by 'the presbytery'; they would wear Genevan clerical dress, and they alone could administer the sacrament. Congregationalists prepared both men and women for the ministry and expected them normally to be ordained within the congregation to which they were first called to minister. (Those like Cadoux who were trained but not called specifically to the pastoral ministry, were at that time not necessarily ordained but were nevertheless accorded ministerial recognition by the Congregational Union).

> Yet it ought never to be forgotten that, according to the Congregational way, he is still essentially a Christian layman, called of God indeed and delegated by his brethren to duties of special difficulty, and solemnly set apart for that purpose, yet not marked off from these brethren by any sacerdotal stamp or other essential distinction of class or caste empowering him to perform

[1] *The Congregational Way* p.17.   [2] *Ibid.* p.18.

functions which they, through lack of that stamp or distinction, are inherently debarred from performing.[1]

Cadoux recognized that not all Congregationalists agreed with him. Some laid greater emphasis on the conformity of the Church to a pattern which they believed was laid down in the New Testament; some placed a much greater emphasis on the sacraments; some laid stress on the significance of clerical dress in symbolising the special status of the ministry. Some stressed the common inheritance of both Congregationalists and Presbyterians in Reformed churchmanship, and the value to both of a joint exploration of that inheritance. Cadoux recognized these different views as part of the variety contained within Congregational 'catholicity'.

The reader of *The Congregational Way* might have been left with a somewhat idealised picture of Congregationalism. However, it was important for the debate that the values of the Congregational tradition should be stated forcefully, by a competent and convinced scholar. The editorial of the *Congregational Quarterly* (April 1946) advised its readers – 'We have commended Dr Cadoux's booklet as an admirable statement of his case, but it is right that before giving a judgment Congregationalists should hear other points of view'. In the end those other points of view prevailed, and the two denominations eventually came together as the United Reformed Church in 1972.

There were many Congregationalists who wished Cadoux's convictions to be heard at the forefront of the denominational councils. Partly for this reason, and partly as a personal honour, the Cornwall Congregational Union asked Cadoux if they might nominate him for the Chair of the Congregational Union of England and Wales – the highest honour the denomination could bestow on any of its members. Sadly he felt he must decline. His health simply would not stand up to the constant travelling round the country which the office would entail, let alone the stress of the controversy in which he was bound to find himself involved.

He was a 'controversialist' to the last. At Mansfield his Reformation lectures gave him the opportunity of the occasional provocative remark. He wrote to Theo on 4 November 1945 about his 'fine class': 'There is a stout man – Canadian, I think – whose face absolutely beams with mischievous delight every time I make a thrust on behalf of Liberal Protestantism'.

Theological controversy was not confined to the lecture room or academic journal. Travelling often offered suitable opportunities. On his way to address the Cornwall Congregational Union in 1945 he had

[1] *Ibid.* p.27.

a long bus journey. He wrote to Ruth (23 September): 'I sat – from Bristol to Exeter – next to a high Anglo-Catholic lady, who, tho' nice, was very prejudiced agst Non-Conformists and in particular down on Cromwell. She had to be dealt with. I needn't say any more than that!'

Joan was sometimes embarrassed by the eagerness with which he launched into argument with fellow-passengers on train journeys. She remembers how, just after the end of the war, he walked into a compartment reserved for American soldiers and sat down (his heart condition made standing for long periods dangerous). When the soldiers arrived, he refused to move; although the military policeman protested to him, the soldiers soon agreed that there was room for all of them. The soldiers then began to play poker. He started to remonstrate with them, managed to change the direction of activity from card-playing to a discussion of ethics, and finished the journey by shaking hands with them amid expressions of warm friendship. He was not thick-skinned, and did not enter into such encounters with enthusiasm; but he was prompted by his sense of duty, and his courteous manner usually disarmed those whom he approached.

In April 1946 he paid his last visit to Bradford, on his way to give two addresses to the Lancashire Congregational Union. Not many days after his return he was taken ill again. Once more he had to abandon his lectures for the term; he spent the whole summer as an invalid upstairs. He was able to write an article, do a little proof-reading and keep up with his reading; and there were plenty of visitors who kept him in touch with college affairs.

By the time Michaelmas term (1946) began he was well enough to resume lectures, so long as a friend could drive him to and fro. Otherwise he was not able to play much part in college life.

At the end of that term, he had one of his happiest visits to friends. It was to the Becks in Caterham. Teddy Beck had been one of his 'boys' in his Sunday School class at Trinity Church, Catford. Now, after a career in business, and with a grown up family (including a son who was already a Congregational minister), Teddy Beck had decided to seek ordination. He had asked Cadoux to give the charge to the minister at his ordination service at Caterham Hill Congregational Church.

Cadoux went to stay with the Becks a few days before the ordination in order to enjoy a rest and to see other friends and members of the family. He visited Joan at Milton Mount, and there met not only some of her teachers but also many of her contemporaries who were the daughters of a number of his former students. He had a happy time with Bernard and his family in south Croydon – 'jolly talk and family jokes'. At the end of her term, Joan joined him for the last day of his stay, before they returned home together for Christmas. It had been a thoroughly happy time.

A great family event was expected any day: the birth of the first grandchild. Harold and Lilian were now living in a small cottage at Long Itchington, near Rugby, where Harold was working for his old firm, British Thomson Houston. Though originally expected on 29 December, the baby did not finally arrive until 24 January – a son. It was an exciting moment. Cadoux wrote to Harold two days later:

We were all tremendously bucked to get your phone news on Friday evening. Rejoicing greatly, we fetched down the family-tree then and there, and solemnly entered up the birth of MICHAEL JOHN. Jim was with us and fully entered into the spirit of the meeting. . . . special message of encouragement and congratul^n to Lilian, and all blessings to the babe. How little he realizes that his is the privilege of keeping the great name of Cadoux echoing down the centuries.

Three weeks later Jim Wickett drove the family over to Long Itchington to see the new Cadoux. It was an occasion of great excitement.

Jim Wickett was now engaged to Ruth. Cadoux did not live to see their wedding, but had welcomed their engagement, and gave them his blessing.

The household was now reduced in size. Ruth was the only member of the family left permanently at home; the lodgers had gone, and Theo and Joan came home only for the vacations. The top floor of the house had now been made into a self-contained flat, which produced some extra revenue.

In that first term of 1947 Cadoux was able to give most of his lectures, but by the beginning of March, he was ill again, this time with pneumonia. He made a partial recovery, enough to become embroiled in a controversy in *The Christian World* about the Congregational-Presbyterian negotiations, and in *The Congregational Quarterly* about his review of H. Cunliffe-Jones' book, *The Authority of the Bible*. In May, he had another spell in the Acland Nursing Home.

The last university function he attended was Encaenia on 25 June, when honorary degrees were presented to a number of distinguished people. He wore his DLitt robe and hood, and enjoyed processing 'thro' admiring crowds' to the Sheldonian Theatre. In the afternoon he met numerous old friends at the university garden party.

That same day he received an invitation to spend a few days with the

Morleys, friends of an old student of his who lived in Bath. He had wanted the opportunity to relax, convalesce, and correct the proofs of *The Life of Jesus,* somewhere out of Oxford. This relieved the household, for Marguerite had just broken her wrist and Ruth was taking her final examinations. Theo came home from Cardiff to help. In Bath he enjoyed the quiet and peace of a beautiful garden, and the hospitality of his host and hostess. Dr and Mrs Morley were used to living to a precise timetable, but even they were a little startled when Cadoux, told that breakfast would be at 8 o'clock, asked that he should have a glass of hot water brought to his room at 7.20; this would give him time, he said, not only to dress and shave, but also to do his regular ten minutes of Hebrew and ten minutes of Greek. His regular, scholarly discipline continued until his strength finally gave out.

From Bath he went on to Bristol for another few days to stay with the Bryan family. Here he met more friends. This stay was clouded by his hearing that Maud, his youngest sister, was very ill and not expected to live. When he arrived back at Oxford station on 9 July, Theo was there to tell him that Maud had died that same morning: the first break in the family since Herbert's death more than forty years before.

Though it would inevitably involve further strain, he was determined to go to her funeral. He and Theo travelled to Tonbridge to pay their last respects to a much-loved member of the family. Maud was warm-hearted, generous, loyal, always grateful to Jack and Marguerite for having taken her in when she and Annabel fled from Glasgow. She had never lost her cheerfulness or sense of humour in spite of many years of deafness and ill-health. Harold wrote to his father in warmly appreciative terms about 'aunt Maud' which Cadoux found 'a very fine comforting letter'.

By the end of July Cadoux was too unwell to attend Michael's baptism at Summertown Congregational Church. He was now confined to bed; a consultant called in by his doctor warned him and the family on 4 August that the prognosis was poor, but said he did not think he was in immediate danger. Consequently, Marguerite went to Portsmouth for a much-needed rest, leaving Theo in charge. On the 13th, however, he became suddenly weaker and realised himself he was near his end. Marguerite returned at once. Late in the evening of Saturday 16 August he died, with Marguerite and Theo at his bedside. His long struggle was over.

Letters soon began to pour into the house from all over the country – over 250 arrived over the next two or three weeks. The Fellowship of Reconciliation, holding its annual conference in Dorset, immediately sent a telegram of sympathy.

One of the most touching messages came by telegram from W. E. Orchard, now a Roman Catholic priest living in semi-retirement in Gloucestershire: 'Want you to know saying Mass for Doctor Cadoux tomorrow'. Their friendship and affection was stronger than any doctrinal barrier.

The funeral was held in Mansfield College Chapel on 19 August. Alec Whitehouse, the Chaplain, conducted the service, assisted by H. R. Moxley, minister of Summertown Congregational Church, and Will Moore gave the address. (The Principal was abroad.) All the immediate family except Joan were there, also Ida and her daughter Noreen, Bernard, and Maud's daughter Annabel, but neither Arthur nor Connie were in good enough health to be able to travel from Glasgow. (It had been one of the sadnesses of recent years that Jack and Arthur had not been able to meet and exchange ideas). A large congregation of Oxford friends and people from other parts of the country came to join the family in offering thanks for Jack Cadoux's life and work.

His body was laid to rest in Wolvercote cemetery; the gravestone bears the words 'Speaking the truth in love'.

Cadoux's life may be described as a theme with variations: the theme was the passion for truth. The variations did not explore very far or very adventurously, for Cadoux formed his ideas early, and they remained the basis of his subsequent research and reflection; moreover he was a remarkably consistent thinker. But we may identify five particular fields in each of which he made an important contribution. His insistence that the actual events of Jesus' life could be known, and that they *mattered*, was an important witness at a time when a number of the most creative theologians seemed to show little interest in them; his documentation of the thought of the early Church in *The Early Church and the World* remains a standard work of reference; *Catholicism and Christianity* was an original and magisterial 'vindication of progressive Protestantism'; his *Ancient Smyrna* is the only detailed study there is of the early history of that city; and his intellectual defence of pacifism provided stimulus and support for many faced with the moral problems posed by war.

As a writer, Cadoux appealed to the reason rather than to the imagination of his readers, and some will have found him too matter-of-fact for their taste. He always presented his arguments clearly, logically and thoroughly. He was never satisfied with facile or superficial thought; as one of his reviewers wrote after his death, '. . . there will always be need for writers like Dr Cadoux to warn us against slurring over differences which go deep and which cannot be settled until they are settled right'.[1]

As a teacher, he was demanding, but he could evoke great loyalty and affection. His most effective teaching and preaching was probably done in Bradford, where he was remembered with affection and admiration for many years. It was in Bradford that a C. J. Cadoux Memorial Lecture was endowed, and delivered annually by a succession of distinguished theologians for nearly 25 years.[2] On the other hand, it was Mansfield College, Oxford, which came first in his own affections. One of his students at Mansfield, Dafydd Ap-Thomas (later himself a theological teacher) recalls that 'to be taught by Cadoux was a rigorous discipline, but what most of us young would-be theologians needed'; Cadoux himself he remembers as 'the kindest and most companionable of men, and hospitable to a degree'. A tablet inscribed after Cadoux's death in the College Chapel ends with the motto, generously suggested by Principal Micklem, in spite of their differences, as a tribute to the life of his erstwhile colleague: PRO REGNO CHRISTI MOLITOR ('A labourer for Christ's kingdom') – fitly acknowledging a life-long devotion to his vocation.

He was extremely sensitive to cruelty, especially physical cruelty, whether to humans or animals (he had hoped one day to write a book on the treatment of animals, regarding it as 'a sadly neglected province in the field of ethics'). This very sensitivity perhaps contributed to his own vulnerability to criticism, and could even result in a lack of sensitivity towards others. His approach to life was intellectual rather than intuitive, academic rather than imaginative, and this limited his insight into the problems of others.

A keen controversialist, he valued friendship even more; many of his friendships were life-long. It hurt him deeply to experience a rift with an old friend; such rifts were few, but it has to be admitted that when they occurred, his own pertinacity made them more difficult to heal. In a social setting, he could show great courtesy, and considerable charm, and knew how to transform an awkward situation.

Family life he valued highly, and placed a great emphasis on the responsibilities of fatherhood; as he venerated his own father (and his teachers) so he evoked deep love and respect from his own children. His partnership with his wife was secure, though like many marriages of its time it suffered from lack of companionship; Marguerite Cadoux had to accept that her husband's time was to be devoted

---

[1] H. G. Wood in a review of *Roman Catholicism and Freedom* (4th edition 1947) in *The Hibbert Journal* April 1948 p.288.

[2] A list is given in Appendix C.

almost exclusively to his work. She was the anchor of his life and made his work possible, yet she received little public recognition; in his later years of recurrent ill-health, she accepted without complaint the burden of sustaining his spirits in long periods of depression. Her cheerfulness and good humour, her sheer common sense, provided the balance without which he might have foundered.

In character, Cadoux was a strong individualist, so that a theological and philosophical scheme which laid great emphasis on the importance of the individual conscience, individual participation and individual responsibility made great appeal to him. He was a born Independent, with the virtues and defects of that allegiance. There was, it is true, something unresolved within his own personality; it seems that he never really found peace of mind. Yet deep down, he had a firm faith in God as Father, and in God's love. The words his own father wrote in his Bible, 'Casting all your anxiety upon Him, for He careth for you', were a constant inspiration and strength to him. He once told Nathaniel Micklem that one of his favourite hymns was 'Just as I am, without one plea'; his theology did not express the whole of his faith.

Amongst the hundreds of tributes his family received, what his old friend Leyton Richards wrote sums up well the qualities for which his friends admired and loved him:

> He was such a doughty warrior for the Truth as he saw it, and I was only one of a great many who turned to him for intellectual leading amid the reactions of recent years. He 'kept the faith' if ever man did, and he 'fought a good fight' unsullied by ill-temper or lack of charity. It is not all of us who do that or are capable of it. And then, for me there was more than intellectual companionship; he was a man to be loved because he himself so loved his friends. I always thought of him with affection, and our too rare meetings warmed my heart as well as stirred my mind. I learnt a tremendous lot from him, and it was a joy to feel that I came to see eye to eye with him increasingly; for he had the scholarship which could justify the positions we held or which could at least defend them in a way to which I cannot pretend.
>
> . . . I mourn with you in Jack's going from us, even though I rejoice in his freedom from the disabilities against which he so bravely and patiently battled. If ever a man – quite literally – 'spoke as a dying man to dying men', it was he during the past years; and his speech has not been without effects which can never be measured. I 'bless every remembrance of him' and thank God for a most fruitful friendship.

Appendix A

THE CADOUX PAPERS

Cadoux left an immense amount of carefully sorted papers. Even after much had been thrown away, there remained a considerable quantity of material which seemed likely to be of interest not only to the family but also to other investigators. It falls into the following categories:

(1) *Personal records:* his diaries (from 1903), letters received (from 1900), his drawings, records of daily reading, schedules of study, lists of church services taken, etc.

(2) *Publications:* correspondence relating to all his major works, and a complete set of his minor publications, viz. articles, contributions to books, pamphlets, reviews, letters to the press, etc. (some 300 items in all), with a chronological catalogue; also a ms. of part of the projected second volume of his history of Smyrna, reaching AD 1230.

(3) *Family records:* information about the history of the whole Cadoux family in Britain (including the branch now known as Hudson or Cadoux-Hudson) and its French origin, as also about other connected families (Temples, Hobsons, Candlers, Asplins); some additions to these records have been made since his death.

The bulk of this material has been made permanently available for consultation in the Bodleian Library, Oxford, under the care of the Keeper of Western Manuscripts. For the time being the diaries and drawings, the ms. of the second volume on Smyrna, a typescript history of the firm of MacAndrews and Forbes, and some items from category (3) above, have been retained by his children. Enquiries may be directed to Dr T. J. Cadoux at 27 Gayfield Square, Edinburgh.

Appendix B

PUBLISHED WORKS OF C.J.CADOUX

I. BOOKS

The Early Christian Attitude to War: A Contribution to the History of Christian Ethics, London 1919.
— another edition 1940.
— reissued New York 1982.
The Guidance of Jesus for Today, London 1920.
The Christian Crusade: A Study in the Supreme Purpose of Life, London 1924.
The Message about the Cross: A Fresh Study of the Doctrine of the Atonement, London 1924.
The Early Church and the World: A History of the Christian Attitude to Pagan Society and the State down to the Time of Constantine, Edinburgh 1925.
Catholicism and Christianity: A Vindication of Progressive Protestantism, London 1928.
Roman Catholicism and Freedom, London 1936.
— Second edition 1936.
— Third edition 1937.
— Fourth edition 1947.
Ancient Smyrna: A History of the City from the Earliest Times to 324 AD, Oxford 1938.
The Case for Evangelical Modernism: A Study of the Relation between Christian Faith and Traditional Theology, London 1938.
Christian Pacifism Re-examined, Oxford 1940.
The Historic Mission of Jesus: A Constructive Re-examination of the Eschatological Teaching in the Synoptic Gospels, London 1941.
A Pilgrim's Further Progress: Dialogues on Christian Teaching, Oxford 1943.
Philip of Spain and the Netherlands: An Essay on Moral Judgments in History, London 1947.
The Life of Jesus, West Drayton 1948.

II. CONTRIBUTIONS TO PUBLISHED VOLUMES

'The Witness of the Church' in *The Ministry of Reconciliation*, ed. H. Martin, London 1916, pp.31-50.
'Congregationalism the true Catholicism' in *Essays Congregational and Catholic*, ed. Albert Peel, London 1931, pp.53-77.
'Zwingli' in *Christian Worship*, ed. N. Micklem, Oxford 1936, pp.137-53.

'The Revised Version and After' in *Ancient and English Versions of the Bible*, ed. H. Wheeler Robinson, Oxford 1940, pp.235-74.

Biographical Memoir in J. V. Bartlet, *Church Life and Church Order during the First Four Centuries*, ed. C. J. Cadoux, Oxford 1943, pp.xiv-lviii.

'What the Cross means to me' in a symposium of that title, ed. H. E. Brierley, London 1943, pp.29-39.

III. PAMPHLETS

An Appeal to the People of the Christian Church (for the Fellowship of Reconciliation), London 1919.

The Meaning of the Cross for Christian Ethics (being the last section of *The Message about the Cross*), Leeds 1924.

The Resurrection and the Second Advent of Jesus, London 1927.

The Possibility of a United Christendom: From the Standpoint of the Congregational Communion (in preparation for the International Convention on the Union of Christendom 1940), London 1937.

The Spiritual Principles of the Reformation, London 1938.

The Congregational Way, Oxford 1945.

IV. ARTICLES

This list includes all C. J. Cadoux's more scholarly articles. A complete list of his minor publications is to be found lodged with *The Cadoux Papers* (see Appendix A).

Abbreviations:

BJRL	*Bulletin of the John Rylands Library*
CC	*The Christian Century*
CQ	*Congregational Quarterly*
ConsQ	*The Constructive Quarterly*
CR	*The Contemporary Review*
Ex	*The Expositor*
ET	*The Expository Times*
HJ	*The Hibbert Journal*
I	*The Interpreter*
IJE	*The International Journal of Ethics*
JBL	*The Journal of Biblical Literature*
JR	*The Journal of Religion*
JTS	*The Journal of Theological Studies*
LQHR	*The London Quarterly and Holborn Review*
MC	*The Modern Churchman*
NA	*The Nineteenth Century and After*
Pr	*The Preacher*
R	*Reconciliation*
V	*The Venturer*

'The Ethics of a Hebrew Lawyer', *I* XII (Jan. 1916), pp.158-69.

'St Paul's Conception of the State', *Ex* 8th series XII (Aug. 1916), pp.135-47.

'Our Lord's Conception of the State', *Ex* 8th series XIII (Oct. 1916), pp.41-9.

Appendix B

'The Implications of Mutual Tolerance', *V* II (Jan. 1917), pp.117-20.
'The Attitude of Jesus to the Jewish Administration of Justice', *Ex* 8th series XIII (April 1917), pp.309-20.
'Christian pacifism and the state', *V* II (May 1917), pp.225-31.
'The chronological divisions of Acts', *JTS* XIX (July 1918), pp.333-41.
'The Christian idea of God and its bearing on human conduct', *V* III (Sept. 1918), pp.269-73.
'The Johannine account of the early ministry of Jesus', *JTS* XX (July 1919), pp.311-20.
'The subjective element in churchmanship', *ConsQ* VII (Sept. 1919), pp.517-30.
'The place of Jesus' ethical teaching in modern Christian life', *Ex* 8th series XIX (Feb. 1920), pp.96-110.
'The crux of the problem of Christian reunion', *V* I (new series) (Aug. 1920), pp.407-12.
'The proposed credal basis of Christian reunion', *JR* I (Nov. 1921), pp.592-607.
'The individual factor in social progress', *IJE* XXXII (Jan. 1922), pp.129-41.
'Anglicanism and reunion – a Freechurchman's Eirenikon', *ConsQ* X (Mar. 1922), pp.1-19.
'The quest for John the elder', *Ex* 8th series XXIII (Mar. 1922), pp.206-20.
'Christianity and the conflict of duties', *CR* no.679 (July 1922), pp.72-80.
'The early Christian Church in Egypt', *ET* XXXIII (Sept. 1922), pp.536-9.
'Should we all be perfect?', *HJ* XXI (Jan. 1923), pp.327-36.
'The Christian concern with history', *JR* III (May 1923), pp.225-37.
'Homer and modern thought', *NA* XCV (Mar. 1924), pp.386-97.
'The spiritual meaning of Biblical criticism', *CQ* II (April 1924), pp.184-95.
'The ten best books on the Synoptic Gospels', *Ex* 9th series II (Aug. 1924), pp.84-93.
'The nature of authority in religion', *R* I (Nov. 1924), pp.189-91.
'The visits of Jesus to Jerusalem', *Ex* 9th series III (Mar. 1925), pp.175-92.
'The Gospel-story and the higher criticism of today', *HJ* XXIII (July 1925), pp.611-21.
'God, history and ourselves: a study of the relationship between historical belief and religious experience', *CQ* IV (April 1926), pp.152-66.
'Judaism and universalism in the Gospels', *ET* XXXVIII (Nov. and Dec. 1926), pp.56-60.
'A defence of Christian modernism', *CQ* V (April 1927), pp.164-72.
'The way of Jesus', *R* V (Nov. 1928), pp.212-13.
'Hesiod, a neglected pioneer-poet', *NA* CV (Feb. 1929), pp.256-68.
'The person of Christ as determining our idea of God', *CQ* VII (Oct. 1929), pp.534-49.
'Catholicism and toleration', *CR* no.768 (Dec. 1929), pp.757-65.
'The Cross in modern life', *CC* Dec. 1931, pp.1649-51.
'Dr B. W. Bacon's views on Gospel-origins', *LQHR* 6th series II (July 1933), pp.289-308.
'What does the Crucifixion mean?', *HJ* XXXII (Oct. 1933), pp.70-80.
'Jesus and the problems of prayer', *CQ* XII (Jan. 1934), pp.29-37.

'The ethics of coercion', *CR* CXLV (June 1934), pp.688-97.

'The doctrine of the Church in the light of Christian history' (Inaugural lecture from the Mackennal Chair of Church History in Mansfield College, Oxford), *CQ* XII (July 1934), pp.284-97.

'The dates and provenance of the imprisonment epistles of St Paul', *ET* XLV (July 1934), pp.471-3.

'Authority in religion', *MC* XXIV (Dec. 1934), pp.509-22.

'The historical Jesus: a study of Schweitzer and after', *ET* XLVI (June 1935), pp.406-10.

'Dr Klausner's estimate of Jesus', *LQHR* 6th series IV (July 1935), pp.306-21.

'The politics of Jesus', *CQ* XIV (Jan. 1936), pp.58-67.

'The liberal-modernist view of Jesus', *HJ* XXXIV (Jan. 1936), pp.288-99.

'The conception of community in the history of the Church', *CQ* XIV (Oct. 1936), pp.503-11.

'A tentative synthetic chronology of the apostolic age', *JBL* LVI (Sept. 1937), pp.177-91.

'The educational use of the New Testament', *MC* XXVIII (Oct. 1938), pp.332-47.

'Mr Kenneth Ingram's views on sex-morality', *CQ* XIX (Jan. 1941), pp.31-40.

'The use of hyperbole in Scripture', *ET* LII (July 1941), pp.378-81.

'The Christian pacifist case', *JR* XXI (July 1941), pp.233-42.

'The imperatival use of *ἵνα* in the New Testament', *JTS* XLII (July 1941), pp.165-73.

'Is it possible to write a life of Christ?', *ET* LIII (Feb. 1942), pp.175-7.

'The present theological cleavage in Congregationalism', *CQ* XX (July 1942), pp.230-9.

'*The Historic Mission of Jesus*: a reply to the Bishop of Gloucester', *CQR* CXXXVI (July-Sept. 1943), pp.186-204.

'Did Jesus foresee his passion?', *ET* LVI (Dec. 1944), p.83.

'The punishing of Germany after the war of 1914-1918', *HJ* XLIII (Jan. 1945), pp.107-13.

'The root of the present tension in theology', *Pr* (Jan. 1946), pp.5-6.

'Dr T. W. Manson's attack on liberalism', *CQ* XXIV (Jan. 1946), pp.25-30.

'The character of the Gospel-record', *BJRL* XXIX (Feb. 1946), pp.269-85.

'The historic Jesus in the earliest Gospel-sources', *MC* XXXVI (Sept. 1946), pp.143-52.

'The religious value of sacrifice', *ET* LVIII (Nov. 1946), pp.43-6.

'Scripture and theology', *CQ* XXV (Jan. 1947), pp.21-6.

Appendix C

C.J. CADOUX MEMORIAL LECTURES

Delivered at the Yorkshire United Independent College, Bradford, until that college's amalgamation with the Lancashire College in 1958, and thereafter at different churches in West Yorkshire.

1948	T. W. Manson	The Church's ministry
1949	H. H. Rowley	The splendour of God
1950	S. L. Greenslade	Toleration and freedom in Church and State
1951	A. R. Vidler	The Christian frontier
1952	Charles Duthie	God in His world
1953	C. E. Raven	English liberal theology
1954	John Baillie	The ideal of orthodoxy
1955	William Manson	The early ministry of Jesus according to St Mark
1956	Norman Sykes	200 years on: Religion and the Churches in England 1756 and 1956
1957	C. Kingsley Barrett	New Testament interpretations of the death of Christ
1958	A. M. Ramsey	The Christian conception of sacrifice
1959	Gordon Rupp	
1960	John Huxtable	Church and State in relation to education
1961	G. B. Caird	The Epistle to the Ephesians
1962	F. F. Bruce	The historic mission of Jesus
1963	Erik Routley	The redemptive obedience of Christ
1964	J. A. Figures	
1965	F. D. Coggan	The spirit of flame
1966	H. S. Stanley	
1967	John M. Graham	Creative conflict: the struggle for Christian meaning in a secular age
1968	Stuart Jackman	
1969	E. J. Tinsley	
1970	W. J. Coggan	
1971	Martin T. Shepherd	

(The author will be grateful to readers who can supply any of the missing titles.)

Appendix D

PUBLISHED WORKS OF
ARTHUR TEMPLE CADOUX (1874–1948)

Essays in Christian Thinking, London 1922.
Jesus and Civil Government, London 1923.
The Gospel that Jesus Preached and the Gospel for Today, London 1925.
Morals for Ministers, by R.E.X., London 1928.
The Parables of Jesus: Their Art and Use, London 1930.
A New Orthodoxy of Jesus and Personality, London 1934.
The Sources of the Second Gospel, London 1935.
Shakespearean Selves: An Essay in Ethics, London 1938.
The Theology of Jesus, London 1940.
The Thought of St James, London 1944.
Songs of Self and God, London 1951.
Onesimus (a play), London 1952.

Index

This index includes the names of most of the persons, places, institutions and publications mentioned in the text. Roman numerals refer to chapters in which names occur frequently. Personal titles are generally omitted.

Abelard, 92
Acland Nursing Home, Oxford, 165, 180, 209
Acton, Lord, 156
Adil Bey, 123
Admiralty, The, 9, 11, 135
Ahmetli, 126-8
Aire, R., 70
Airedale College, Bradford, 29, 72, 74
Ali, Mr, 126-8
Alva, Duke of, 187-9
Andrews, H. T., 66
Angus, H. F., 39f
Anselm, 92
'Appeal to all Christian People', 90
Appeal to People of the Christian Church, 68f
Ap-Thomas, Dafydd, 212
Arkell, Henry, 11, 22
Asplin, Dorothy, 46
Asplin, Elizabeth Harriet: see Cadoux
Asplin, Florence (née Wright), 46
Asplin, Marguerite Mary: see Cadoux
Asplin, Thomas, 46
Athenaeum, Bradford, 72, 79
Athens, 122

Baggs, Fred, 7, 97
Baker, Philip (Lord Noel-Baker), 52
Bampton Lectures (1915), 92; (1920), 89
Barnes, E. W., Bishop of Birmingham, 106
Barth, Karl, 151f, 154, 159f, 166, 194
Bartlet, James Vernon, 30-3, 42f, 49f, 81, 102, 110, 114-17, 131, 134, 147-9, 154, 162, 179, 183

Bartlett, Percy, 118
Bate, R. S., 7
Beck, Edward O., 60, 208
Bell, G. K. A., 51
Bembridge, Isle of Wight, 135
Benson, Oxfordshire, 41, 116
Berry, Sydney M., 138
Bethune-Baker, J. F., 66
Binsey, Oxford, 34
Birmingham, 80, 90f, 176f
Blackfriars, Oxford, 180
'Blackheathens', 144, 146
Blackwell, 168f, 174
Blelloch, D. H., 59
Bligh, Harold, 17
Bligh, Wilfred, 60
Blott, V. E., 59
Blunt, A. W. F., 139
Bodleian Library, Oxford, 29, 96, 148f
Boer War, 10f
Bouquet, Alan C., 7
Bournville, Birmingham, 91
Boyd, John Francis (Sir Francis), x, 149, 164
Boys' Brigade, 10, 14-22, 34f, 42, 44, 52, 150
Bradford, Yorkshire, 29, 38f, 67-9, VI, 114-16, 141, 155, 157, 163, 191, 208, 212
Bradford Congregational Association, 136
Bradford Free Church Council, 136
Bradford Grammar School, 71, 99, 143
Bradford Theological Circle, 80, 139
Bradford Weekly Telegraph, 72
British Museum Reading Room, 98

Index

British Thomson Houston, 164, 203, 209
British Weekly, 100f, 129
Brown, Annabel Maud, 80, 97, 176, 210f
Brown, James, 39, 80
Brown, Maud Irene: *see* Cadoux
Brunner, Emil, 152, 159, 194
Bryan, F. C., 59, 210
Buja, near Izmir, 125
Bultmann, Rudolf, 194
Bunker, Alfred, 26, 35, 56
Bunker, Harold, 35, 56, 61
Bunyan, 184
Burney, C. F., 89
Butterfield, Herbert, 187
Byron, 53

Cadman, W. H., 146f
Cadours, Haute-Garonne, France, 1
Cadoux, Adolph, 1
Cadoux, Anna (née Kelly), 13, 18, 20
Cadoux, Arthur Temple, 2, 4, 6, 8f, 11f,
    19, 22f, 26, 35f, 38-40, 42, 47, 60,
    62, 84, 99, 101, 103f, 133-5, 138f,
    143, 191f, 211
Cadoux, Bernard Temple, 5, 8f, 12-14,
    17-21, 39, 53, 56, 97, 121, 125, 209,
    211
Cadoux, Cecil John, major publications:
    Ancient Smyrna, 3, 22, 96, 116, 129f,
        142, 149, 164, 192, 211
    Biographical memoir of J. V. Bartlet,
        50, 179
    Case for Evangelical Modernism, The,
        151, 157-63
    Catholicism and Christianity, 86, 89,
        101f, IX, 132, 135, 152, 156, 164,
        185, 192, 211
    Christian Crusade, The, 83, 87f
    Christian Pacifism Re-examined, 58,
        XIV
    'Congregationalism the True
        Catholicism', 134
    Congregational Way, The, 205-7
    Deuteronomy (colloquial translation),
        116, 134
    Early Christian Attitude to War, The,
        63-6, 83, 100, 171
    Early Church and the World, The, 100f,
        164, 211
    Guidance of Jesus for Today, The, 78,
        81, 84-7, 109, 132f, 191
    Historic Mission of Jesus, The, 148, 165,
        183, 190, XVI

Life of Jesus, The, 190, XVI, 210
Message about the Cross, The, 92-4, 167,
    172
Philip of Spain and the Netherlands,
    184-90
Pilgrim's Further Progress, A, 184f
*Resurrection and Second Advent of Jesus,
    The*, 102f, 200
Roman Catholicism and Freedom, 156f
'Spiritual Principles of the Reforma-
    tion, The', 163f
'Witness of the Church, The', 63
'Zwingli', 147
Cadoux, Charles, 3
Cadoux, Constance Emma (Mrs A.
    Brown Kelly), 2, 5, 8, 13f, 18, 38f,
    42, 44, 53, 80, 134, 139, 181, 211
Cadoux, Edward Henry, 2
Cadoux, Elizabeth Harriet (Bessie, née
    Asplin), 22, 38f, 42, 44f
Cadoux, Emma (née Temple), 2f, 5, 98f
Cadoux, Ethelwyn Alice (Effie), 2, 5,
    135
Cadoux, Harold John, 61, 67, 95f, 99f,
    116, 135, 141, 164, 168, 176f, 203f,
    209
Cadoux, Herbert William, 2, 5-8, 11-14,
    18-20, 97, 210
Cadoux, Ida Mary (Mrs Frederick
    Neve), 2, 5, 8, 18, 20, 23, 35f, 39, 42,
    55f, 61, 80, 97, 99, 115, 134, 176,
    211
Cadoux, Joan Mary (Mrs Dennis
    Armstrong), 134, 141, 165, 177f,
    182, 203f, 208f, 211
Cadoux, John Henry, 2
Cadoux, Lilian Violet (née Humble),
    203f, 209
Cadoux, Marguerite (née de Hochepied),
    97, 121
Cadoux, Marguerite Mary (née Asplin),
    44-7, 49f, 53-6, 60f, 67-71, 95-9,
    115f, 119, 134f, 138f, 176-8, 181f,
    203, 210, 212f
Cadoux, Matthew, 1f
Cadoux, Maud Irene (Mrs James Brown),
    5, 8, 13f, 18f, 39, 80, 91, 97, 116,
    121, 133, 176, 181, 210
Cadoux, Michael John, 209f
Cadoux, Mrs (née Maclean), 1
Cadoux, Ruth Mary (Mrs James
    Wickett), 98, 116, 134, 141, 165,
    177f, 182, 192, 203f, 208-10

222

Index

Cadoux, Theodore John, 60f, 95f, 99, 116, 133, 135, 141, 155, 164-8, 176f, 179, 181, 185f, 192f, 203f, 207, 209f
Cadoux, William Henry, 1-8, 97f, 121, 135, 178, 212
Cadoux, Yolande, 97
Cadoux-Hudson, 1
Caerleon, 118f
Calvin, Calvinism, 31, 147, 160
Camden College, Sydney, 137f
Campbell, R. J., 25
Canada, 18, 21
Cardiff, 204
Carlyle, A. J., 68
Caterham School, 100, 164
Catford, London, 6, 15f, 25, 34, 36, 42, 51, 60, 80, 143, 150
Chaffinch, The, 20
Champneys, Basil, 29
Cheshunt College, Cambridge, 117, 138
Chingford, Essex, 38, 98
Chipping Norton, Oxfordshire, 59
Christian World, The, 101, 112f, 115, 132, 135, 138, 146, 152, 154, 162, 183
Church Quarterly Review, The, 198f
Clayton, John, 4
Coleridge, 53
Coltman, Claud, 41
Coltman, Constance: see Todd
Conference on Christian Politics, Economics and Citizenship (COPEC), 88, 169
Congregational churches, local:
  Belvedere, near Erith, Kent, 22
  Benson Free Church, Oxfordshire, 67, 96
  Blackheath, London, 146
  Bowdon Downs, Altrincham, 115
  Broomhill, Glasgow, 84
  Carr's Lane, Birmingham, 28
  Caterham Hill, Surrey, 115
  Church in the Grove, Sydenham, London, 17, 22, 24, 56
  City Temple, London, 25
  Colchester, 34
  Cowley Road, Oxford, 45
  East Boldon, near Sunderland, 38
  Emmanuel, Cambridge, 30
  Farnworth, Lancashire, 75
  Greenfield, Bradford, 80, 135f, 163
  Greenock, 99
  Harpenden, Hertfordshire, 69
  Highbury, Cheltenham, 48

Highgate, London, 30
Hungerford, Berkshire, 34, 60, 62
Kingston-upon-Thames, 45f
King's Weigh House, London, 49f, 90f, 99, 101
Lyndhurst Road, Hampstead, London, 104
Paxford, Gloucestershire, 34
Saltaire, Shipley, Yorkshire, 70
Summertown, Oxford, 34, 144, 204, 211
Trinity, Catford, London, 10, 14f, 22, 46
Warsash, Hampshire, 2
Warwick, 41
Wethersfield, Essex, 2
Witney, Oxfordshire, 34
Congregational College, Edinburgh, 67
Congregational Pacifist Crusade, 119
Congregational Quarterly, The, 103f, 132f, 162, 185, 207, 209
Congregational Theological Conferences, 104, 116f, 149
Congregational Union of England and Wales, 42, 73, 119, 134, 145, 163, 205-7
Constance, 50
Constantine, 64, 100
Constructive Quarterly, The, 90
Cornwall Congregational Union, 207
Countesthorpe, 3
Cromwell, 208
Cross, F. L., 162
Croydon, 3-5, 97
Cullercoats, Northumberland, 99
Cumnor, Oxford, 142
Cunliffe-Jones, H., 162, 209

Dale, R. W., 28
Darby, Evans, 51
Darlaston, George, 22-4, 35, 56, 67f
Davies, R. Trevor, 187-9
Davies, W. A., 38
Davies, W. T. Pennar, 31, 181
Dehn, Günther, 159
Divinity Road, Oxford, 55
Dodd, C. H., 41, 56, 67, 77, 87, 89, 91, 97, 100, 104, 113, 117, 131, 134, 137, 147, 178, 196
Dr Williams' Scholarship, 37
Driscoll, Francis, 182
Driver, S. R., 32
Dryer, Oliver, 69

Duff, Archibald, 74f
Dunkirk, 52-5, 62, 177

East Anglian Congregational Ministers'
 Summer School, 116
East Boldon, near Sunderland, 38f, 42,
 44f, 55
Edinburgh, 1
Edinburgh University, 72, 76f, 136
Egypt, 177
Eichstorff, Dr, 3
Elisavetpol, the Caucasus, 13, 20
Encaenia, 209
Ephesus, 125f
Eppstein, Katie, 14, 125
Eppstein, Maurice, 3, 5, 125, 129
Erasmus, 156
Erdelyi, Martha, 80
Escott, Harry, 77f, 135
Essays Catholic and Critical, 110, 113f
Essays Congregational and Catholic, 134
Eurich, F. W., 72, 137, 140
Expositor, The, 62f
Expository Times, The, 193
Eynsford, Kent, 42, 44

Fairbairn, Andrew Martin, 22, 29-31, 72,
 74, 180
Falding, F. J., 73
Fellowship of Reconciliation (FOR), 51f,
 55, 58-63, 68f, 78, 80, 95, 117-19,
 166-8, 210
Finland, 177
Forest Hill, London, 9f, 19f, 27, 46
Forster, W. E., 71
Forsyth, P. T., 24
Franks, Oliver Shewell (Lord Franks),
 147
Franks, Robert Shewell, 104, 112f, 134,
 147
Free Church camps, 42, 44, 120
Free Church Fellowship, 38, 55, 61
Friend, The, 52
Friends' Ambulance Unit (FAU), 52-5,
 57, 61f, 168, 176f, 203
Friends, Society of (Quakers), 2, 51f, 56,
 58f, 72, 84f, 91f, 109f
Fuller, Horace, 15, 60

Gardner, Lucy, 51
Garvie, A. E., 24
Gaunt, Margaret, 68
Geikie, J. C., 23

Germany, 23, 165, 168f, 203
Gibbon, J. Morgan, 101
Gillett, Margaret, 59
Glasgow, 10, 13, 18, 39, 42, 84, 99, 211
Glasgow University, 138
Glover, Sarah, 28
Gore, Charles, 32
Graham, Richard, 59
Grassington, Yorkshire, 92
Gray, George Buchanan, 30, 32f, 42, 114,
 131
Gray, Herbert, 118
Greece, 177
Greek Evangelical Union for Seamen, 4
Green, T. H., 28
Grieve, A. J., 39, 67
Griffith-Jones, Ebenezer, 73-5, 84, 103,
 117, 132, 134, 136, 139, 167, 174
Grote, George, 56, 61
Grubb, Edward, 110
Guiffray, Mrs, 128
Guildhall, London, 2
Guillaume, Alfred, 39
Gwatkin, H. M., 26

Hackney College, London, 24, 38
Hadfield, J. A., 97-9
Haile, A. J., 33
Hall-Houghton Prizes, 36f, 39
Halliday, Fearon, 51
Hanson, John, 125
Harnack, Adolf, 22, 25, 31, 64, 82-4, 98,
 160, 198
Harris, Joel Chandler, 96
Hart, Greville, 7
Hase, Karl von, 106
Hatch, Edwin, 82
Haworth, Sir Arthur, 106
Hayes Common, London, 15
Hayling Island, Hampshire, 5, 135
Headlam, A. C., 88f, 198f
Heiler, Friedrich, 29
Henry Rogers Essay Prize, 35
Herford, Vernon, 59, 91
Hibbert, G. K., 110
Hibbert Journal, 112, 191, 211f
Hill, Wynnie, 19, 23, 37, 56
History, 190
Hitler, 166, 169
Hochepied, Lison de, 125
Hochepied, Marguerite de: see Cadoux
Hodgkin, Henry, 50f
Hooker, Richard, 162

Hope Hill, near Shipley, Yorkshire, 71
Hornus, Jean-Michel, 66f
Horton, Robert Forman, 104
Hoskyns, Sir Edwin, 151, 194f
Hoyles, Mr, 10
Hügel, Friedrich von, 113
Huguenots, 1
Humble, Lilian Violet: see Cadoux
Hungerford, Berkshire, 60
Hunter, A. M., 178, 192

Iffley, Oxford, 96
Ilkley, Yorkshire, 119
Ilkley Moor, 71
Inge, W. R., 106, 109f, 112
Ingram, Kenneth, 185
Inkpen, Berkshire, 60, 150, 177, 181f
Interpreter, The, 93, 191
Isaiah, 197
Isle of Wight, 7, 15, 35, 42, 44, 135, 150, 165
Italy, 39f, 169
Ithaca, 122
Izmir: see Smyrna

Jerome, 77
John Rylands Library, 117
Jones, Rufus M., 110
Journal of Religion, 90
Journal of Theological Studies, 66, 190, 195

Kaye, J. Allan, 59
Keats, 53
Kelly, Adam Brown, 13f, 18
Kelly, Anna: see Cadoux
Kelly, Constance Emma: see Cadoux
Kemal Ataturk, Mustafa, 120f
Knox, Wilfred, 107

Lake, Kirsopp, 102
Lambeth Conference (1920), 88, 90;
(1930), 169
Lancashire Congregational Union, 208
Lausanne, 143
Lausanne, Treaty of, 121
Lawrence, Mr, 125
Lawson, A. Clifford, 33, 39f
Lawson, E. J., 33
Lecky, W. E. H., 188
Leeds Mercury, The, 120
Leeds University, 83f
Lewis, John, 174

Lewisham High School, London, 46
Lightfoot, R. H., 148
Lock, Walter, 88f
London Peace Society, 51f
London University, 7, 21f, 26, 28, 36f, 45, 49, 62, 129, 191
Lowe, John, 195
Luther, Lutheranism, 31, 147, 149
Lynton, Devon, 204

Macalpine, Bernard, 33, 41
MacAndrews and Forbes, 2f, 14, 18, 21, 122, 126
Macgregor, G. H. C., 138, 168
Maclean, Miss: see Cadoux, Mrs
Madariaga, Salvador de, 190
Magnesia-ad-Sipylum (Manisa), 128
Malkinson, L. J., 135f
Manchester College, Oxford, 41
Manchester Guardian, The, 124, 164
Manchester University, 117, 131, 178
Manning, Bernard L., 163
Mansfield College, Oxford, 2, 7, 16, 22, 24, 26, 111-v, 72, 75f, 80f, 88, 97f, 106, 114-17, 119, XI, XII, 151f, 154f, 162f, 165, 168, 178-81, 192, 203, 207-10, 212
    Chapel, 29, 37, 143-5, 147, 154, 178, 180, 211f
    Junior Common Room (JCR), 29f, 37f, 40f, 151f, 162f, 178
    Senior Common Room (SCR), 33, 49, 55, 57, 139, 144, 152
Mansfield College Magazine, 37, 66, 75, 87, 112f, 183, 198
Mansfield, Elizabeth, 28
Mansfield, George Storer, 28
Mansfield House Settlement, Canning Town, London, 50
Manson, T. W., 137, 139, 146f, 158, 178, 183, 195, 198
Margate, 7
Maritain, Jacques, 186
Marsh, John, 178
Martin, A. D., 132f
Martin, Henry, 135
Martin, Hugh, 63
Martineau, James, 109
Mathew, Gervase, 180
Mathews, Basil, 61
Matlock, Derbyshire, 42, 44
Matthews, A. G., 147
Mauvezin, Gers, France, 1

Micklem, Nathaniel, 30, 33, 35, 104, 129, 131f, 134, 136-9, 144-7, 154f, 162, 180, 211-13
Micklem, E. Romilly, 146f, 178
Military Service Tribunals, 58f
Mill Hill Prize, 35
Milledge, Sydney, 15
Milton Mount College, 204, 208
Minster, Kent, 15, 44
Moberly, R. C., 191, 194
Modern Churchmen's Union, 104
Moffatt, James, 30, 32, 67, 147
Möhler, J. Adam, 163
Montauban, Tarn-et-Garonne, France, 1
Monfort, Gers, France, 1
Moore, Will G., 149, 211
More, Sir Thomas, 156
Morgan, Herbert, 68
Morley, Dr and Mrs, 209f
Motley, J. L., 188
Moxley, H. R., 204, 211
Muncaster, Eric, 33
Munz, Mrs F., 165
Mussolini, 121, 166

Nantes, Edict of, 1
Nathan Whitley Travelling Scholarship, 39
National Sunday School Union, 116
Netherlands, 187-9
Neve, Frederick G. P., 8, 56
Neve, Ida Mary: see Cadoux
Neve, Noreen Mary, 211
Neve, Ronald Frederick, 61
New College, London, 24, 32, 73
New, Edmund, 59
New Forest, 135
Newman, Sir George, 52
Newman, John Henry, 108f, 113, 156
New Statesman, The, 112, 114
Nicene Society, Oxford, 148
Nicholas, David, 56
Niebuhr, Reinhold, 166
No-Conscription Fellowship, 58
Non-Collegiate (later St. Catherine's) Society, Oxford, 29f
Norwich, 119
Nuridin, Mr, 126-8
Nuttall, Geoffrey F., 185

Officers' Training Corps (OTC's), 167
Oldmeadow, Ernest, 113
Oman, John, 89

Orchard, W. E., 35, 38, 41, 50f, 53, 60, 63, 89-92, 99, 101f, 211
Orient Trading Corporation, 4f
Origen, 65f, 77, 170
Origen Society, Oxford, 148
Oudjari, the Caucasus, 5, 8
Oxford, 24, 26-9, 55, 69, 80, 96, 114-17, 129, 131f, XII, 178, 180, 192, 203f, 210
Oxford Chronicle, The, 58f
Oxford High School for Girls, 141, 178
Oxford Joint Advisory Committee, 58
Oxford Magazine, The, 129f, 151, 162
Oxford Society of Historical Theology, 31, 62, 139, 148
Oxford University, 27, 111, 102, 143, 147f, 152, 164, 181, 187, 204, 209
Oxford University Pacifist Association, 168

Paddington Infirmary, 45f
Paddington Station, 45f
Palestine, 177
Parry, Kenneth, 147
Pastors' College, London, 4
Paul, 43, 62, 161
Peace Pledge Union, 167f
Peacock, Roger, 15, 20f, 135
Peake, A. S., 117
Peel, Albert, 134, 138, 162
Penguin Books, 193
Pergamum, 128f
Perry Hill, London, 46f, 97
Pfleiderer, Otto, 22
Philip II of Spain, 184-9
Philpott, R. W., 7
Polycarp, 123
Pomeroy, Vivian T., 80
Pope, Ambrose, 75
Pope, Infallibility of, 111
Poperinghe, Belgium, 52-4
Porchester, Hampshire, 15
Port Meadow, Oxford, 34, 142
Portsmouth, 10, 135
Presbyter, The, 179
Presbyterian churches, local:
  Crouch Hill, London, 50
  Enfield, Middlesex, 38
  St. John's, Forest Hill, London, 14
Presbyterians, 204-7
Price, Ernest J., 75, 136, 162
Priestman, Mr, 54
Purley, Surrey, 97, 116, 121

Index

Quakers: *see* Friends, Society of
Queen's College, The, Oxford, 148, 164, 204

Rabagliati, Dr Andrea, 72
Rashdall, Hastings, 92
Raven, Charles E., 88
Rawlinson, A. E. J., 110, 112
Reading School, 8f
Redmire, Yorkshire, 95
Rees, Dr J. R., 54
Rees, Ronald, 33
Regent's Park College, Oxford, 146, 178
Reunion Society, Oxford, 148
Review of Reviews, 23
Réville, Albert, 25
Rhodesia Transport Ltd., 8
Richards, Leyton, 62, 95, 115, 132, 138, 213
Ritschl, Albrecht, 31, 74, 81f
Robbins, Keith, 51f
Roberts, Richard, 35f, 50f, 63
Robinson, H. Wheeler, 137, 146f, 178, 180
Robinson, Theodore H., 52f
Rogers, George, 4
Rollin, Charles, 23
Rome, 40
Rotherham, Yorkshire, 73
Rowley, H. H., 60f
Royden, Maude, 51
Rugby, 59, 164, 203, 209
Runacres, H. R., 59
Ruskin, 23, 40, 121

Sabatier, Louis Auguste, 25
Sadler, Sir Michael, 78
St. Andrew's League, 44
St. Anne's Society, Oxford, 178, 204
St. Catherine's Society, Oxford, 30, 164, 187
St. Dunstan's College, Catford, London, 6-9, 23, 97f, 143
Salisbury, Frank, 69
Salt, Sir Titus, 70
Saltaire, Shipley, Yorkshire, 70
Salvation Army, 17
Sanday, William, 26, 31, 68, 82, 91, 148
Sardis, 126
Schweitzer, Albert, 83, 193
Scott, Dr Levi Prinski, 3
Scottish Free Church, Glasgow, 15
Selbie, Robert Joseph, 57

Selbie, W. B., 24, 26, 30f, 33, 36, 39-43, 45, 47, 49, 52, 55, 57, 59-62, 67, 96, 104, 114f, 117, 131, 134-6, 144f, 155, 179f
Selwyn, E. G., 110, 113
Serampore College, Bengal, 52
Serbian Relief Committee, 57
Sèvres, Treaty of, 120
Shalbourne, Wiltshire, 150
Sheldonian Theatre, Oxford, 44, 164, 209
Shelley, 53
Sheppard, Dick, 118, 167
Shillito, Edward, 147
Shipley, Yorkshire, 68, 70, 80
Shipley Glen, 71
Short, Charlton, 15, 17, 23, 55f, 150, 182
Shrubsole, Stanley, 15, 20, 24, 41, 48
Siegmund-Schultze, Friedrich, 50
Silcoates School, Yorkshire, 120, 149
Simmonds, P. G., 57
Simon, D. W., 73
Simons Bros., Messrs, 5
Sleningford Road, Shipley, 68, 70f
Smith, William A., 15
Smyrna (Izmir), 1-4, 18, 22, 38, 96, 116, x, 142, 168, 203, 211
Society of Free Catholics, 90f
Somme, Battle of the, 57
South Africa, 8, 12, 22
Southmoor Road, Oxford, 26f, 49
Spain, 187f
Spanish Inquisition, 187
Spring Hill College, Birmingham, 2, 28f
Stamford House School, Croydon, 5
Stanton, V. H., 109
Stewart, Charles, 97
Stock Exchange, 2
Stokes, Mr, 122
Stopford, Robert J., 54
Strand School, King's College, London, 9
Streeter, B. H., 148, 195
Student Christian Movement (SCM), 38, 42, 44
Sunday School classes and camps, 10, 14-17, 21, 23, 25-7, 34, 42, 56
Swanwick, Derbyshire, 27, 35, 38, 42, 44, 50, 55, 60, 107
Sy, Belgium, 38
Sykes, Norman, 190

Tablet, The, 113, 135

Taunton School, 132, 164, 167
Taylor, Vincent, 195
Temple, Beatrice, 5, 8
Temple, Emma: *see* Cadoux
Temple, Josiah, 2
Temple, William, 88
Terrell, Herbert S., 54
Tertullian, 77
Theology, 107
Thomas, J. M. Lloyd, 90f
Thompson, Dr, 54
Times, The, 157
Times Literary Supplement, The, 187
Tod, Marcus Niebuhr, 129f
Todd, Constance (Mrs Claud Coltman), 40f
Tolstoy, 10f, 18, 51
Tonbridge, 8, 18, 35, 39, 42, 55, 97, 176, 210
Travers, Walter, 162
Trinity Hall, Cambridge, 50f
Turner, Ralph, 76

United Reformed Church, 207
University College of North Wales, 157
University College of South Wales, 204
Unwin, Stanley, 102, 106

Venice, 40, 121f
Ventnor, Isle of Wight, 7, 135
Venturer, The, 57f, 89
Verdant Green, Adventures of Mr, 96

Wales, Prince and Princess of, 18
Walsh, W. T., 187-9
Watson, E. W., 68
Westminster College, Cambridge, 116
Whale, J. S., 113, 115, 137, 147

Wharfedale, 70f
Whitehouse, W. A. (Alec), 178, 211
Wickett, James John, 192, 209
Wickings, Harold F., 77f
Wigley, T., 146
William Deacon's Bank, 2
William of Orange, 187, 189
Williamson, Grace, 121-3, 125f
Wilson, William E., 92
Wodehouse, P. G., 144
Wolvercote Cemetery, Oxford, 211
Wood, Herbert G., 91
Woodbrooke Settlement, Birmingham, 59
Woodstock Road, Oxford, 139, 141, 176
Woolf, Leonard, 174
World Alliance for Promoting International Fellowship, 50
World Conference on Faith and Order, 143
Wormwood Scrubs, 60
Worth Park, Sussex, 204
Wright, Florence: *see* Asplin
Wytham, Oxford, 142

York, 84, 98, 120
Yorkshire Post, The, 83f, 126-8
Yorkshire United Independent College, Bradford, 39, 67-9, VI, 84, 112, 114, 116, 132, 136, 139, 148, 163, 191
Young, Geoffrey W., 54
Young Men's Christian Association (YMCA), 57
Ypres, 52f, 57
Yuill, Edward, 38, 60, 98, 120

Zwingli, 147